Thinking Like
An Entrepreneur

by Peter I. Hupalo

Library of Congress Catalog Card Number: 99-90329
ISBN 0-9671624-6-7 (softcover)

Printed in the United States of America.
Softcover Edition 2004

http://www.thinkinglike.com

HCM Publishing
P.O. Box 18093
West St. Paul, MN 55118

Table of Contents

Preface

Welcome! I'm glad you purchased *Thinking Like An Entrepreneur*. This is a book of my personal musings of entrepreneurship and what is most crucial to success in building and growing your own company. This book will help you *learn to think* in ways that will enhance your chances of succeeding as an entrepreneur. It is also hoped to be an enjoyable read, and, yes, in a way, it is a self-help, power-of-positive-thinking tome. I hope it will be inspirational to you, giving you new ways to think about your life, what you want to do with it, and, more specifically, how to generate that all-important, overly-desired thing called money.

How we as individuals think about any given topic must invariably be influenced by our personal philosophies and prejudices. How we approach understanding something is inseparable from who we are as people. It is inseparable from what we have learned or what we have been taught. In some cases, for personal growth, the big hindrance is not learning more, but, rather, unlearning what we have been taught or conditioned to believe. Knowledge gives us new ways to think about how we want to live and what options are available to us. The overriding goal of this book is to show you the option of entrepreneurship.

What we can intelligently comment about and use as meaningful examples depends upon the fields we know. This invariably leads me to have a heavy focus upon the fields of computer programming and CBT development; direct mail and freelance consulting; and self-publishing and multimedia entrepreneurship. Yet, the book will aid future entrepreneurs regardless of the industry you contemplate— so, whether you start a computer consulting company, a dating service, an Internet based company, a retail store, or a garbage removal company—you will find solid, fundamental business philosophy to guide you toward success. This book focuses upon the fundamentals of business success and how they are interrelated. It focuses upon the "Big Picture" and will help you be sure that the enterprise you start has a workable business model behind it.

This book is written for people who don't have a background in entrepreneurship and company formation; for people who have not had exposure to this area as they grew up, but who are now contemplating starting a business and might be looking for general business-philosophical advice. Yet, the book goes into sufficient detail to be useful reading for people already familiar with business. For example, Chapter 8 on expectation values—which I adopted from basic quantum mechanics as a method to evaluate business opportunities—and Chapter 16 on compounding—which shows how wealth compounds within a business—will help even the most experienced business person. This book will distinguish the most desirable characteristics that your start-up business should have. Maybe, my deepest hope is that this book will encourage a few people to do something they otherwise might not have done, and, somewhere inside, they will remember this book. They will remember me. Maybe, that's all we can ultimately ask for in our lives. Good luck in your entrepreneurial endeavors!

Chapter 1.
Don't Get Bernoullied

Most people are afraid to take a chance. More than anything else people learn to fear failure. If you ever watch children, you will see, often much to the chagrin of their parents, they are not afraid to make a mistake. They are not afraid of appearing foolish. Of course, as we age, we become more self-aware. And, especially, we become much more aware of how we are perceived by others. We allow this to influence what we attempt to do with our lives. There is also a horrible fear of losing what we now possess that often paralyzes us from reaching for more.

Daniel Bernoulli was the first mathematician to try to evaluate how people make investment decisions, not just from a risk/return basis, but also from a basis that considers how we *feel* about the investment, how we emotionally value the investment. Today, Bernoulli's work is known within the investment field as "utility theory." What he found and what is true of most people is that we value each succeeding financial gain less and less than the one just before.

To illustrate, consider being given the "investment" opportunity that follows. It's a fair coin toss. Heads you win and tails you lose. As you know, you have a 50% chance of winning and a 50% chance of losing. If you participate in this "investment" 10 times, you will, on average, win about 5 flips. There will be some variation in this number. Some people might win only 4 flips, while some will, maybe, win 6 or 7 flips. This is just a standard deviation. It doesn't mean you are lucky or unlucky, although, if you want, you can look at it this way. It just means there is a variation in the outcomes. The important point is that, on average, you win one half of the flips. If you were to participate in, say, 1,000 flips, rather than 10, the amount you would expect to deviate from the average number of wins of 500 would be smaller when compared as a ratio to the total number of flips. But, don't worry about that. It's unimportant here.

What you should be asking is "What's the payoff, and what's the risk?" In other words, if you win, how much do you win, and, if you lose, how much do you lose? Here is where most people start thinking to themselves, "Well, to be a fair game, I expect to win an amount equal to the amount I wager." In other words, if I said you could win $10, you might expect you would have to bet (and risk losing) $10. This is a natural tendency to evaluate break-even scenarios coupled with knowing the outcome is 50-50. You really don't expect to win more than you are wagering. You expect that all things will probably even out—not in your favor, but not against you either. We should not think this way. It is not at all true that all things "even out." Some contests put you at a decided disadvantage, such as going to a casino, whereas other endeavors, such as investing in carefully chosen and reasonably-valued stocks, put you at an advantage. I'm not saying that the break-even point isn't of special concern. It is, but that's later.

The point is that you do not yet know how much you must risk or how much you might reasonably hope to make (or, win, in our gaming case). You have not been told. Of course, in real life, you would need to research a given potential opportunity and try to come up with reasonable estimates of both how much you might make and how much you must risk. But, back to our game. I don't like stressing people out, so I'm not going to make you wager anything! If the coin comes up heads, you get $10. If it comes up tails, you get nothing. Not bad, eh? In fact, if you can find such an opportunity in the real world, jump on it. The goal would be to get as many tosses as possible. If, for example, you were given 10,000 tosses, this would mean you could expect to win about half of them or about 5,000. You win $10 on each of those heads, so you expect to make about $50,000. Notice the key word I'm using here: EXPECT. You expect something based upon a reasonable estimate of the scenario. You don't hope. You don't dread. You expect. It's all very mathematical. Do the math; get the answer. You're not emotionally involved. You might be excited at the prospect of making money so easily, but that's not the same as trying to bias your estimate of the tossing outcomes. Here's how you calculate your expectation value:

Expected amount = ($0 X 5,000) + ($10 X 5,000) = 0 + $50,000
= $50,000

On 5,000 flips you expect to win nothing, $0 times 5,000 which is the big goose egg. But, on the other 5,000, you expect to win $10 and get $10 times 5,000. There is another way to look at this. How much do you expect to win on the average throw? Well, you already know you expect to win $50,000 and you know that there is a total of 10,000 throws. 5,000 of them pretty bloody useless to you! So, doing the division, you get $5 per throw as the expected amount you make per throw. Why am I dwelling on this? It may seem simple, but it is very important. We could write the above line in another way:

Expected amount = ((50% X 0) + (50% X $10)) X 10,000 throws
= $50,000

Of course, you could evaluate this on a per throw basis. And, you would see for one throw that the expected winnings are $5.

Expected amount = ((50% X 0) + (50% X $10)) X 1 throw = $5

There is an important generalization of this equation, which can be expressed as follows:

Expected amount = Σ (probability of a given outcome)(amount acquired for the given outcome)

Where the summation symbol (or Σ) just means we must sum over all possible outcomes. Calculating expectation values is discussed in detail later and is very important to understand. For now, though, let's assume you are only given one toss of a two-sided coin. If it comes up heads, you win the $10; tails, you lose nothing. If someone were to offer you this deal (neglecting skepticism that there is a catch or the game is somehow rigged), you gladly accept the deal. What do you have to lose? Nothing. What do you have to gain? $10. You can be emotionally happy to have such a deal. But, other than that, emotions don't enter into the analysis of the desirability of this game. Unless, of course, you believe coin tossing will somehow corrupt you as a person!

But, now, I'm going to make the situation more difficult for you. I'm going to give you a choice between two versions of this game. Version 1 is just as above. One coin toss. You win $10 on heads; lose nothing on tails. Version 2 is one toss. On heads, you win $20. But, on tails, you *lose* $10. Think about this for a moment and ask yourself, "Which choice would I take?" When you have answered that in your own mind, continue.

Welcome back. If you have just read through without thinking about the above question (and, I know, there are some of you out there!), please go back and think about it before continuing. It is a good chance to understand something about yourself. You may have realized that the choices, for all practical purposes, are the same. As shown above, the expectation value of the first version is $5 for one throw. The expectation value of the second version is the same:

$$\text{Expected outcome} = (\$20)(50\%) + (-\$10)(50\%) = \$10 - \$5 = \$5$$

This is the cold, hard mathematical analysis. From a desirability standpoint, Version 1 and Version 2 are equal as opportunities. Depending upon your mood, you may have chosen Version 1 or Version 2. After all, $10 (or $20) isn't really a lot of money. There is little emotional reason to favor one version over the other. It is precisely because of the small amount involved that many would take Version 2, although they might not realize this.

Now that you are familiar with expectation values, I want to give you one more choice. Whenever you can calculate a reasonable overall expectation value outcome for an investment situation or a business idea, you should. It can help you in your decision making. I assume that will be the first thing you do in evaluating the game below.

Version 1: Heads, you win $40; Tails, you lose $10.
Version 2: Heads, you win $10; Tails, you lose nothing.
Which do you take? What are the expectation values?

The answer is that Version 1 has an expectation outcome value of

Expected outcome = (50% X $40) + (50% X -$10) = $15.

Version 2 has an expectation value of $5. You clearly would want to take Version 1 in this case. Its expectation value is three times higher. This is all well and good. Emotions don't really come into play. But, now, let us start dealing with some larger values. Same coin-tossing game. Answer honestly.

Version 1: No flip required. You instantly win $50,000.
Version 2: A coin flip. Heads you win $100,000.
            Tails you win nothing.

Think about your answer. The expectation values are the same, and this is just an exercise. So, like the wise student in the class, you could just point out they are the same, and, so, the choice doesn't matter. But that won't get you anywhere. And, yes, young grasshopper, the choice matters a great deal. Treat the situation as real. Pretend you have really been given this choice by someone. Which do you *want*?

It's not an easy decision, is it? Not for most. You need to start thinking about your life and what you will do or could do with the money. Maybe, you wanted to go to college but didn't have the money. $50,000 would cover your costs (at some universities this is still true). You might say, "I'll take the $50,000." On the other hand, maybe, you've been wanting to buy a new $80,000 sports car, and you think, "Gee, I'll take the chance for financing the entire car. I'll take Version 2." If you chose Version 2, then, most likely, you don't consider $50,000 to be a lot of money. Maybe, you've built a multimillion-dollar company already, and $50,000 more or less just doesn't matter. For most people $50,000 matters. Most people will choose Version 1 and the guaranteed $50,000. You start thinking about what the money can do for you and start spending it (mentally, at least!). The thought of losing what you already have (or know you can get) becomes significant. Simply put, you value the first $50,000 more highly than you value the next $50,000 that Version 2 gives you above and beyond Version 1. In any case, both versions have the same expectation value, and, from a purely mathematical point, they are equivalently desirable opportunities. Let's change the game slightly.

Version 1: No flip required. You instantly win $100,000.
Version 2: A coin flip. Heads, you win $300,000.
                      Tails, you win nothing.

The first thing you should notice is that you like this choice much more than the previous game. At the very least, you will win $100,000 which is the best you could have hoped for in the previous version comparison. So you should be a happy camper! But you still need to make a choice. Which do you take? Think about it before continuing.

The expectation value for Version 1 is $100,000. The expectation value for Version 2 is $150,000. So, mathematically, Version 2 is the better opportunity. Nonetheless, Version 2 is also the more volatile investment. There is a 50% chance you wind up with nothing. Ick! Who wants that? $100,000 is considered a lot to most people. They wouldn't want to lose it. Most people would take the $100,000 and run. Yes, they might wonder, "Would I have won the flip?" They might even ask the person offering the opportunity "OK, I've taken the $100,000. But, I really want to know. Will you flip anyway, just for fun?" Pretending it was "the flip," maybe, they will feel they have made the "right" choice, if the noncounting flip comes up tails. Maybe, they will curse themselves, if it comes up heads. In any case, what might have been doesn't really matter, does it?

Now many reading might be thinking, "I'm smart. I see that Version 2 is the better opportunity, and I'd take it." You might feel only dumb people would take Version 1. This is simply not true. Invariably, life circumstances must affect your decision. Suppose, for example, you had a sick child who needed a special surgery to live that costs $90,000. Is Version 2 superior then? There is a 50% chance your child will die, whereas Version 1 guarantees your child's life. Simply put, Version 1 is the hands-down winner in this case.

The crucial point is that the desirability of an investment does have an emotional component that is meaningful. To simply rule out the emotional value of the outcomes is wrong. This is what Daniel Bernoulli saw. The emotional value of the next $200,000 accompanying Version 2 is not as great as the emotional value of the first $100,000 for many people. You might still be thinking, "I'd take Version 2." That's OK. In this case, mathematically, it is the better opportunity. Maybe, you tend to be more of a risk-seeker. Let's do another one:

Version 1: No flip required. You instantly win $200,000.
Version 2: A coin flip. Heads, you win $1,000,000.
Tails, you win nothing.

Which do you take? Hmm…A tough call? Mathematically, Version 2 is better. It has an expectation outcome of $500,000 which is more than double the expectation value of Version 1. On the other hand, you might start thinking, "Gosh, there is a lot I could do with $1,000,000 that I couldn't do with $200,000." Early retirement comes to mind. You might not be able to retire on just the $200,000, but the $1,000,000 assures it. You might well choose Version 2. I think many people would choose Version 2 for two reasons: One, it has by far the better expectation value; and two, a psychological threshold has been reached. The one million dollars represents a level of wealth people aspire to attain, but see no way to achieve. Not easily, anyway! But this is an easy choice. Consider the next one:

Version 1: No flip required. You instantly win $1,000,000.
Version 2: A coin flip. Heads, you win $10,000,000.
Tails, you win nothing.

Which do you take? Why? There is no one correct answer. Version 2 is by far the better mathematical choice with an expectation value of $5,000,000 which is five times greater than the expectation value of Version 1. Yet, on the other hand, maybe you're thinking, "There really isn't much I want to do with $10,000,000 that I can't already do with $1,000,000." That's valid reasoning also. Maybe, the value of the next nine million dollars above and beyond the first one million dollars just isn't great enough to risk losing the first million dollars. Maybe, you could imagine multiplying the above values by a factor of ten. Is there anything you really want that you can't buy for $10 million dollars that you could buy for $100 million dollars? Would a factor of five, or even ten, in better expectation value justify taking the version where you might wind up with nothing? I'll say more about this in the next chapter.

Our analysis, so far, is incomplete. It neglects two facts. First, there is a known tendency for people to feel they need more as they acquire more. Studies have asked people how much more money above and beyond what they currently posses would they need to feel financially secure. Poorer people tend to feel they need far less money, overall, than people who have more money. And the people with more money tend to often feel that they need *much* more to be secure. What this means is that if you already have $10 million dollars, you might be thinking, "I really do need the $100 million. After all, I really need a new yacht. And, I've been wanting to buy a jet-fighter plane for fun." This tendency of wanting more material goods as your capacity to buy them increases is one factor that keeps many people relatively poor. Income is not the same as retained wealth. There will always be people who have little retained wealth, because they are always buying more. I'm not saying you shouldn't want more, but you should be aware of what exactly you want and why. If you find that you are constantly increasing your spending to match your income, you should ask yourself, "How will this affect my wealth in the future? How well off will I be in retirement? What if I were to lose my income?" These are important questions to ask yourself, if you ever wish to achieve a high level of wealth relative to what you have now.

Yet, while poorer people tend to think in terms of savings, i.e., how much can I save if I don't buy this or that, people who do well financially tend to focus upon increasing revenue or earnings. While there will always be a limit to how much money you can save clipping grocery coupons, there is no practical limit to one's income. This is crucial.

This brings us to the second issue, that we have neglected in the above analysis, and which is, in fact, the purpose of this chapter. I have discussed Bernoulli's realization that people are more sensitive to losing what they already have than in gaining more, and, in particular, each succeeding financial gain increment is valued less highly than the one before it, even though the dollar amounts of the increments are the same. The problem is that this fear of loss kicks in very early and well before a person achieves an amount of financial security that really makes the person happy.

How many people do you know who hold jobs they do not like, but will not give them up for fear of losing a job that pays well or has great benefits? How many people will spend their lives never really doing what they want, and, in the end, wind up with neither a sense of having done what they wanted nor having achieved any real financial security? What prevents them from taking the small risk to do something that they really want? They view it as a long-shot, big risk that probably wouldn't turn out well for them, anyway. They are Bernoullied! That's what I call it. They are so afraid of losing what little they have that they don't even stop to evaluate the real expectation values of various situations in life. They not only miss factors of five or ten or greater opportunities, while sitting on what they feel are good-paying jobs, but they aren't even able to evaluate the probabilities of various outcomes. They don't evaluate them, maybe, because it involves work, or maybe, because they know that if they take the plunge and start their own company, then there is a chance of losing what they already have. Never mind that they don't have a clue what the chances of incurring a real loss are. Never mind that the potential financial upswing is often so large that it would allow them to achieve that one thing they seem so obsessed with—financial security. They are Bernoullied! They are thinking in terms of worse-than-the-worst-case that is highly unlikely. The fear of loss prevents them from undertaking a rational study of the opportunity. The fear of loss prevents them from taking any action at all. It is psychologically safer not to pursue the opportunity.

And here is, maybe, the biggest "secret" given in this book. The only people who have achieved any real financial security (neglecting the few odd-balls who become famous as actors or athletes or who win the lottery or who inherit a lot) are those who have built their own companies. Think of the people you consider financially secure. Bill Gates? Steve Jobs? Michael Dell? Rick Born? All of these people have achieved their wealth via building a business.

"Who the hell is Rick Born?" you ask. He's the founder of Minnesota-based Born Informational Services. For every well-known entrepreneur, like Bill Gates, there are hundreds of company founders who have achieved financial security, measured in the millions of dollars, whose names you would never recognize. In many cases, you wouldn't even be sure of what their company does exactly. It's not that they are really any smarter than you, but they have taken the chance of starting their own business, and they have succeeded.

The real question is: What are my chances of success in building a company? This is an impossible question to answer in general. It depends upon several factors including your personal characteristics, the opportunity, and your resources to pursue the opportunity. Common wisdom has it that most businesses—four out of five is a regularly bandied about number—fail. It is assumed that failure brings total loss of everything to the extent that the failed entrepreneur finds himself standing on a bridge contemplating jumping. And, there isn't even a guardian angel in the conventional view! This common wisdom is, like most things taken for granted, incorrect. A truer statistic is that the typical manufacturing company has about a 50% chance of succeeding. I believe the success rate for information-based companies, i.e., multimedia, computer consulting, etc... is even higher. When a good opportunity is combined with a management team with a bit of experience in the industry, the chances of success are actually quite good. Yet, due to the human tendency to worry more about a loss than embrace a potential gain, most people grossly overestimate the chances of failure, and they imagine "losing everything" even though that possibility is remote. Entrepreneurs are more likely to evaluate the situation based less upon emotional aspects and more upon expectation values.

Industry factors play a significant role in determining relative business failure. Put simply, if you start a low-margin, high-turnover business, like retailing, apparel or opening a convenience grocery store, or, God forbid, a restaurant, your odds of survival are relatively slim. This is the type of business that tends to strongly favor the established competitors. Great companies that achieve significant growth do exist in these industries. McDonald's had to start somewhere and sometime! In fact, the founder went to school not too far from where I am sitting right now! So, I don't want to overtly discourage you, if you really know what you are doing in one of these fields. But fatalities in these industries are much higher. Be forewarned. Why not choose to start a business that has higher profit margins and other factors that are more in your favor? The first and most crucial decision you will make, when starting a business, is choosing the type of business you will enter. Choose wisely.

What also tends to contribute, I personally feel, to the relatively high failure rate of these low-margin start-ups is that these fields are often entered by people who say to themselves, "Gee, I don't really know anything about any business, but a restaurant seems simple enough." This is usually a bad sign. For it leads to the second contributing factor of many business failures. That is a lack of experience in the field. While there are scores of people who had no knowledge of an industry, when they entered it with a start-up company, who are now dominant players in the industry, I don't think this invalidates the message. If possible, get some experience in the industry before you start a business in that industry.

I remember talking to a guy who had started his own photography studio fresh out of college. He was doing what he wanted and doing well. I asked him how long he had been working in his own studio. He said twenty years and that he hoped to work another twenty years. It blew my mind, at the time, that some people had twenty years of experience in a field and wanted to be in it another twenty years. I asked him if he had any regrets, and he said he wished he had gotten some experience before starting his own studio, as it would have prevented many costly mistakes and aggravation. So, even people who jump on the idea or the dream with no experience often echo the same motto of "Get some experience first."

Finally, it should be pointed out that many of the businesses that fail to succeed do not really succeed at fully failing either. They just sort of fade away. The owner never really makes a lot of money, but he doesn't lose any money, either, or at least not nearly as much as most people fear. Most people think in terms, "If I fail, I'll lose everything. My house, my car…" This is usually not true. Often, all you will lose is a few years of career building and, maybe, some savings that might have accrued to your retirement account. Even a failed venture will probably not cost you "everything."

So, let's use expectation values one last time to conclude this chapter. I don't want you to forget them! Using them is not completely valid, because all we have are very rough guesses. But in business, that's often all you have. You need to make some decisions with incomplete information. So, here you are. You want to start your own business, but you fear failure. You've given some real thought to what you want to do. Let's also assume you have some experience in the industry of your proposed business. You're a hard worker, and you'll give it your best. "What are my chances?" you ask. Using the above statistic of a 50% chance of survival and considering that all you will probably lose in the worse case is a few years of career promotions, it seems that you really risk very little. Maybe, you will need to work a few more years before retirement, the number of years you were puttering with your didn't-quite-work-out-business. That's if you fail. But what if you succeed? You might well achieve a wealth measured in the tens or even hundreds of millions of dollars. A few million dollars is not at all an unconservative estimate of the potential upswing. It's quite reasonable. And, who even needs that much? Maybe, all you achieve is just a slightly higher level of financial security than the average employee. You are your own boss. You have far more control over your own destiny than the average employee. Do you take the chance? Or, are you Bernoullied?

Chapter 2.
You're Not That Far Behind Michael Dell

I write this chapter as my own personal philosophy about money. We all have some philosophy about money. Many people never contemplate their philosophy. Yet, it has a major impact upon how they live, the decisions they make, and how they relate to money. You should ask, "What are my views about money? How does money relate to my life? Is there anywhere in this topic where my thinking, maybe, should be shifted?" Sometimes, just examining the way you look at something helps give you a perspective that can lead to a more fulfilling life. And, of course, if you develop good money habits, you might just want to compliment yourself on your money intelligence!

The first point is that money is important. There is just no getting around it. We live in a capitalistic world. In fact, I believe that capitalism and democracy go hand-in-hand. If you are not in control of what you produce, then you are a slave. That's not to say that you might not choose to sell your services to an employer in exchange for a wage. It's just to say that you have the choice. Maybe, you choose to work for no one but yourself. You want to produce something on your own to sell, cutting out the middleman of the employer. You want to take it to the consumer streets. Your ability to make this choice is intimately tied to your ability to control your own life, to choose your own destiny.

Money, to most people, represents one of four things: 1) power, 2) status, 3) security, or 4) freedom. People who seek wealth for either 1) or 2) maybe would benefit more from some good personal self-help books, rather than this tome. Sure, they could adopt a thinking that aids them in making more money, but, ultimately, it really won't give them what they want, or they will be too blind to ever realize that. Power doesn't follow from having money. You could have hundreds of millions of dollars, and, still, any two-bit-third-world dictator has more power than you do. You can feel powerful, but to many you will just seem self-centered and pompous.

Seeking status via wealth is much more common, and, I guess, status is a form of power, or, at least, a feeling you have power. Maybe, more a sense of being important. Of being "Better than the Jones's." Again, if status is your real goal, then I think you will ultimately not be happy no matter how much you achieve financially. In a sense, if you are after 1) power or 2) status, you really need to mature. Both of these represent not wealth, but either a desire to control others or else to be accepted and approved of by others. Neither of these is really a good characteristic of a successful entrepreneur. If you must control others and exert dominance over them, then you will drive other people away. People won't choose to be around you. They won't want to interact with you, and they won't want to be employed by you. It's difficult to build a company, if that's the case.

If, on the other hand, you are constantly seeking others' approval, then it will be difficult for you to really break the mold and choose your own path. In Chapter One, I discussed why many don't try to build their own businesses. They are afraid of losing what they already have. Part of that is the fear of losing status. They don't want to be labeled a failure, as having less status. They don't want to drive a less expensive car, if their business doesn't succeed, so that they can recoup retirement savings lost while they were trying to build a company. Many don't want to drive a less expensive car even during the first few start-up years of their company! They want the status they currently have. If you are equating your personal worth as a human being with your financial worth, then it will be especially painful to suffer a defeat. Many people reading this will say, "Of course, I don't equate my worth as a person to the amount of money I have." Yet, at some deep psychological level, they will. This is not meant as a personal criticism, but just as food for thought to help you think about what money really means to your life.

If, however, you are seeking 3) security or 4) freedom, then, I think, this book can help you. In a way, I see 3) and 4) as intertwined. I feel this is really, at root, the only way to view money. I have known lots of people who wanted security. That's not at all unreasonable. There are few feelings worse than financial stress. Constantly worrying about paying bills and staying out of debt is simply not fun. If you must worry about it, you might as well worry about it at the company level rather than at the personal level.

As a company starts up, there is often the same feeling of, "How will I get all these bills paid when they are due? Will I have the money?" Even if you are making decent profits on your sales, there is the question of timing of the payments you owe in relation to the money that is being paid you. This is referred to as "cash flow" and is an important issue for any business. Even if you *will have* the money, your creditor wants the money *right now*. Certain businesses are less problematic in this regard than others. But, things might need to get worse, before they get better. Seldom will a business start and smoothly sail to financial freedom and security. Often, things will get worse, initially. However, at a certain point, if you are successful, you might find that fear of cash flow is no longer bothering you. You have financial reserves. You have "breathing room." In fact, you will have more financial security and freedom than if you had not taken the plunge to start your own company. Whether you are prepared to go through a potentially turbulent psychological period to achieve possibly higher financial security is a decision only you can make.

Many believe that the ideal time to attempt to build a business is when the lead entrepreneur is about 25 years old. If you are much younger, you might well lack not only the experience but also the maturity. If you are much older, it is more difficult, as by this age, most people have families to support and spend time with. Much more is at risk. You have dependents. If you fail, you will have less time to recoup retirement savings lost during the years that you tried to build a business. If you are in this latter category, your decision whether or not to start a company is more difficult. But, there is always the option of looking for a way to enter a business part-time and in a lower-risk way. It is easier if your spouse agrees with your decision to start a business and you have a second income to fall back upon while the business is started. Surviving the start-up years, when the business isn't generating a livable income for the entrepreneur, is often the biggest concern an entrepreneur has. Further, energy and enthusiasm can be lower as you get older, because you have had more battles with the world and you are aware that not everything will always turn out the way you had optimistically hoped. Yet, experience and maturity will be in your favor.

If you are married, it is absolutely essential that the decision to start a business be discussed and decided upon mutually. Many marriages have been ruined by diverging wishes in this area. Even in cases where a business has been wildly successful and it seemed the two people were suited to each other, I have seen divorces. I can't explain this. Maybe it's just too tough to live and work together at the same time. You get on each others' nerves. Everyone needs space. I mention this just so you are aware that, even if you succeed financially, this by no means implies that your life will be happier or better than it was before you attained wealth.

But, then again, I remember a friend telling me he once worked for a company which, in an attempt to increase manager productivity, sent three of its managers to participate in one of those reevaluate-what's-important-to-your-life-get-away-retreats. I don't remember the details, but it was like an excursion into the mountains or some such thing. The goal was to push the managers physically and mentally to the point that they really felt they might die—to make them confront death and their own mortality and, hopefully, in so doing, learn what's really important to them (if you watched *The Game* with Michael Douglas, you'll get the general idea). Well, anyway, the three managers returned from the trip and were grateful for the experience. It really did get them to think about their lives. Two of the managers immediately resigned from the company that sent them and began their own business—in competition with their former employer. The third manager did stay with the company, but, immediately upon his return, divorced his wife.

I fear many people believe that money will drastically change their lives for the better. You will be better looking, more respected, more intelligent, have a better love life, and, in general, be all-around a better person. That simply doesn't happen. You will be the same person. Some people expect more. But, let's assume you are psychologically prepared to accept your new status as nouveau riche! "Not a problem!" you say, "I want security and financial freedom."

Wealth building is like chess or football in that playing too defensively will often not lead to the security you desire. Being too cautious will prevent the attainment of the security you desire. Sometimes, you must take a risk. It's a case of the best defense being a good offense. I tend to think of this as outrunning risk. By pushing yourself early on to build a company, you can achieve a high level of financial freedom that could not have been achieved in any other way. If you are not a natural-born risk taker (and, I include myself in that category), coming to this realization will give you a new way to approach the issue of financial freedom and security.

Many people desire financial security and freedom, but don't really know how to achieve this goal. They feel that if they don't inherit or win a lottery, that wealth, for them, is unlikely. This is not true. Most of the wealthy people today have created their own wealth by starting and building a business. And, most of those who do inherit wealth, inherit wealth created by one of their ancestors who built a business. Almost all wealth today is the direct result of entrepreneurship. Most people who lack entrepreneurial role models don't tend to think in terms of "What can I do to make money?" but, rather, they ask the question, "Who will hire me and pay me a wage?" That's sort of putting the cart before the horse. Why must someone hire you for you to make money?

We all tend to have preconceived ideas of how our lives should flow and what we will do with our lives. Different people have different expectations about their futures. From my experience, it seems to be correlated with the level of wealth a person is exposed to as a child. The environment influences attitudes about what is considered "successful." I have seen relatively poorer people consider "success" to mean getting some skills at the local technical college and, then, moving on to a job that pays $30,000 a year. Now, I'm not knocking this, if this is what the person wants. But, I also see other individuals, who are no more talented, but who were raised in slightly more affluence and who were expected to go to college and become engineers or lawyers or doctors. To them, success is getting a four-year degree and making $60,000 a year. In both cases, the person will usually achieve his goal, but little more. It seems that the level of financial success all these people will achieve is intimately tied to what they believe is "out there" for them as far as career options. More rare are people who grow up in entrepreneurial environments. Often, these people think that they should be able to build a successful company. While they know that attaining huge wealth is always a bit determined by the luck of being in the right place at the right time with the right product or idea, they tend to think that if they work hard and make fundamentally good business decisions (not brilliant ones mind you, just good) that they should be able to build a multimillion dollar company. And, they build a successful company.

In the extreme case, there is IPO fever (Initial Public Offering, this is when a company goes public and becomes traded on the stock market). Usually, this fever hits people who know several individuals who have taken companies public. They've seen it done so many times that there is no mystique about the process anymore. It becomes an issue of building a company that is marketable to venture capitalists and, then, to retail investors. You start to think, "Gosh, I know more than so and so, and he did it, so I can too. Hmm…but, what if his company going public was a fluke? But, then, so and so also did it…" Sometimes, there is a whole group of fifteen or so people, who all know each other, and they're all thinking the same thing! Each one is scheming, "Well, I should, at least, be able to get some venture capital firm to back us to the tune of one or two million dollars. Then, we'll have an initial public offering and raise $10 million dollars. And, the company will, maybe, be valued at $100 million dollars on the stock market. The venture capitalists will cash out much richer, and, so, they'll want to do it. In the end, I'll, maybe, own 20% of the stock and will be worth $20 million dollars. Of course, all this should happen within three years or so." And, guess what? Several of those people do take a company public! And, what separates this person who is now worth several tens of millions of dollars from the person with the vo-tech degree who is working as a multimedia designer for $40,000 per year? It's not skill. It's not talent. It's not intelligence. It's largely a matter of the perception of what's "out there" for the person to achieve. Of course, connections to people in the venture capital business don't hurt any either!

Because people think differently about money, they achieve different results. The key defining point of an entrepreneur, I believe, is that they tend to think in terms of "What opportunities are out there? What products or services can I create that other people will pay money for?" Once they have an idea, some just jump in and try it. But most, before actually trying it, give the idea a serious and honest evaluation of feasibility. They ask the questions, "How much will it cost me to produce my product? What are my big expenses? What will be my ongoing expenses? How long will it take before the business can support me financially? If I fail, how much will I lose? If I succeed, how much might I earn? What is a reasonable level of success to expect?"

Notice that many of the questions get back to the ideas of Chapter One. About thinking in terms of risk and return. About trying to honestly quantify the most likely outcomes. This is not only a powerful decision-making tool for businesses, but once a person starts thinking in these terms, it is difficult not to come to the conclusion that entrepreneurship is, financially, at least, the preferred career choice. This does not mean that, once you find a business idea that is reasonable, you must follow it. You should ultimately ask, "What do I want to do with my life? What kind of thing do I want to do?" You do not need to find "the best" opportunity out there. There are many great ideas that will be competing for your attention, before you choose the type of business you want. Ultimately, you need three overlapping factors.

The first factor is a business that is financially feasible, i.e., one where you can sell the contemplated product at a cost that will lead to reasonable profitability. This is relatively basic business analysis, and you will master this by the time you've read this book. The only difficulty lies in making an accurate and honest assessment of potential sales.

Secondly, you need to want to do the business (or product). It has to be something you desire. Best of all is something about which you feel truly passionate, a field that really interests you. I am convinced that many businesses that just fade away start as good opportunities, but the entrepreneurs who start them lack a passion for the endeavor. It's easier to stay with something you love. And, the longer you stay with a viable business idea, growing it, the more likely you will achieve financial success.

Third, you need to choose an undertaking of which you are capable. Sometimes, the idea really is a good opportunity, and, yes, you really feel passionate about it, but nonetheless you do not really have the resources or the ability to undertake the venture. If you want to start a manufacturing company and you estimate you need $10 million dollars and you simply cannot raise the money, then, this might not be the business for you at present.

Many people believe that money or lack of skills is their limiting factor. They feel they have a great opportunity and are passionate about it, but they just don't have the skills or the resources to undertake it. In many cases, these people are incorrect. They have failed to think through their options. In particular, if you feel you are talent or skill limited, read Chapter Three, "Men Are Cheaper Than Guns." If you feel you are financially limited, read Chapter 11, "Risk Shifting and Pursuing Larger Opportunities," and, especially, Chapter Four about bootstrapping. It may still be true, however, that you are unprepared for the venture or that you will be unable to marshal the needed resources.

Let's assume you've found a business opportunity to pursue. You are building a company. As you see your wealth increase, you might well lose touch with just how much is enough. Entrepreneurs have built and sold out companies for millions of dollars and, then, been heavily criticized by people for having made a bad decision when selling their company. In particular, they "should have gotten much more" for the business. There is no doubt that entrepreneurs who build a company to the size that it can go public (sell shares to investors on the open stock market, so-called IPO's) will make far more money than those who sell their businesses earlier to other companies. But not everyone wants to build a company to a size that makes it a viable public company. Not everyone wants the responsibility of managing a public company. A great cartoon I remember is of two guys sitting at a bar. They are debating the purpose of life and money. One says something like, "The purpose of life is to earn enough money so that earning money is no longer the purpose of life."

Until you have financial security, money will be an issue. But, beyond a certain point, "Who cares?" This is one area where poorer people often tend to have a better understanding of life and money than some wealthy people. If money is really the purpose of what you do, what do you do when you have enough? In particular, I ask the question, "How far behind someone like Michael Dell (or Bill Gates) are you financially speaking?" This draws the usual response of "Huh?" In other words, how much does he have that you do not? Most people would answer the differential is in the billions of dollars. Technically, they are correct. But that's not the whole story. The real question is "What can he buy that you cannot that you believe will contribute meaningfully to your life?" If you are worth, say, $10 million dollars, what is there that you cannot buy that you could buy for, say, $100 million dollars? Don't just seek to name something that costs more than $10 million dollars, but ask, "Is this something that will really benefit my life? Do I really want it?" Usually what people name, if they name anything at all, is just some status symbol that really won't contribute to the enjoyment of their life. We can always up the ante, and ask, "What is there that you cannot buy for, say, $100 million dollars that you could buy if you had a billion dollars?" If your goal is to become the richest person in the world or make a Forbes' list, you have probably lost touch with just how much is enough.

You are really no more than, at most, a few tens of millions of dollars behind even Bill Gates, when you consider the question of *importance* of the financial differential. It's really more of a yes-no or zero-one boolean logic. Either you feel financially secure, or you do not. Either you can buy the things you desire, or you cannot. Either you feel you are financially free, or you do not. How much other people have or "Keeping up with the Jones's" (and, especially, the

Gates's!) is meaningless. Never forget that. You're not that far behind Michael Dell or, even, Bill Gates himself!

Chapter 3.
Men Are Cheaper Than Guns

I often hear two interesting comments. Both demonstrate a misunderstanding of the role of knowledge and intellect in business, more specifically, the needed knowledge and intellect of the lead entrepreneur in a start-up company.

The first comment is usually said by relatively bright individuals, or, at least, individuals who feel they are relatively bright! It is something akin to, "I'm smarter than Michael Dell (or Bill Gates or pick your successful entrepreneur), so I'll be able to build a more successful company than Dell." In many cases, these individuals are highly talented in a difficult computer programming language like C++ or Java. Nevertheless, their companies often never really get off the ground, and they go back to computer consulting. Yes, they make a good deal of money consulting—measured in the low hundreds of thousands—but they don't achieve their dream of the multimillion-dollar company. Why is this?

The answer is simple. How talented you are as a programmer will not determine how successful you will be in building an informational services company that grows to significant worth. In particular, to grow requires doing more. Writing more code. Creating more software. This is especially true in the specialized solutions provider category. By this, I mean companies that are hired by other companies to create specialized custom-written software. What these companies produce is computer programming code. One person, no matter how good a programmer, can only do so much. There are only so many hours in a day, and you can only spend so many of those hours doing any given thing, including programming. This sounds simple, I know. But, many miss the point.

What is worse, once a business is started, the founder instantly finds that there is a whole slew of other company-related demands that take time—administration, sales, and marketing, for example—which don't even involve creating the product to be sold, computer code in our example. So, our ace programmer is left with, maybe, 1,000 hours a year of a 2,000-hour work year in which he can write code. This is a significant limit to the amount of product that can be created by only one person.

This brings me to the second comment I hear even more frequently. It goes something like this, "I can't possibly start a business. I simply don't know enough." Sometimes, this is true. But, often, the comment comes from someone who has years of experience in a field. A good question for such a person to ask himself[1] is: "When will I know enough?" Then ask, "What more must I learn before I am ready?" Occasionally, there will be a few definite, concrete things you must learn to function in a given industry. Some generalized business study is very useful. By all means go and learn it.

But what happens most often is the person begins making an all-skills-encompassing list that would take a lifetime or more to master. You think, "How can anyone build a successful company? I will never know enough! All those company founders who created hundred million dollar and billion dollar companies must be geniuses to know so much." SECRET INSIGHT: This is just not so. Many of the founders of even billion dollar companies are not really any brighter than you are. Many of them believe they are brighter! But it's a case of the tail wagging the dog. Most people who build hugely successful companies are quite understandably highly confident and, in time, will start to believe that it is their inherent intelligence that was instrumental to their success. More on this later. The primary question is: How did they build a company that has such vast intellectual capabilities?

---

[1] In general, I will use male nouns and pronouns to mean any person, male or female, for gender is really immaterial to all issues discussed in this book. Everything applies equally to both sexes.

Let's take a simple example of a guy who wants to start a multimedia production company. By this, I mean a company that produces interactive CD-ROMs, maybe, Internet web pages, and, maybe, computer-based training for other companies. If you are not familiar with these areas, don't worry about it. It is not necessary to know exactly what this terminology means in order to fully understand this example. Let's say our entrepreneur is named Henry. Henry does know what the above terminology means. In fact, he also knows just what software can be used to create the above content.

Henry makes a list of "What I Need To Learn." The list includes Java, JavaScript, C, C++, Director, PhotoShop, Premier, Authorware and Sound Edit. He thinks, "OK, I need to be a good programmer. I need good artistic skills. I'd better be able to communicate clearly in writing. I'd better know something about sound and video editing. Some 3D modeling could come in useful. I should probably also know a bit about music scoring, and I will probably need to use some video within the CD-ROMs and computer-based training (CBT), so I'd better learn basic videography, also."

Poor old Henry has a big job ahead! But, he persists. He learns it! And, he creates his first complete multimedia piece. And, it sucks! Bummer. Well, Henry was a good programmer, better than most. But his artistic skills sucked, and it showed in his creation. His video was better than he initially expected, but it wasn't really that good, either. Henry simply could not do it all. No matter how hard he tried, he was just not mastering all of the areas he needed. He thought about going back to work for someone else. After all, that seemed so much easier!

My advice to Henry is to take a break. He's earned it. Go watch a movie. In fact, make it *The Magnificent Seven* with Yul Brynner. It's a great story. This little Mexican town is being pestered by bandits who take what little crops the town can produce. Further, the bandits are just downright rude when they visit. So, the little town collects what little money it has, presumably hidden from the bandits, and it goes to another slightly larger town to buy guns, so that the little town can defend itself. In their search for weaponry, the town representatives meet up with Yul Brynner, who, they hope, might be able to sell them guns. After all, Yul is a pretty tough-looking guy.

They go to Yul, and ask him, "Will you help us buy guns?" Yul listens to them, and he responds, "Why buy guns? Why not buy men? Men are cheaper than guns."

Never forget that line. If Henry really understands this line, he won't look at things the same way. If Henry wanted to be a consultant and "do it all" himself, then, his list of learning topics would be valid. But, why spend any time trying to master PhotoShop, a graphic arts program, when you are not an artist to begin with? You can find people to hire who are artists and who know it. If you can't justify hiring someone full-time, maybe, you could hire someone part-time. Maybe, you could scout the local technical colleges to see if any students would be interested in an internship. They gain experience and a reasonable entry-level wage, and you get a chance to evaluate their skills. Maybe, you already know someone with the skills you seek. Keep your eyes open and build contacts. Make lists of people who have skills that might be useful to the type of company you want to build.

Even if Henry learns PhotoShop well, does it really matter? Not if he is interested in *growing* his company. He can only do so much. Beyond some point, he will need to delegate, even if he is a master of the area under question. When you seek to hire others, you should always look for people who far exceed you in a given area that is important to your company. Even if you aren't putting people on staff, be sure to build contacts with these people, anyway, in case you ever need help.

I recall reading that, on average, any given person in the world is at most seven steps away from any other person in the world (no, this isn't one of those Stephen Covey things). This means that they know someone who knows someone who knows someone... four steps later...who knows the person. You just need to find the chain! Of course, this will depend upon how many people you know. The more contacts you have, the better. But, who cares about contacting a given person? The fact is that any person is usually only one of many people who can help you. If you need a top-notch person in, say, C++ computer programming, there are many great candidates. If you need a great salesperson, there are many of those also. You just need to be able to identify them. This means your chain of seven people is drastically reduced. Within one or two contacts, you should be able to find someone who suits your needs.

You, as the founder of your business, identify the skills crucial to your company's growth. To an extent, you can choose what skills are crucial by varying the type of business you form. If you start a company to write custom software for larger companies, then, yes, software programming is a crucial skill within your business. But, let's say, instead, that you start a matchmaking service (fixing up people with romantic interests, rather than making the matches that burn when struck). Is programming a crucial skill? The answer is: "I don't know enough about the business to tell you for sure, but my guess is no." If you have a dating service, using computer matching of individuals, maybe programming is a crucial skill (after all, it's the computer pairing the people up!), but, if you have a more personal service, matching people based upon personal interviews with someone on your staff, then, I would say the crucial skill is the ability to communicate with and understand your clients. It's more of a personal psychology skill. I will say more about choosing a business suited to the skills you want to see utilized within your company in the chapter on personality and business choice, but I want to reemphasize that *you* must *identify* the skills.

You cannot just say, "I want to start such-and-such-a-type of company, and I want these skills to be the ones used by my employees…" It doesn't work that way. To an extent, the industry you are in and the type of "work" your company does will determine these skills. If you believe one set of skills is required, when in reality an entirely different set of skills is required, you will run into problems.

In the ideal case, you will know someone you trust who has successfully built a company similar to the one you contemplate, a mentor, to help you understand what skills are most needed. The best mentor is someone who has not only built a company similar to yours, but who has also grown sick and tired of the industry and has sold his company. This person will not view you as competition. Be aware that not everyone will be interested in helping you or becoming part of your network of resources. That's OK. Just move on and seek other contacts. Despite hiring employees, and even if you have a good mentor, you will need to be the one to pass judgement on any business issues that significantly affect your company. You can never delegate that responsibility.

If your company grows larger, a good Board of Directors, consisting of people knowledgeable in the industry, can be a very valuable resource. You want people who can contribute to your organization. Many people want to hire people like themselves. Some business people hire people who, they feel, are "subordinate" to their own abilities. They want to hire people less talented than they are. Maybe, they have a fear of being outdone, of not looking as good as the employee. This is a good way to sabotage your company. Whenever you make a new hire, ask yourself, "What does this person bring to the company? In what area is this person superior to the people currently on staff?" You should hire people better than you.

Diversity of ability and skills is a huge benefit of having employees. But, how should you go about hiring? When you start out, there really is no need to post positions in newspaper employment sections and similar places. Don't you already have enough suitable candidates among the people you are currently networked with? This is a big advantage of a small company. As your company grows, you will need to post jobs or make them commonly available, rather than just recruit from you current contacts. That is a difficult area. When and if you reach this size, hire people adept at making good hiring decisions. A good recruiter may be your most valuable employee, especially if your employees have significant contact with your customers or clients.

Most experienced Human Resources (HR) people tend to be very conservative in terms of whom they will hire. They are aware of the potentially huge cost to the company of making a bad hire. They are *especially* aware of how the bad hire will reflect upon the judgement of the person doing the hiring! This is a simple example of risk and reward. If the HR person takes a chance and hires a questionable candidate, and the candidate becomes a great employee, there is little benefit to the HR person. It is the hired person who will get all the accolades! But, if the questionable candidate doesn't work out, then everyone, including the HR person's boss, will say, "What were you thinking, hiring this guy? He obviously was a bad hire." As a rule, people don't make decisions that can only lead to little benefit for them, but that could lead to considerable downside risk for them.

This hiring mentality is exactly what you need in many industries. If you are hiring people to work in a warehouse, there is little benefit to not weeding out people who might be a problem. The HR people look for a reason *not* to hire the person. If they find one, that person won't get the job. The chances that the person not hired would have been a stellar employee means little. The difference between a great worker and the average worker is not really that large. So, why take any chance hiring questionable candidates? In growing technology companies, this overly conservative approach of HR people can sometimes be a problem. Here, the difference between the most productive employee and the average employee can be huge. And, many of the best hires are a bit unique.

When I wonder about a given company's ability to grow through hiring, I am now asking myself, "If good Will Hunting applied for a job with this company, would he get it?" For those of you who don't know who Will Hunting is, you need to relax a bit more. Go rent a video called *Good Will Hunting*. In many cases, the company would pass on Will. Lack of experience, a dubious history, etc…would knock him out of the running for a job. Now, true geniuses are rare, but I know of cases where multiple companies passed upon hiring questionable candidates and the individuals went on to work for other companies and, instantly, became the companies' best programmers. One person, making $40,000 per year, outdid five experienced programmers, each making $100,000 annually. Was it a risky hire? Maybe. Was it a good hire? Definitely. The person's pay went up considerably, but the person was still a bargain.

Despite all I said about the value of growth via new employees, some of you might say, "Gosh, I just don't want the hassle of having employees. I'd rather go it alone." That's OK, of course. I'll say more about it in another chapter. But, what I said about developing a network to rely upon still applies. If you are too cut off, you will have trouble.

There are some crucial skills you should acquire before starting any business, areas with which you must at least feel somewhat comfortable. First, there is the area of human interaction. You must be comfortable speaking with other people. Enjoying it is best of all. Selling, in one form or another, is really an entrepreneur's best skill. Let's take the case of a company that will do computer consulting. It will send out programmers to help companies write code to manage their business better. The real key to this business is not the programming ability of the lead entrepreneur. In fact, several individuals with relatively few programming skills and little programming knowledge have built such companies. The real key is twofold.

One, you must find client companies to buy your product. This involves selling. Promotion. Maybe, taking a demo around to companies to show what you can do for them. There was a regular renaissance in this specialized-solutions-computer-consulting-programming field when Visual Basic appeared. Visual Basic made it fast and easy to create simple application programs for businesses. Many people, who were not programmers, saw how quickly a consultant could write code useful to their company. One day a consultant was at their company. The next day, there was a simple prototype of the application program that the company desired. The person assigned to work with the consultant thought to himself, "Hey, our competitors would really like this program. In fact, it would be easy to sell it to them. And, we have lots of competitors." Often the company employee who saw this teamed up with the consultant to build a custom-solutions-programming company serving a specific industry. Some of these companies have grown to have market values in the hundreds of millions of dollars, while other such companies were sold along the way, leaving the founding entrepreneur rich. In most cases, the lead entrepreneur was not even a programmer.

As demand grew and it was clear the company could sell even more slightly-modified versions of the same solution (application program), often, the computer programmer could no longer keep up. What happened was natural. And, it brings us to the second key in building such a company. That is hiring enough programmers to write the code. This is certainly not a technical skill. You don't need one iota of programming ability in your blood to seek out and hire programmers. It's more of a human resources job. So, you see, it's very possible for a nontechnical person to build a technical company.

Incidentally, as long as we are discussing this example of a custom-solutions provider, I should point out that such a company can grow from start-up to millions or tens of millions or even hundreds of millions of dollars in worth very quickly. All it really needs to grow is: 1) selling its product; and 2) hiring programmers to create the product. These are the only two things that can limit the growth rate of such a company. If you can add new clients and if you can produce what the clients want, you can expand quickly, incredibly fast, in fact. This is a great business model. You sell a high-end service; you hire people to perform the service; and you collect a good chunk of the payment for the service as the service is rendered or soon after. As you go, you gain experience and reputation which strengthen your company.

Most people are used to thinking in terms of manufacturing companies, which have a significant investment in plant and equipment. To produce widgets, you need widget-making machines. And, they cost a lot, $500,000 apiece, in fact. Each machine can only make 10,000 widgets a year. Not that the machines are unionized or anything, but they can only work so fast. You have one machine, and you are selling 9,900 units a year. Next year, you think you can sell 12,000 units. Well, gosh, you need another widget machine. And, maybe, a machine needs its own building. That means you need another building. Now, if the company is making $400,000 a year selling the 9,900 widgets, then, obviously, you can't internally fund the new machine from current one-year earnings. You could seek financing, but that means that the bank from which you borrow has a say in your growth. There won't be any growth, if they don't lend you the money!

Maybe, the overall economy is bad, and the bank won't lend you the money for the new machine. If you are a start-up company to begin with, your chances of getting bank financing are slim. And, even if you got it, you would probably pay a high interest rate. You don't want that. Because the expansion of the industrial company must involve significant capital investments and the growth in added capacity often must exceed the immediately recognizable sales increase, industrial companies have capital barriers to growth which information-based companies do not. Similarly, service companies, such as a dating service firm or a money management firm, are not really capital intensive. They tend to be "people businesses," where the most valuable company asset, next to reputation, consists of the employees and what they can do.

Because of the large number of businesses that can be started today that are not capital intensive, it really is the age of the entrepreneur. It's not like I imagine it was in the early 1900's when capital was the essential ingredient favoring the already rich in building new businesses. I will discuss this in the next chapter.

One final skill every entrepreneur must know is basic accounting and simple, financial decision making. You must know how to use numbers to not only track how much you are making, but also as input to evaluate possible directions you might take your company. Is Product A or Product B a better product for us at present? Questions like this crop up in every business, no matter what the industry. A few college classes in accounting or some self-study is really essential for all entrepreneurs who wish to attain a reasonably high level of success. Some things just can't be delegated. You must achieve a relative comfort with numerical decision making. This is not at all difficult, but it is essential. The rest of this book will take you far in that direction.

Chapter 4.
Intellectual Capital
and Bootstrapping

In this chapter, the term intellectual capital refers to not only intellectual capital but also creative capital or service capital—anything, in fact, that can be used to create wealth that does not involve plant, equipment, machinery, buildings, or other tangible assets. Today, intellectual capital is often the source of wealth created by companies. It is also the primary reason many companies can experience phenomenal growth rates. As mentioned previously, companies that must invest capital in plant and equipment will be limited in growth because of limits in available capital regardless of whether the capital comes from bootstrapping or from financing.

When building a start-up company, I would always tend to favor non-capital-intensive businesses. Service businesses. Businesses that create intellectual property. Not too long ago, a new company started up in Minnesota to compete with Harley-Davidson. The brothers who started this company were able to raise a good level of financing due to favorable stock and business market conditions. The survival rate for manufacturing companies that start at such a size is quite good. The company was touted as being in an excellent growth area—high-end motorcycles. While this may be true for the present and for even the past decade, it is not fully true, in general. In fact, the company name they chose, Excelsior-Henderson, once belonged to another manufacturer of bikes that did not survive along with many other such companies. Sole survivor Harley-Davidson remained. In other words, the high-end motorcycle business is more appropriately described as a cyclical area rather than a growth area. A bull stock market and economy tends to blur these distinctions. Further, promoters of such stocks (of IPO's) tend to encourage the false label in order to generate more investors for the company. Now, I'm not knocking Excelsior-Henderson. They seem to know what they are doing and have hired excellent people in the areas of engineering and business to help them. In this way, even manufacturing companies benefit from intellectual capital and experience, as well as physical assets.

But, if the stock market had not been so conducive, would the brothers have been able to raise the money to start-up from scratch? Certainly not as a public company. Would, on the other hand, a company, such as the dating service, It's Just Lunch, have been able to start? Yes. This is because the dating service is not a capital-intensive business. When you start a capital-intensive business, you are subjecting yourself far more to the vagaries of the general economy. While all types of businesses will suffer from a poorer economy, the ability to start a capital-intensive business might entirely depend upon the economy. Because of this, I strongly encourage entrepreneurs to give heavy preference to businesses that are not capital intensive. Many students of entrepreneurship tend to disagree with me on this one. They say choose the type of business you want, regardless of capital factors. Some businesses will, invariably, demand larger initial capital investments, and the entrepreneur must simply accept this. So, rather than choose another area or try to rescale a business that can't be rescaled, or effectively started at a smaller size, just seek external financing, i.e., equity investors.

I can't help but feel this view is, at least partly, based upon the easy availability of capital due to the bull stock market of the late 1980's and 1990's. My response to them is always, "What if you can't raise the capital? Suppose you write up your business plan, and everything is feasible. But, what if you still can't raise the capital?" You could try for several years to fund your start-up. Ultimately, whether or not you start would be a decision dependent upon someone else, the investors who back you. I would much rather have a business, which I could begin bootstrapping to a larger size, than be sitting and waiting for someone else's approval. Remember, four years could easily take you from a start-up to a self-sustaining business entity. In fact, in four years, your company could be worth millions, or even tens of millions of dollars, without ever raising a dime in equity financing.

You could respond, "Ah, but raising capital really is just selling a product (selling the idea of the company) like any other. And, if you have a good product, you should be able to find someone to sell it to." But, let's assume you don't really want external investors, i.e., equity capital. Or, like me, you are skeptical about being able to raise capital under all conditions. In this case, you must fund the venture yourself, and it seems obvious that you should avoid capital intensive businesses. This means that you should look to service companies or companies that create products that do not require large factories, machinery, etc..

But, what if you really *want* to build a motorcycle company? Bootstrap, but not fully within one type of business. Here is where many entrepreneurs tend to think in terms of projects, in terms of "What can I do now?" They know where they want to be in, say, ten years or what type of thing they want to be doing, sometimes. But, that is not always immediately possible. You choose a path that will get you where you want to go, a path that will better position you to do the thing you want to do. Most businesses do not continue to do only what they initially did. They evolve. They change. Opportunities will appear, and your company can change to pursue them. Change is good. Change is growth. New products will replace old products. Sometimes, there is a master plan. Other times there isn't.

But, don't fall into the trap of accepting society's "career paths." People will tell you, "To succeed at this, you must to do this. And, then, you must do that. To get into this field, you must to do this." That's just bunk. You must give sincere thought to the path you will follow. You must have some knowledge of the general industry you wish to be in for this to work. I can't say, "Do this, and you will succeed." It depends upon the industry, which is one reason mentors are good. They can show you the nontraditional paths within a given industry. One area I do know is the computer programming field. Many people want to enter the field of programming or network administration, because it is an in-demand field, at least as I write this, and they want to earn good money. That's understandable. What are some good entry methods?

Well, a degree in computer science is great. But, what if you don't want to spend that much time in college? No problem. Take a few classes in network administration at the local community college. That will give you some exposure. In particular, try to build some recommendations. Look into the various "certifications," such as Microsoft's Certified Systems Engineer. Basically, you take tests (and, give money to Microsoft. Would you expect them to have it any other way?) and, by passing those tests, you show that you know something about Microsoft's products, such as Windows NT. Best of all, look into what you can do for your present company. Could you help out the MIS staff? Would another smaller company, one that doesn't really want to pay the bucks to get a "real" network administrator, hire you to do simple stuff that could build your skills and give you experience in the field? This is all very common advice to a newbie network administrator and it is, by and large, valid.

However, look at the real purpose of the above actions. This really falls into two parts: One, trying to learn new skills that are needed, but that you don't already possess; and, two, getting those skills somehow *recognized* or *certified*, in effect, showing *others* you have the skills. A computer science degree is probably the best way to say, "Hey, I know what I'm doing in computer science. They wouldn't have given me the degree if I didn't." With most universities, this is true. Despite all the bad press about college graduates who can't read or write, most graduates do tend to know more than people without degrees in the area. Occasionally, the university or the people selling the skill training will become so focused upon making money that an entire supporting industry will develop to teach people the minimum they need to know in order to obtain the "certification." This happened with Novell NetWare, a network operating system. Books, courses, CBT, etc…sprang up to allow people to pass the tests, never mind getting a real understanding of what was being done and why. But, let's just pass the test. Get the important certification. Get a good job and worry about being able to actually administrate a network later. Students considered the training a success if they passed the tests. What happened is that companies in the know tended to devalue the importance of Novell certification. Maybe, it meant you knew something. Then, again, maybe not. It was viewed with more skepticism. The real losers were the students who had the certification and really did know something, but who were classified with the other "paper CNEs" (Certified Network Engineers).

Everything I've said is valid, if you want to be hired in the network administration field. The astute reader might even see why it would be more valuable to favor Microsoft's certification in preference to Novell's. But, what if you want to build a company in this field? How much of the above really applies? Well, learning skills needed is always good. It's pretty bad, if you run a company offering network consulting, and you know nothing about Windows NT. But, as pointed out in the chapter, "Men Are Cheaper Than Guns," you don't need to (and can't) know it all. So, while we can agree that Point One still has value, what about Point Two, getting our skills recognized by others? Is this important?

As a consultant, you might say, "Yes, obviously, it's even more important than as an employee." But, let's neglect this. In many ways being a computer consultant sucks. When you send out a computer consultant, the company is interested in the experience of the person you are sending and in your company's reputation to always send out highly-skilled people. The hiring company doesn't give a rat's ass about what you *personally* know about Windows NT, unless, of course, you are the one going out on the job. Let's assume you have higher aspirations in building a larger company. How important is being validated by others?

A hint. No doubt the best entry-level certification is a full computer science degree. How many founders of companies in the computer industry have computer science degrees? Hmm. Well, Bill Gates dropped out of Harvard. Steve Jobs and Steve Wozniak, the cofounders of Apple Computer, dropped out of several colleges. Larry Ellison, founder of the leading database company, Oracle, dropped out of college. Rick Born, founder of Born Informational Services, has a few technical college classes under his belt. That's all. Michael Dell dropped. The list could go on and on. How can all these founders of information-programming-based companies not have computer science degrees? And, yet they succeed!

The crucial factor is these entrepreneurs were thinking in terms of "What product can I create to sell to others?" rather than in terms of "How can I show others what I know, so they will hire me?" Traditional career path advice is heavily slanted toward showing others what you can do without actually doing it. Traditional paths are concerned with winning acceptance from others. "Yeah, he knows what he's doing. He got straight A's and great recommendations. Let's hire him." Traditional career path advice is slanted to the belief that you need to convince someone else to "give you a chance" to succeed.

Yet, when you buy a product, do you really ask which individual produced it? Usually not. You go by reviews of others, reviews of the *product*, not reviews of the creators, not, usually, even reviews of the company creating the product—although the company's reputation might influence your decision. A person only has so much energy to expend in life, and you must decide where to expend it. It's fun and reassuring to have multiple projects in the hopper, various ideas you contemplate pursuing, different things you are working on or learning. But, once you start down a particular path, you can only split your time in so many ways before you wind up sabotaging yourself. Have you ever tried to do too much at one time, and, as a result, you didn't do well at any of the things you were trying to do?

In a college computer science program, you will learn dozens of different aspects of computer programming, most of which won't be applicable to what you will do in the "real" world. Taking a dozen classes and using what you learned from only two is not a good return on your investment of personal time. Once you start creating a product, chances are you will need to learn many things that weren't covered in any class, anyway. You may as well spend your time learning the things, as needed, to create your product.

Entrepreneurs tend to focus upon creating the best product they can at the time and, then, marketing it. That is the priority, not impressing others with their qualifications to enter the field. It's really a question of knowing what is really important. Is doing it important, or is showing off important? Show off by doing! While most people tend to think in terms of "If I work hard enough and do a good enough job, then, I'll be recommended for a promotion," as the best career path, entrepreneurs think, "How do I get where I want to go? How can I bootstrap myself up?"

For those unfamiliar with the term "bootstrapping," I should probably define it. It refers to "pulling yourself up by your bootstraps," starting with whatever you have to work with and building from it. Compounding it and shaping it, so that you work toward your goal. Maybe, a better, visual way of thinking of this is trying to elevate yourself higher and higher. Imagine trying to get a whiffle ball out of a tree. You can't reach it. You tossed another ball up there to knock it down. But, now, the second ball is trapped up there also. You look around to see what you could stand on. What you see is a picnic table and benches. You bring one of the benches over. But, it's not high enough. So you bring over the table. It's not high enough, either. But, then, you stack the bench on top of the table, and, Walla, you can reach the balls. That's bootstrapping in a nutshell.

Our visual example is bad in that it gives the impression that bootstrapping is inherently unstable. If we were to put the second bench on top of the first, which was on top of the table, we might not feel comfortable standing on it. We don't want our creation to come toppling down. Especially if we are standing on top of it! But, the stability with which you build the base is totally unrelated to the concept of bootstrapping. Some entrepreneurs bootstrap rapidly, giving little thought to the stability of the base. They expand their business as rapidly as they can. They keep little in reserve. Others tend to be more cautions. They are sure the base is secure before they start adding to it. Some are so conservative, they fear the base is never stable enough, so despite having made it solid, they continue working upon the base and never get to the second platform of the pyramid.

Bootstrapping means using whatever resources are at hand to go in the correct direction, to make what progress you can. Many non-entrepreneurs don't really see how bootstrapping can help them. They say, "Yeah, I see I could do that. But, so what? What I really want is just so far away I'll never get there by bootstrapping." Then they never exert the effort to make progress at all. That's not unreasonable from their perspective. It is fundamental risk/return analysis! Why do something, if you don't see any gain from it? But, they are making a major error. They miss the fact that bootstrapping often involves the *compounding property*. By this, I mean, that as you make each incremental gain, that gain becomes the base from which you can make newer gains. This is the same principle as compounding money through reinvestment. It's not always easy to see just how far you can go. You see the limits, but you miss the compounding nature inherent to business and bootstrapping. And, yet, this compounding nature of bootstrapping is exactly how most businesses are built to a substantial size. Once you understand the compounding property, you will understand how businesses grow. I cover compounding in detail in Chapter 16.

Regarding business, whiffle balls aside, bootstrapping means using current earnings to reinvest in producing more products, either more of the same product or entirely new products.[1] You sell your products and generate some profits. This all occurs over some time period we will call the interval cycle, or compounding cycle, or cash flow cycle. What exactly you choose to call this cycle is unimportant. What is important is to know that it exists. There *is* some time period over which products are produced, marketed, sold, and the sales revenue is collected for that set of products. Then, the process can start all over with slightly more money to produce more products to sell.

Let's suppose you have invented a new board game called, "Lifer." Producing Lifers is easy. You outsource manufacturing of the board and the player pieces to a fictitious company called, "We Do Games." You will market the games yourself via direct mail, the Internet, and various advertisements. Suppose that We Do Games tells you it can

---

[1]Some people will see that, maybe, I should more properly use the term cash flow rather than current earnings. I don't want to make any distinction between which term is more proper or best at present, nor even to distinguish between the two. I think for most nonbusiness people, the term, current earnings, will most clearly convey the idea I want to express. Getting into cash flow is counterproductive at present.

produce 1,000 Lifers for $5,000. That sounds high, but Lifers are really complex with lots of special pieces, and you can't find a better manufacturing price from another source. Further, you know that to set up a plant to actually build Lifers is too high a cost for you. Even if you could fund the manufacturing shop yourself, you are not sure you can sell Lifers, and, so, you decide it is safer, at the onset, at least, to outsource manufacturing. So, your cost to manufacture a Lifer is $5. This is referred to as your cost of goods sold (cogs). Other costs that are properly allocated to the individual game units could also be included in cogs, such as any shipping charges We Do Games charges you when they ship you your 1,000 Lifers. We will assume the cogs of a Lifer is $5 which is just the total production cost divided by the number of units (Lifers) produced. You can only afford to make 1,000 Lifers.

You decide you will price your Lifers at $20 retail. Maybe, that's a bit high. But, it is a high-quality game. You might do some price testing to see what people are willing to pay for your game and set your price accordingly, later, but, for now, you need a price, and you've chosen $20. The big day comes, and your Lifers arrive. You have 1,000 Lifers in your garage and starry-eyed dreams of competing with Hasbro, Mattel, and the other big toy and game manufacturers. You try to market your Lifers, and, immediately, you discover the following: 1) Internet sales just aren't happening. No one wants to send you his credit card number over the Internet just to buy a Lifer. They don't know you. They don't know your company. They pass; 2) Your direct mail plans, also, just aren't working. You are not generating enough sales to recoup your promotional costs. So you nix both the Internet and direct mail as marketing channels. And, they both seemed like such good ideas!

However, there is some good news on the Lifer front. A couple of the chain stores have agreed to try selling your game, and the few units they put on the shelves sold out. They want to order more. Now, they only pay you $10 per Lifer. The other $10 of the Lifer's retail selling price is the retailer's mark-up. The retailers have a 50 percent cogs ($10) for Lifers relative to their selling price of $20. You have a cogs of $5 which is only 25 percent of the retail selling price of $20.

But, as you only collect $10 per Lifer sold, your cogs ($5) is also 50 percent when compared to the actual revenue a Lifer sale generates to you ($10). We will ignore all the other costs associated with selling Lifers. In particular, there is no order fulfillment cost allocated to shipping the Lifers to the retail seller. Nor is there any allowance for overhead, etc. We want to keep the example simple.

The net result is that you sell your 1,000 lifers. The retail store pays you $10,000. You paid your manufacturer, We Do Games, $5,000 so you made $5,000. Not bad at all. That's a 100% return on your initial investment of $5,000. Not even a bull stock market would ever give you such a rate of return on your investment within a year. You should be pleased. But things are even better than this. For the retail stores are clamoring for more Lifers. And, a crucial neglected fact is, "What exactly was the period over which my business investment compounded to a 100% return?" Now, if we are in time-lapse photography, and it is ten years later, before you have sold your 1,000 Lifers, I have bad news for you. Your Lifers suck as an investment. Sure, you got a 100% rate of return, but it took you a decade to do it. That amounts to only a seven percent annual rate of return. But, that isn't what's happened. It didn't take a decade to sell your 1,000 Lifers. It only took 6 months. So you really don't have a 100% annual rate of return. You have a 100% rate of return within 6 months. Your compounding interval is 6 months or half a year, not one year. You might want to give this some real thought. This is a crucial aspect of business and is discussed more on the chapter on compounding.

Now, even the most basic analysis shows you that you are compounding your money at a rate of at least 200% annually. For you could use your initial investment sum of $5,000 to buy 1,000 Lifers and sell them over 6 months (which you already did), then turn around and buy 1,000 more Lifers 6 months later (the present actually, as you have been selling Lifers for 6 months now) and sell them over the next 6 months. That's 2,000 Lifers sold in one year, and you have made $10,000 on your initial investment of $5,000 in exactly one year ($10,000 return on $5,000 is 200%). This shows that the compounding interval is just as important as the rate of return. Compounding intervals for small and start-up companies vary, obviously, but usually are much shorter than one year. Compounding intervals tend to be shortest for non-capital intensive businesses and businesses which have high gross and net margins.

But things are even better! For our simple analysis above actually neglects compounding entirely. This is because it makes no use of the money made on the initial $5,000 investment as reinvestment funds to produce even more Lifers. Remember, 6 months down the road, you not only have your initial investment of $5,000 returned to you (which you can turn around and spend to invest in another 1,000 Lifers), but you also have the profits made on the first set of 1,000 sales. That amount was $5,000 if you recall. What this means is that you can order not 1,000 Lifers on your second production run, but rather, you can order 2,000. This is because you have your initial investment of $5,000 and, now, you also have the profits on the first set of sales which is also $5,000. You have $10,000 to reinvest in more Lifers. A Lifer costs $5 per unit to produce, so you can produce 2,000 of the little buggers.

So, assuming the Lifer market demand is there, within the year you could have sold a total of 3,000 Lifers—1,000 from the first production run and 2,000 from the second production run. You made $15,000 which is a 300% return on your initial investment within one year. Your initial investment of $5,000 was enough to produce not just 1,000 Lifers in your first year, but it was enough to produce a total of 3,000 Lifers, which had a total production cost of $15,000. This is the power of compounding as applied to business activity. It is an immense force. As long as the market demand for your product is sufficient, you can keep reinvesting the money made on previous sales to produce more units to sell. Never was more money put into the company. There was no new so-called equity financing or borrowing in addition to the initial $5,000. The growth was the result of bootstrapping. More correctly, the growth was really the result of being able to sell more and more Lifers, but the capital to produce the Lifers came from reinvestment of earnings.

Notice, at the end of the year, you have $20,000 which is just the sum of your initial $5,000 and the $15,000 profit you made throughout the year. Because your money doubles every six months and there are two such periods within one year, at the end of the year, you have four times your initial amount. So, as long as the Lifer demand remains, you will multiply whatever capital you start a year with by a factor of four to determine how much capital you end the year with. So, you could calculate that at the end of your *second* year, you will have four times $20,000 or $80,000 in equity.

As a preview to compounding: If there are n compounding periods within one year, and you compound your money at a rate of return given by R (expressed not as a percentage, but as a decimal) for each of these sub-year periods, then, within one year, your money grows to become the initial amount times $(1+R)^n$. Here R=100% or expressed as a decimal just 1, and n is 2. The factor $(1+R)^n$ is 4. This is equivalent to a one-year 300% rate of return whose multiplying factor is calculated as $(1+3)^1$.

Reinvestment of earnings is how real growth businesses get most of their financing. It's not by selling more and more stock to investors. It's not by borrowing more and more money from lenders. Yes, those are ways to increase your working capital, but to really grow involves generating more and more sales. With those sales come profits to be reinvested which are used to…generate more sales. Now, neglecting the effect of taxes, you can see how businesses can grow rapidly. In particular, we have shown that our business creating Lifers is generating a 300% annual return on the initial investment. Suppose the company could continue growing like this for five years, i.e., there is no market limit to growth for this time. The initial $5,000 investment would grow to $5,120,000. In eight years, the amount would become $327 million dollars! That's not a typo. That's $327,000,000. In ten years, the amount would compound to $5,243,000,000. Five billion two hundred and forty three million and change neglected. In twelve years, the amount would be $83,886,000,000 or eighty-three billion eight hundred and eighty-six million and change neglected.

The above should serve to convince you of the importance of compounding and bootstrapping in building a business. If you ever really want to build large levels of wealth, this is worth understanding. If there are aspects you don't understand, reread it, again and again.

Read the chapter on compounding. Maybe look at a mathematics book on investing or seek out a college class that covers this. Now, obviously, our hypothetical company could not continue growing like this forever. Probably not even for five years, in fact. After all, only so many people will buy the Lifer game. Further, as the company grows, it will find itself taking on overhead expenses. Are you going to pack and ship all those Lifer games yourself when sales are in the millions? Where will you store all the inventory before it is shipped to the retailers? In practice, there will be constraints on a company's growth. Often, it will be the level of sales you can generate with a given product. You will be market limited. If Lifer sales started floundering, it would be smart to start trying to come up with other games to market. You would already have the retail channels lined up. The retailers would know you are a serious business person they have worked with before.

Now suppose that in our idealized example, Lifer sales do continue unlimited, and the costs and the profits are as above. At some point, your success would be noticed by other entrepreneurs and business people. They would think to themselves, "Lifers really are profitable. Maybe, we should be in the Lifer business." Suddenly, there is another company producing Lifers. The games they make are exactly like yours, but rather than charging retail stores $10 per Lifer, your new competitor is only charging $9. Where will the retailers buy Lifers from? The other company, of course! The only way for you to get back the lost sales is to charge less, say $8 per Lifer. But this means you are only making $3 per Lifer profit now. Your growth rate will be lower. But, your situation is even worse. Your competitor drops their Lifer price to $7. You drop your price to $6. You are only making $1 profit per Lifer now, only one-fifth of what you were originally making. The Lifer business is getting really tough. "But, at least, it won't get any worse," you think.

Your competitor drops their price to $5 per Lifer. "They can't do that! That's insane. They won't make any money." But your competitor has found a way to manufacture Lifers for $4 apiece rather than $5. To be competitive, you now need to lower your Lifer production costs. If you can't do this, you're out of the Lifer business. Lifers have become a commodity. They are available from several sources, and the only factor that really distinguishes your Lifers from your competitors' is price. You don't want to be in a business where the low cost competitor wins. It's tough to survive, let alone make money and grow. What you want is a monopoly on the Lifer game market. And, you could have gotten it. You could have copyrighted your game. Then, you alone would have control over how Lifers were sold. No other company could just move in and start selling Lifers exactly like yours.

Copyrights and patents give you *proprietary* products. Proprietary products are products that for whatever reason are exclusively controlled by one company (technically, several companies could share patent rights, but that's a nit-picky detail that doesn't concern us). If the market demand exists for a product, and the product is not proprietary, you will have great difficulty bootstrapping to a much higher level of sales. You could only produce 3,000 Lifers in your first year without external financing. This doesn't change if the demand for Lifers is 300,000 per year.[2] If the product is *not* proprietary, your competitors and the market will not simply wait as you bootstrap yourself to riches! Someone with more capital will fulfill the 300,000 orders, and they will become the dominant player in the Lifer industry. Never mind that *you* were the one who showed that the Lifer market existed in the first place! With a proprietary product and huge demand, you will be in control. You will probably be able to raise the working capital to immediately fulfill all the orders. Even if you cannot raise enough money to fulfill all the orders, at least, you would be able to raise your selling price. Some retailers would be willing to pay more to get the much in-demand Lifers! They will charge the end buyer more.

[2]Notice, I'm not saying why you can only produce 3,000 Lifers in one year. This is just our assumption. Saying that you can only produce 3,000 Lifers in one year is equivalent to saying that your compounding cycle is six months. It might be that the retailers only pay you every six months, or it might be that you can only schedule two production runs per year. The possible limitations upon how many compounding cycles will fit into one year is discussed in detail in Chapter 16.

Each Christmas, there is at least one hot, hard-to-get toy everyone seems to want. And, some parents pay ungodly amounts for one. If the market demand for Lifers remained strong, you could bootstrap yourself to riches if you had proprietary control. Or, maybe, you could just sell your proprietary rights to another company that could produce all the little 300,000 Lifers. You might collect a royalty for each sale, or maybe a significant one-time payment, or maybe some combination of the two. Controlling an in-demand proprietary product gives you options, and it allows you to keep your prices and, hence, profit margins high.

Notice, I said a proprietary product is one that is exclusively controlled by one company *for whatever reason*. It could be legal copyright or patent protection that gives the company exclusive control, but the product could essentially be proprietary due to other factors.

The common example is the trade secret product. No one else has the secret decoder ring or the secret recipe to make the product. You guard that information with your life! If no one else can do what your company can do, you have a monopoly on the market. You have a proprietary product. Some companies like Coke-a-Cola really play this up. However, there is no product, that once on the market, cannot be reverse engineered, understood, and reproduced. In fact, even with full legal patent protection, there are few products that cannot be analyzed by your competitors who then turn around and replicate the underlying *idea* of your product. Pure trade secret protection isn't all it's cracked up to be. It is usually only naive companies who believe that they have a stranglehold on some body of knowledge. In fact, it usually works in the reverse direction. The best entrepreneurs, upon seeing a good opportunity, know that they must act fast or else someone else will beat them to the market with their own version of the product or idea.

Some entrepreneurs realize the above, but they figure, "Maybe we can't prevent others from copying us, but we sure can be the front runner, the pacesetter, or the leading company in our industry. We will innovate so rapidly that no one can keep up." This is a tough, tough road. Innovation alone will not lead to success. However, it can lead to a reputation. One form of proprietary product that does tend to work is proprietary ownership based upon *reputation*. Clients or consumers buy your product due to the company's strong reputation or name brand recognition. This is especially true for companies which provide services, and it is the reason you should try to build a great reputation for your business. Clients will pay more for a service, if they feel that the company providing the service is one of the best.

There is one case where you can effectively get the benefit of a proprietary product, protection from competition, for, at least, a period of time, despite having no actual proprietary control. This is the case where the demand for the product is so immense that demand exceeds the total capacity of all the companies capable of producing the product. In time, the business will become competitive and difficult, but for awhile, there will be no competitor limiting your growth or profit margins.

The Lifer example chosen is a difficult product to classify in that even though it is a manufactured product, its manufacture is being outsourced. How would you classify such a product? Is it a manufactured product, or is it more of an intellectually-created-informational product? Is it a bit of both? You might think I'm dwelling on a trifle of a point. But it's not a trifle. It's important. Where is the value of this product? Where was the value created? Why was this product such a good choice for bootstrapping? For use in our example? What are good characteristics of a product for a company that wishes rapid growth via bootstrap financing? What difficulties might the product run into? Give some thought to these questions before moving on to the next chapter.

Chapter 5.
The Importance of Margins

The last chapter left you with questions, a whole lot of them. This chapter will answer them. Lifer was a good product because 1) it sold! and 2) it had low overall production, marketing, and fulfillment costs per unit relative to the price for which it was sold. We never gave the company that invented Lifers a name. I guess, when you get busy with selling, some things get missed! Well, since the product Lifer did so well for us, let's call our company Lifer Limited. Yes, it will be a corporation.[1] So 2) is more properly stated that Lifer had low production costs per unit relative to the price for which it was sold by Lifer Limited. We are not concerned here with the retail price that Lifer sold for on the shelves. We are concerned with the actual revenue it brought our company, Lifer Limited. Another way of saying 2) is that Lifer had high gross profit margins. Equivalently, we can say the cogs for the product Lifer is a relatively small ratio of the price Lifer Limited collects for it.

Every product or service sold has some production or fulfillment cost associated with it, the so-called cost of goods sold (cogs). Gross profit margins refer to the percentage of your sales price that you keep after cost of goods sold is deducted. With Lifers selling for $10 to the retailers, your sales price is $10. Your cogs was $5 per unit (the manufacturing cost). Hence, your gross profit margin on Lifers is

---

[1] Whenever you see the terms Limited, L.T.D., Corp., or Incorporated, they refer to a special type of business entity called a corporation. There is nothing really special or mysterious about corporations, regarding day-to-day operations.

50% ($5/$10 x 100, where the 100 is required to convert to a percent). Now, for a real company, other factors can and will enter into cogs. In particular, if there is some shipping cost associated with the units being sent to you, then this cost should be added to your total cogs. For example, if We Do Games charges you $100 to ship your order of 1,000 Lifers, then you could calculate your gross margin as follows:

$$\text{Gross Margin} = \frac{100 \times (\text{Total Sales Price} - \text{Total Cost})}{\text{Total Sales Price}}$$

Total Sales Price is the total revenue you collect for the "bag of goods" in question. For us, "bag of goods" would be the 1,000 Lifers. Total Cost is your total cost to acquire the "bag of goods" which is the $5,000 manufacturing cost plus the shipping cost of $100. Notice that the factor of 100 is present to convert from a fraction into a percentage. It doesn't really matter if you calculate in terms of fractions or percentages, as long as you know what the terms mean.

$$\text{Gross Margin} = 100 \times (10,000 - 5,100) / 10,000 = 49\%$$

From this value of gross margin, you can quickly see what your cogs *per unit* is. Because you are selling your Lifers for $10 apiece and the gross margin is 49%, you make $4.90 per unit sold, and your cogs must be the difference between what you make as gross profit and your selling cost. Hence, cogs per unit = $10 - $4.90 = $5.10. Your cogs has risen by ten cents per unit. This makes sense, if you think about it. For your costs have risen by the shipping charge of $100. You have 1,000 units to amortize this cost over. Hence, your costs rise by $100/1,000 = $0.10.

Now, there are other costs involved with selling Lifers which we have neglected such as overhead. The question is which costs should be added to cogs? The first guess might be, "All costs that apply to selling the product." This is not fully correct. There are some costs which from a logical standpoint cannot be properly allocated to cogs. These are expenses which really do not relate to any particular product. For example, if you have a building to store and manufacture your games, how should the rent be allocated to the individual units? Although you could do it, it really serves no purpose. The rent is a larger cost of keeping the business running. To try to allocate it to individual units will just confuse the issue. The cost really doesn't relate to individual units. In general, when doing business-financial planning, your goal should be to accurately portray how your business is functioning. You want your financial analysis to mirror how expenses are incurred. This is the only way you can get a handle on expenses, i.e., to know where the expenses are coming from. If you know this, you can make better business decisions.

While there are more complex accounting ways to try to evaluate a business, such as activity-based accounting, for most endeavors just breaking costs into those clearly associated with the product (into cogs) and those not clearly associated with the product is more than sufficient. As a rule, if your business doesn't seem feasible using the simpler methods of financial analysis, it will not become feasible when you do a more sophisticated analysis.

There is always the danger of the "hope" factor entering into your analysis. As you plan a new product, you really want to see it succeed. You hope it works. That is good. That is OK. What is not OK is deceiving yourself about the true costs involved. Nor should you overpredict sales. Sales potential is usually difficult to estimate with accuracy, but there is little excuse for not having accurate estimates of your costs. In particular, your cogs. This just involves researching the costs that go into your product. If your cogs is a strong function of sales volume, the per unit cost usually dropping with increasing volume, then, you should know your cogs as a function of sales volume for any reasonable sales volume.

Now you might ask, "But what about the other costs like overhead?" Clearly, we must recoup and allow for these costs. In particular, there is some amortization necessary, in the sense that sales must be sufficient to offset these costs. However, these costs are not merged with cogs. Rather, they are subtracted after cogs is calculated. Assume Lifers Limited has $2,000 in overhead.

Below are Lifer's income statement calculations.

Total Sales of Lifers 1,000 units at $10.00 apiece is	$10,000
Cogs for the 1,000 Lifers	- 5,100
Gross profits from sales of 1,000 Lifers	4,900
Expenses not accounted for in cogs	- 2,000
Net profits before taxes	2,900

Notice that overhead and costs amortized into cogs take a heavy toll on the overall profits. Before, we were assuming profits of $5,000 for every 1,000 Lifers sold. Now, they are reduced to only $2,900. Such is Life. Net Profits are the "bottom line" (because they appear at the bottom line of the income statement), and they also allow us to calculate the net profit margin. The net profit margin is calculated just like the gross profit margin, except that now all expenses are allowed for, rather than just those costs that could be clearly allocated to cogs. In our example, our net profit margin is 29% (2,900/10,000). That's not bad! It's quite good, in fact. A common question new entrepreneurs have is, "What are typical gross and net profit margins?" There is no hard and fast answer. This is heavily dependent upon the type of business, i.e., what industry it is in. It often also depends upon the size of the business. Smaller businesses often can maintain higher gross and net profit margins. The best way to estimate *your* margins is to decide upon what you feel is a reasonable selling price for your product. Assume a reasonable production run. Then, research the direct costs of that production run, the costs directly associated with the product, i.e., cogs. Finally, to estimate net margins, subtract an estimate of all the costs incurred that do not properly belong to cogs. Be sure not to overlook any significant costs!

This brings us to the key observation of this chapter. The above analysis is not really anything special. You can find similar analyses in thousands of business books. Anyone who has operated a business will be familiar with the calculations. There is no magic there. Anyone can learn it. What is not always recognized is the importance of margins. By this, I mean the importance of margins in growing, compounding, and bootstrapping a business. Don't just think of margins as some calculation you can make *after* you are selling a product. If you are only doing these calculations *after* you are selling a product, you are missing the point. These calculations can be used to help you evaluate the desirability of any given product. The best entrepreneurs always do such analysis. It helps them choose the most desirable and profitable product to produce. Before I continue, I must point out one technicality. In the above, I calculated net profits before taxes. But taxes are a real expense. You must pay them. They are not an expense in the usual sense. You only pay them when you make a profit! From a product evaluation standpoint, you neglect taxes entirely and calculate net profits before taxes. If you think about it, the taxes you pay on any profits you make should not enter into any decision about which of two given products represents the better opportunity.

You can also allow for taxes and calculate net profits after taxes. In business literature and income statements, this is often referred to as net profits. In other words, net profit is an overloaded word. Some use it to mean one thing, while other people use it to mean another. Some use it to mean profits before taxes. Others use it to mean profits after taxes. There is not much you can do about this, but it will never be a problem if you simply ask the question, "Are we talking about net profits before taxes or net profits after taxes?" If you are contemplating buying a business or investing in one, knowing what the term means is crucial. In most cases, you should be able to tell from the income statement. Just look for an expense line that corresponds to income taxes. When you are doing the calculations yourself, as in evaluating a potential product or calculating how much your business made in the year, confusion should never arise. You know which one you are calculating! By writing "before taxes" or "after taxes" you help eliminate confusion later. Always use the explicit expressions.

Let's conclude our Lifer example by calculating net profits after taxes are paid. We will assume a tax rate of one-third or 33.3%. As you recall, we made $2,900 before taxes. So our tax will be $2,900 x 33.3% or $965.70. I guess the lesson here is that taxes suck. They really reduce the amount of money you make. Your net profits after taxes are $2,900 - $965.70 = $1934.30. This amounts to net profit margins after taxes of about 19.3%. Our income statement is as follows:

Total Sales of Lifers 1,000 units at $10.00 apiece is	$10,000
Cogs for the 1,000 Lifers	- 5,100
Gross profits from sales of 1,000 Lifers	4,900
Expenses not accounted for in cogs	- 2,000
Net profits before taxes	2,900
Tax Expense (33.3% tax rate)	- 965.70
Net profits after taxes	1934.30

We have said the most valuable use of these calculations is in evaluating product desirability and those calculations always involve pre-tax amounts. So, why did I want to explicitly show the after tax calculation? It has crucial value. For this is the truest measure of the "bottom line" amount of money that you make in a given venture. Recall that in the last chapter the large levels of wealth were computed with artificial values. We just, for simplicity, used gross profits. We neglected overhead and taxes. But, in real life, the possible bootstrapping-financial rate of growth will be calculated using profits *after all expenses including taxes*. In other words, the amount of money you have, after paying taxes, is what you have to reinvest and grow your business for the next year. Now, I know there are some out there asking, "Hmm…but couldn't I find a way to defer the taxes and pay them later? By doing so, I'd have the full amount of money to use for reinvestment in the business." My answer to this is, "Yes." You can find ways to effectively defer taxes. However, I would be very, *very* careful here. It is a horrible feeling, knowing that you have a substantial tax bill due, but don't have the cash to pay it. You made the profits, but your money is all tied up in Lifers and other games. Bad situation. Trust me, you don't want this. You can't just send the government several boxes of Lifers as payment in full for your taxes!

You might decide it best to just bite the bullet, pay the taxes, and forego all the fancy tax-deferral tricks. Accept the fact that, when you are making money, you will be taxed. Pay the taxes and move on with your business. I have heard of cases where a business was going well, and the entrepreneur was really financially sharp in reinvesting profits in a tax-deferred way. Then, one day, the jig is up. The government wants some money. A lot of money. "But, I don't have it," the entrepreneur says. That's the end of the business. It wouldn't have happened, if the entrepreneur simply had been "honest" in paying taxes. Sincere entrepreneurs don't waste time playing with tax gimmicks. My rule of thumb is, "If you can go to jail for it, it's probably not worth it. If it can close your business if it doesn't work, it's probably not worth it."

Now, if you were to go back and use 19.3% as your semi-annual rate of compounding rather than 100%, you might be quite disappointed. You won't be worth billions of dollars in a few short years by selling Lifers. Bummer! That does not invalidate the point made in that chapter. Compounding growth is a tremendous force, and reinvestment of earnings to bootstrap to higher levels of sales is the best source of growth capital for your business. The correct compounding rates to use are the true after-tax net profit margin rates (19.34% semi-annual return is a 42% annual rate of return). The reason why it would take so much longer to earn an equal amount of money, using a 42% annual rate of return, rather than, say, a 300% rate of return is because of the mathematics of compounding. There is about a factor of seven difference between these two compounding rates! And, because compounding is exponential growth, the amount of money you will have is not merely reduced by only a factor of one-seventh. It is reduced much, much more. Yet, we only added a few more modest expenses to our income statement. What is the lesson here?

The reason we could grow Lifer Limited so fast, when we were earning profits of $5 per Lifer, was that with each Lifer sold, we could use the $5 earned to produce another new Lifer to sell. When we accounted for all expenses, we had roughly a 20% margin. This meant that we had to sell five Lifers in order to have the funds to produce another new Lifer to sell. Suppose we had made $10 profit per Lifer, and it still only cost $5 to manufacture and sell one. Then, we could reinvest in *two* new Lifers to sell for every one we sold. At heart, this is the reason why high overall profit margins are desirable. For every item or service sold, you get back a sizeable profit to reinvest. Because the cogs is relatively low, you can reinvest rapidly to produce more units to sell. Your level of wealth compounds much quicker. The only way to maintain high net profit margins is by maintaining high gross profit margins.

I never answered the question about typical net profit margins for businesses. While it is true that profit margins really are unique to any business, there are general industry margins representative or typical of what companies in any given industry earn. Let's look at a few examples. All the margins discussed below are net-after-tax profit margins. First, consider a common retail seller or manufacturing company. Dell Computer would be a representative. So would stores like Wal-Mart (we will neglect the fact that these are much larger businesses than the typical start-up. In fact, start-ups can often maintain higher margins). For these businesses, 5% is a reasonable estimate of margin. Now 5% is way below the margins we were dealing with above for our Lifers. Yet, 5% is sort of the "standard" profit margin which business thinkers keep in mind. Many companies have decent growth and never achieve better than 5% margins. This means that for every $5 your company earns you must generate $100 in sales. You must sell twenty times your product to have enough to recreate one of your product! Ouch! Such companies often leverage their growth by making use of trade credit, debt, or equity financing. This way they can finance more of their product to sell. Trade credit is most typical. Yet, this is inherently dangerous. There is nothing wrong with trade credit, or financing, but when you are forced into it to grow, it is a weakness of the business model.

Even worse are companies in, say, the grocery business. Here margins can become only 1% or 2%. Some mail-order companies find, through catalog sales, they can sell more and more of their products. However, they cannot maintain a decent margin. They might only get a tenuous 2%. Apparel manufacture is another industry where, despite high gross margins, the net margin is often only a few percent. This is because most of the mark-up in price is given to the apparel retailer. "So, the retailer is the one getting rich," you say. Not quite. The retailer needs this mark-up to cover the overhead of keeping a large floor area store open. Often, the apparel retailer also only has a net margin of one or two percent. Restaurants are another game, where in Sylvester Stallone's immortal words in Rocky, "You are almost certain to wind up a bum." Restaurants have low overall margins simply because you need to sell a hell of a lot of $2 hamburgers to pay the rent.

I always think of these businesses as a man standing with a little tin cup and reaching out over a ledge into Niagara Falls to get a drink of water. If all goes well, he'll get his drink of water. Most of the water will just pass by. And, because of the rushing torrent, much of what enters his cup will get displaced by the huge flow of water hitting his cup. He will pull his cup away half empty. But, if he reaches too far or loses his balance, he will be carried away with the torrent of water. Going down the raging falls will, of course, kill him. Oh, yes, and I haven't mentioned that many other people, seeing the huge, clear, gushing stream of water, will also run to the ledge with their tin cups. There will be a lot of pushing and shoving as everyone tries to get close to the edge by the water. Some will be trampled right off the ledge! Someone will look at all the people with the little cups and say, "Fools, all that water, and all they bring are cups." This person goes and grabs a huge pail, gets his position on the ledge, and watches his pail fill up thinking, "I've got this mastered." Then, all of a sudden, his pail is heavy, his arms tremble, and he simply can't hold onto his pail anymore. It's too late to just drop it. The momentum has overcome the time needed to come to that decision, and he too is carried to his doom.

Low margin businesses are the same. What happens if you are earning a "solid" 2% on your sales? You need $100 in sales to generate a measly $2 in profits! This implies your costs of doing business are $98—or almost 100% of sales! What happens if your overall costs increase by, say, 2%? Basically, your profits are wiped out. You truly are in the business only for the fun of it! What if your costs go up another couple of percent? Ick. You are losing money. That can only go on so long before, what is the technical term they use for it?... oh, yes, bankruptcy, scandal, shame, a guardian angel to make you realize that money really isn't all there is to life! What if sales drop and your expenses stay about the same? This often happens in businesses with large plant and equipment or to businesses that have large retail floor space and large relative overhead as a percentage of sales. Low margin businesses tend to be hit hard by bad financial times. They often tend to be cyclical with the economy.[2]

Now, let's consider the other end of the margin spectrum. Consider a software company that creates various programs to sell to consumers. Often, such companies can maintain 10%, 15%, or even better net margins. A big cost is the payroll of experienced programmers. Yet, they can be added relatively easily in good times. Unlike most capital expenses, where you buy the item up-front for a huge amount, which will only be amortized over a period of time

---

[2] For those stock investors looking for "turnaround" businesses in which to invest, this is not always bad. Such investors are sometimes called bottom feeders. They look for companies whose earnings are only temporarily, it is hoped, depressed, but whose earnings can rebound, if the company can rein in costs, or if the sales improve, as they could coming out of a recession, for example. Most investors abandon such businesses in droves, when bad times hit. Often, the stock price falls drastically. If the company does recover, or "turnaround," the stock price often goes up five or ten times or more (for example, Dell Computer stock went up about 100 times from 1993 to 1998 as the company went from "struggling" to "growth" in the eyes of investors). More conservative "buy and hold" investors tend to favor businesses with higher margins. It is hoped these companies will be more resilient in bad times and that they will grow more rapidly due to their higher margins. If they had chosen lower-margin companies, not only would growth likely be less over a long holding period, but such companies are, as explained above, inherently less secure investments (waterfall analogy). So, one type of investor will find most of his great buys in these low-margin companies that I am critical of, from an entrepreneurial view. It is crucial to distinguish between being a capital investor in a business and the founder of a business. Founders should always, in my opinion, favor the high-margin business. Some knowledgeable investors will chose low-margin businesses under certain conditions.

after the purchase (or you could finance the purchase and absorb interest expense on your financing), you usually pay staff bi-weekly. There is no financing cost. No large, up-front payments. Microsoft is the best example of such a business. Microsoft had about 24% net margins the last time I looked. For such a large company, that is phenomenal. High margins are the result of Microsoft having a virtual monopoly on the personal computer operating system market. High margins are the reason Bill Gates is the richest man in the world today! Twenty-four of every hundred dollars Microsoft generates in revenue comes to the bottom line! This would never happen for, say, a boat-building company or a restaurant.

But, these margins are not unheard of for fast-growth, informational-based businesses—for companies that focus on information, ideas, creativity, and even service areas rather than manufactured goods. I have seen service businesses, such as high-end, personal dating services, maintain such high margins (No, it's not that kind of a service! Just the sort that innocently matches up lonely engineers or computer programming geeks with potential mates). Let's recap. Significant growth in wealth is usually the result of bootstrapping, of reinvesting earnings to grow earnings. Larger gross margins and the resulting higher net margins mean a larger percentage of the revenue to reinvest in the growth. Growth rates can be higher. There is no need for equity financing, nor for extreme borrowing, to finance growth. The growth can largely evolve from internal financing. If conditions change for the worse and expenses increase, high-margin businesses can absorb the increased costs and still remain profitable. Low-margin businesses, under similar conditions, will probably *lose* money.

Yet, when a person says, "I want to start a business," and I ask, "What kind of a business?" they often respond, "A restaurant. Maybe, a retail store. Maybe, I should think about a grocery store. After all, people will always need food." What this means is, "Gosh, I haven't really thought about it. These are the types of businesses I frequent, and they don't look that hard to run." What they need to do is go though the analysis of estimating expenses. Get a handle on the cost of the goods involved. Get a handle on what kind of overhead the business will require. Get an estimate of profit margins. Study the margins of existing businesses in the industry you are contemplating. And, at the most basic level, understand that high margins are your friend. Many people, who feel they could run a retail store, would feel totally out of their league trying to build a computer consulting company. But, reread the chapter, "Men Are Cheaper Than Guns." You can't know it all, not in any industry. Understand, that choosing a low-margin business, because you don't feel "qualified" to run a higher-margined business, is often the exact recipe for failure. If anything, high margins allow room for errors. If you want to start a typically low-margin business, because that is really the type of business you want and are really excited about, then, by all means, go for it. But, know that control of costs is crucial and aim to be one of the higher-margin businesses *within* your industry.

I'm glad some people don't make the optimal business choice. They choose low-margin businesses. It seems to me, if everyone were truly focused on making the best mathematical decision in choosing the business they started, no one would enter the industry of food processing—the whole industry is low margin, from getting food from the earth or animal to getting it into the mouth of the consumer. No one would enter the apparel business, either. Not manufacturing clothing, nor retailing it. Everyone would be building a software company or a service business. We'd all basically be starving and naked, but we'd have lots of great software for our computers! I really don't ever want to see that happen! So, just be advised, I have a personal interest in not discouraging you too much from low-margin businesses!

Chapter 6.
The Need To Generate Good Revenue Per Sale

OK. You've decided you'll let some other misguided entrepreneur worry about keeping us clothed and fed. You're after money! You're after growth! You can't stand the thought of trying to build a low-margin business. You're having bad dreams of waterfalls. You are a high-margin convert. Instantly, you think, "I could sell Widget Z mail-order. I know I can price them at ten times my cost. I know the market niche that will buy them, and I know how to reach this niche." Problem. Widget Zs only sell for about $10 per unit. Sure, they only cost you a buck apiece, and you have high-gross margins, but will you be able to retain high overall net margins? With most lower-priced products, even if the gross margin is extremely high, that cannot be converted into high net margins.

The reason is that each product sale only can contribute so much to paying overhead and marketing costs. Some people speak in terms of product *contribution*. This term is used differently in different circles. Direct mail marketers are most concerned with contribution allowances for mailing costs. I'm assuming Widget Zs are small. Maybe, they can be shipped for $3 per unit. That's 30% of your selling price taken just to ship the product! Your shipping charges are three times your production costs!

Of more concern are the marketing costs associated with getting someone to want you to ship him the product in the first place. Suppose only 2% of your niche market chooses to buy Widget Z from you, when you mail them a promotional, direct-mail piece. Hidden and missed by most people who dream of direct-mail riches, but who haven't really studied the industry, is the huge marketing cost of direct mail. This is because you are marketing not only to those who buy your product, but you are also absorbing costs to market to those who choose not to buy your product. The actual sales generated must amortize both costs.

Let's assume you are sending out your mailings at a postage cost of $0.30 apiece. This might seem high, but not unreasonable. Let's assume your cost of envelopes and paper is also $0.30. We are allowing for some color brochures, but nothing too fancy or too large. Again, your cost will depend upon quantity produced, but we don't want to get into this. We will assume no other marketing costs, so we have an in-the-mail cost of $0.60 for each marketing piece sent out. Those who have done direct mail might argue that this cost is too low. They will say, "Yeah, but to really sell, we want to add a lift letter, and we want to add this and this, probably." Others will say, "This is too much. You can be more frugal. Send it bulk rate, blah, blah, blah." But, let's go with the estimate. To produce 100 mail-marketing packages costs $60.00.

We have already said that only 2 of every 100 people sent this mailing choose to buy your widget. Each one sells for $10 so you collect a grand total of $20. Now, obviously, this is a sorry state of affairs. Just in marketing costs alone, you are losing $40 for every two sales. That's $20 per unit. We haven't even added in shipping costs of $3 per unit. The grand, stinking result is that you are losing $23 per unit sold. Oops! We forgot the cost of the product itself, $1 per unit! So, we are losing $24 per unit. If the cost of the product itself is so low, relative to your other costs, that you can for all practical purposes neglect it, that is a good sign that you might have a problem with contribution! And, we have totally neglected any processing or fulfillment cost to fulfill the order.

What has happened here is that each unit sale provides so little contribution that we could get into real trouble if we only thought in terms of gross margins. What little contribution exists is consumed by our promotional costs. Net margins do show us that our endeavor is bad. But another way to get to this conclusion is simply to stay focused upon contribution. Think of contribution not in terms of margins but dollar amounts available to cover various expenses not included in cogs. You can also think in terms of contribution to profit. How much profit, measured in dollars, do I make with each sale? Finally, if you know you can maintain decent gross margins, keeping contribution high is the same as trying to generate significant revenue per sale.

What we have succeeded in showing above is what all direct-mail marketers know. You can't really use the mail to sell products that have too low a price. Over the years, the minimum reasonable price you could consider for direct mail has increased. There is a more general principle that says, given a product price, only certain marketing methods are available for that product. Some marketing methods are simply too high-end. Consider the opposite side of the spectrum. Your company sells inventory management software to other companies. In particular, you have spent your career understanding inventory control, and you have produced a program that allows mid-sized businesses to track their inventory efficiently. You can tweak the basic program into a semi-customized solution for a given business which cannot just adopt your program directly.

Now that you are selling your program for $50,000 as a semi-custom solution, direct mail is no longer a limit. In fact, personal consultative selling is viable and recommended. This, of course, means you send salespeople around to companies to demonstrate what your program can do for their business. Some people would say they have contribution to burn. I never think of it this way. But, when you are making more money per product sold, more marketing options tend to be available to you. You will probably be *forced* into higher cost marketing channels. After all, few businesses will want to buy your $50,000 specialized solution from a crummy thirty-cent flier you sent them! You will probably wind up using direct mail to generate leads for your sales team.

You simply lack marketing means to promote low-priced products to a niche market. Even if marketing were not an issue, order fulfillment and processing costs would kill you.

Now, let's put marketing costs aside entirely. Let's assume Widget Z Company has done an incredible job. They have found a way to increase the Widget Z sales price, without sacrificing sales or adding marketing costs, so that each unit somehow produces a whopping $1 per unit profit. Children, don't try this at home! The product still only has a contribution to profits of $1 per sale. You need a heck of a lot of sales to make any real money. Just to equal one sale of the inventory-management program above, you would need several thousand sales of Widget Z. Although it is true that it is easier to sell lower-priced products than higher-priced ones (if for no other reason, more people can afford them!), it is rarely true you can reasonably hope for the level of sales you need to profit from the differential. In other words, you are almost always better off going with the higher contribution product and a smaller number of sales.

I can think of cases where this hasn't been true with regard to shrink-wrapped software sold directly, non-customized to the consumer. Some prices are just too high, and there will be market resistance. But, in general, I believe that you will almost always be better off selling higher-priced products. Give yourself the contribution to work with. This allows you to "succeed" with a smaller level of sales. You cannot price your product unreasonably high and just hope a few gullible fools will buy it. But, if you can justify the cost of your product, and if the market will bear the cost, being the "high end" player in an industry is a good goal. Aim to sell *expensive* products.

You can sell products for more, if you can clearly demonstrate the value of your products to the buyer. Think of the inventory-management example. If you were unfamiliar with business, you might think, "Why in the hell would anyone pay $50,000 for a computer program?" The reason is that, by allowing more effective management of their inventory, companies can reduce their carrying costs of goods in storage. They can order and manage inventory more profitably. They can prevent "running out" and losing sales. In marketing such a product a key point would be to try to get a handle on just how much money the company could save. If you can demonstrate that their investment in the software will quickly pay for itself, and, then, it will start saving them money, that is a strong purchasing advantage.

People tend to be greedy creatures. If you show them how to make or save money, you are a world ahead in marketing. You want their purchasing decision to be a "no brainer." This is especially valid, if you are marketing to businesses. Marketing your product to other businesses is, in fact, a great avenue. Businesses tend to have more money to buy things than individual customers. Further, businesses are ongoing. It is easier to build long-term relationships. Rather than aiming for a one-time sale, you work to establish an ongoing relationship with the business and make many sales to it. Few individuals would pay $50,000 for a software program.

For some reason, when most people think of starting a business, they tend to think in terms of marketing, not to businesses, but rather to individuals. They also tend to think in terms of low-cost products, hence, low contribution products. I think this tendency stems from the person not taking himself seriously as a business person. They think, "Why would a company buy products from me? I'm only me. But I could sell lower cost products to individuals. After all, no one knows that it is I selling them, and it's not like this is an expensive product." Entrepreneurs tend to think in terms of finding the best opportunity, which often involves the higher contribution product. Again, I want to reemphasize that contribution refers not to percentage margins but rather dollar amounts brought into the company with each sale.

It is true you will have a more difficult time selling a business a $50,000 or a $100,000 program than you would have in selling Widget Zs to consumers. You will really need to have a good product, and you must believe in your product. This is crucial. Best of all is a list of satisfied customers who want to recommend your services to your next prospective client. Sometimes, people confuse trying to choose higher contribution products with just trying to up the price on a current product. This is not the same. In particular, you should never raise the price of your products above what you feel provides a decent value to the buyer. If you do not feel your product represents a bargain at the price you desire, you will probably not be successful or happy as an entrepreneur. If you are simply trying to exploit some segment of market naivete, you are no better than a simple confidence man who is trying to run a scam.

There are really two reasons not to do this. One, you will not be successful. Two, you will not be happy with yourself when you wake up in the morning and look at yourself in the mirror. What do you want to be known for? Some person trying to peddle some overpriced, poorly-made, and generally useless product? Or someone who creates and sells something sincerely appreciated by others? Successful entrepreneurs believe in their products. This gives them a huge advantage when marketing their products. It is much easier for them to convince others of the product's worth when they feel it sincerely.

Do you remember a salesman who you felt was insincere? Maybe, a used car salesman? Do you remember a feeling that this person was trying to milk you for all he could? How did you feel toward him as a person? Did you enjoy doing business with him? Would you do business with him again? In personal selling, customers do pick up an impression of what the salesman really believes. The sad fact is that such salespeople do exist. Further, that approach is encouraged by some companies. I think of these businesses as cutthroat businesses. There is no concept of relationship marketing. There is no concern with keeping a sold customer satisfied. There is only the concern of getting as much as possible right now. Gouge the customer. What happens when you adopt this approach is that you can never achieve a level of growth and stable success. You are implicitly relying upon a steady stream of new customers who have not done business with you before. Usually, they are people who were dissatisfied with another company in the same industry! "Damn. I'd never go back to that car dealership. They just tried to screw me." And, then, the person goes to another dealer and feels the same way. Customers wind up jumping between many businesses and never being satisfied with any of them. Yet, the businesses survive because there is a steady supply of disgruntled customers who are refugees from their competitors!

The problem is that any newcomer entering this type of industry can compete with you instantly. For you have created no positive reputation or customer loyalty. You are not getting referrals from your past clients. Such a business is destined to remain in a start-up mode forever. Once you adopt a "I need to scrap for my existence, and who cares about the consequences" attitude, you will always be searching for new customers, not to grow, but just to survive.

Most businesses, if they succeed in staying actively in business for three or four years, will experience much less chance of failure in the succeeding years. They may choose to sell their company. They may retire. But, they know that, somehow, they are more secure now than they were during the more stressful, start-up years. Their business is more stable. There is closer to a feeling of, dare I say, serenity. Con artists will never know that feeling. That is just.

Many start-up business people, I believe, really do want to offer a good deal for the consumer. But yet, they fear they cannot provide the "best" product, when compared to similar products already in the market. They want to offer value, so they reduce the price of their product. They reason, even if they can't produce the best product, they can, at least, provide a product that is a lower-cost alternative to the existing products. I have mixed feelings about this. On the one hand, I really want to commend people who want to offer value and encourage them on their direction. On the other, it must be pointed out that consumers are not totally rational. There is a tendency to correlate price with quality. Many people will almost instinctively feel that higher-priced products are better. These people are looking for a surrogate for quality, and they feel price works. It doesn't.

As an example of this, I recall classes in network administration. This was a very hot field in the mid to late 1990's. Wages were high. Benefits good. As more and more people realized this, a whole slew of companies were started to provide training in the field. Some companies charge upwards of tens of thousands of dollars for a several week class. Yet, I know of similar classes, as good or better, taught at local community colleges for a couple hundred bucks. I'm sure you could come up with examples where cost and quality have not been, in your own experience, related at all.

The difficulty is that, by pricing your product at the lower end, even though you currently can feel good about the value you provide, it probably will be difficult to raise your prices as your product improves. Consumers tend to measure prices from the bottom up. They tend to remember the lows they paid for something. They don't like going back up! There is a feeling of "Why should I pay more now, when I could have gotten it for…?" Never mind the product improvements. I mention this because I have seen companies who wish to establish themselves as a higher-end player—but they know they don't have the current resources to compete with existing companies in terms of the quality—try this let's-raise-prices-as-we-improve. They succeed as companies, but never seem able to raise their prices to where they honestly feel they could or should be relative to the competition. I don't have any good answers for this one. All I can recommend is that you not automatically believe you can raise your prices at will, even if it seems justified.

Chapter 7.
The Internet and Commerce

The Internet will revolutionize commerce. That is certain. It already is having a major impact. Companies like amazon.com and cdnow.com are successfully competing with stores like Barnes and Noble and Musicland that have existed for decades. Brokerage firms, even the so-called discount firms, like Charles Schwab, are finding companies like e-Trade able to offer flat rate commissions for stock trades that are measured in tens of dollars rather than hundreds of dollars. The brokerage discounters are no longer the best deal in town. I have no doubt, within a few years, nearly all financial transactions will occur on-line. Other companies have sprung into existence with businesses that wouldn't have been dreamt of years ago. Companies like Yahoo, whose product is a search engine to help people find information on-line. The Internet offers smaller and start-up companies a huge advantage they didn't have years ago. Anyone can put out a web page. And, in so doing, they can offer their services to the world. Yet, traffic on the web is intense. Unless you learn a bit about Internet marketing, your page will likely be lost in the crowd. Even if you know a great deal, it will be difficult to get attention in the years to come.

The first thing to realize about the Internet is that it is not magical. We will see the standard business life cycle trajectory that we saw with industrial companies and that we later saw in the computer industry. The Internet industry will mature. The rapid growth will slow. Pricing pressures will affect all the players. The Internet is not properly an industry. At base, the Internet is a whole bunch of computers hooked up together to what is called the world-wide-web.

Not all computers are hooked up all the time, as anyone who has tried to locate very many web pages can testify! But millions are. A whole new industry has grown to create Internet content, develop web pages, deal with issues of computer network security, and provide tools to Internet users and content developers. Throughout the 1990's the stock market has been very generous in funding Internet companies. Just having "Internet" in the company name has been a boon to selling stock.

Most entrepreneurs, especially those who work in the computer industry, have unrealistic expectations of what the Internet offers them. Like any new industry, there is an abundance of hyping the industry by people who benefit from it. Not only the Internet companies, themselves, but mostly the venture capital companies whose goal is simply to sell stock to investors. Too many young programming students feel they will be able to create a billion-dollar company in two or, at most, three short years! After all, isn't this what Netscape, Yahoo, Amazon.com, and many others have done? No. These companies have achieved stock-market valuations in the several billions of dollars. That is not the same as creating any real wealth at all. It doesn't mean that the stocks are reasonably valued, based upon earnings. Much of the so-called newly created wealth is really just hot air.

There is an expression that John Train uses in his book, *The Craft of Investing*, which I just love and which applies perfectly. It is referring to companies who profit by taking other companies public and selling grossly overvalued shares to naive investors. When speaking among themselves, the people who profit this way say, "When the ducks quack, feed them." This is exactly the attitude of some Internet companies going public and the venture firms that are supporting them until they go public. It is not a creation of wealth, but rather a transfer of wealth from the individual investor to the people taking the company public that occurs.

Don't get me wrong, I'm all for the stock-market-put-your-capital-where-you-want system. Many great companies get funds to grow through the stock market. Microsoft, Dell Computer, and countless others come to mind. But I really do have a problem with people who exploit the stock market via untenable IPO's (Initial Public Offerings, stocks going public for the first time). This is not entrepreneurship. It is closer to a confidence game and is unethical, even though it is legal. I know of at least one company founder who has "created" a billion-dollar Internet company and really doesn't give a rat's ass as to whether or not the company survives or prospers. He didn't really even care about what the company product was. Just that it be Internet based. His goal was to sell his shares as soon as he could and pocket the cash. That was his intent going into the venture, and that was his goal at the end. When the company is bought out by some other business, I won't be at all surprised. The initial, individual investors in the business will take a clubbing. I'm not speaking of the venture capitalists, who planned to get out right away, but rather the unsuspecting, private investors who hold the stock via their mutual funds or in their private portfolios, who incorrectly believe they are holding a great, long-term investment.

In one other case, I'm convinced the founder of a billion-dollar Internet business did the same thing. I kept thinking to myself, "Why the hell would he leave a lucrative field (the one he was in at the time) and choose to build a business of a type that invariably will have low margins? It makes no sense. He must have seen a dozen better options." Oops! He took the company public. I overlooked that. If you get a few billion in stock to sell when you want, I guess margins really aren't an issue. Maybe, nothing in this book is really an issue. It's not building a business you're after, but rather, just getting a lot of money, Selling stock for real-hard-currency-cash. It's a redistribution of existing wealth. It's selling the idea that makes such people wealthy, not executing the idea and actually making the idea profitable in the market. (This is, by the way, an example of risk shifting to the extent that a very tough opportunity to exploit becomes a high-payoff, no-risk deal for the "entrepreneur." The founder will get huge rewards, no matter what happens. Success or failure of the business is immaterial in that regard.)

Maybe, I shouldn't take this so personally, but it really galls me. At times, I have a real loathing for the financial industry that encourages this attitude. I have even less respect for these IPO "entrepreneurs," who criticize entrepreneurs like Bill Gates. Most of them aren't fit to lick Bill Gate's boots. And, I'm not a big Bill Gates fan!

So, to new programmers who want to be entrepreneurs, understand that the billion dollar amounts you hear associated with Internet companies are something that relate to generous stock market valuations. It is an enigma. These market conditions don't last forever. Yet, there are many real Internet businesses, generating real sales and real earnings, who have bootstrapped to being multimillion-dollar businesses. It is a tremendous growth area, and opportunities do abound.

The days of the HTML (HyperText Mark-Up Language, which specifies how a web page displays) designer company are coming to a close. You need more, if you want to develop professional web sites. In addition to HTML and the newer DHTML, JavaScript and Java at the very least must be mastered by your company. You must also have a handle on database design and implementation. Most people today want not so much fancy graphics as they want information. They want to be able to order and customize goods from a database. Look at the web sites of companies like Gateway 2000 or Dell Computer, and you will see what I mean. Web page design is no longer a one-person job, but is breaking into two areas: 1) content and graphics; and 2) programming and database responsibilities. Continued learning in this field is crucial. Newer companies, like Net Perceptions, are attempting to merge psychological evaluation of those visiting a web site with marketing and programming to do more targeted marketing. This is the natural evolution of the marketing area known as direct mail.

I really intend this book to have a long-term scope, i.e., to be applicable for all time and to be more of a business-theoretical tome. Because of this, I contemplated not discussing the Internet, Internet businesses, and the state of affairs in the late 1990's. Yet, I feel almost like I am documenting the current state of business. The Internet will change drastically and in ways no one can see. Those entrepreneurs working to develop the Internet or develop services for the Internet really are at the cutting edge of a new area of entrepreneurship.

But, you don't have to be an Internet developer to benefit from the Internet. In fact, with most technological inventions and improvements, it is often the case that those who benefit the most are not those actually struggling to develop the new technology, but those who see simple business ideas that can exploit the new technologies. Companies like amazon.com and cdnow.com are good examples, people who see how more traditional industries can be upset and how a newcomer can at least gain a foothold in the established industry. Often, whole new industry categories are created. You might not even have an industry name for what you contemplate doing! You might be the first! In this case, all my griping about studying and getting some knowledge of the industry obviously is hooey. There is no existing industry to study! But, you can look to industries that are similar to what you intend to do.

Consider the videotape rental business. Before the advent of VCR technology, this business didn't exist. Many entrepreneurs made money with their own video rental shops. Those who saw the potential and acted early had an advantage, but if they wanted to know about the industry, they didn't have anyone to ask. What they could have asked themselves was, "What is this business I'm trying to do? How does it make money? What are the underlying principles involved? What similar businesses could I learn from?"

They would realize they were, first and foremost, trying to build a sales and/or rental business. Maybe video rental was new, but the basic concept is very old. Similarly, once you know how you want to use your web page, you can seek out other companies using the Internet in a similar way. Examine their web site. What is good about it? Bad? If you were one of the company's potential clients, would you keep coming back? Mimicking those who are successfully doing what you contemplate can be very effective.

As a marketing tool, the Internet can be used to sell your products and services on-line. If your products or services aren't readily sold on-line, the Internet can be used to make your customers aware of your services—all of your services. Your web page should have a detailed index of your web site that makes navigation simple. You want people to be able to quickly see (as in looking at the table of contents of a book) what is available through your web site. Remember the HT in HTML stands for hypertext. Users should not have to go through any linear progression of your web pages in some order that you determine is best for them. They will stop looking at your page and go to another web site, maybe one of your competitors. Make it easy for users to jump quickly to wherever they want to go.

The Internet is a media of change. Many users will quickly notice that a page says, "Last updated June 5, 1997." Users are wary of dated content. Many assume newer is better. The most dynamic web sites are now updated almost instantaneously. Now, a small start-up company does not want to spend a lot of time updating its web site. Yet, if it remains the same, many will stop returning to your web site.

How does a company like Yahoo generate revenue? Advertising. In fact, if enough people visit your web site regularly, your site can actually acquire a financial worth to other advertisers who are interested in your niche. I'm not a fan of selling advertising on your web site, unless your intent is mainly to generate revenue precisely in this way. Your site should clearly focus upon *your* products. You don't want other companies' advertisements distracting your viewers. But, what if you say, "My products don't change often, how can I keep the site current in the eyes of the viewers?" The answer is to make your site a valuable resource to your clients.

Web sites that have an abundance of useful links to related sites are often bookmarked by viewers. They want to be able to come back and explore the large number of useful links that lead them to other interesting sites. This is important. If your site is not a resource, a person may visit once and then move on—forever. As long as you have users occasionally stopping by to see what's up, you have a chance to influence them. All the links should be related to your business. If you sell cigars, you could have links to other sites dedicated to cigars, but don't include a link to your favorite rock band. That has nothing to do with cigars, and most users, who came to you because of cigars, will not be interested. Doing this sort of thing makes your site look cheap and amateurish. This is fine for a personal web site, "All about me and what I like." But it's not justified for a company. It is OK to have one link saying "about us," which gives more information about your company, and that page could have links to a brief description of each of the key people associated with your company.

If your skills and experience are a crucial factor in encouraging clients to do business with you, if, for example, you are a consulting firm and you want to show off the strength of your consultants' resumes, by all means have such pages (the trend today is not to list your consultants' resumes on-line. Why make your competitors' recruiter's job easier?). But, don't just throw all these links on your opening web page. Have them linked only to your "about us" page. Do not confuse this with what I said above about allowing your viewers to access any part of your web site easily. They are not contradictory. You want to organize content in a way that does not bombard the viewer with huge levels of detail about topics in which they are not interested. Use your index as a jumping off point to more detailed content. Don't make every arbitrary link you can!

Another reason not to throw a lot of detailed content on the screen at one time is because large web pages take more time to load in the viewer's browser (that's the computer program on their PC's that allow them to view your web page). It is well-known that many viewers simply will not wait for your page to display. They will just go elsewhere. If you are hiring a web-design company to create your web page, look for the above factors in their design. Don't accept a design that requires a large download of detailed graphics. This is a sure sign of an amateur designer. In all of this, never forget that it is the content that is the key. All of the design, all of the behind-the-scenes coding of your page is not what is most important. It is the content. If you have good content, you will have a good site. If your content is lacking, no amount of skilled programming will help you.

Do allow clients to contact you directly via your web site. Have a link or links by which they can contact you via e-mail. And, as in all correspondence, respond promptly, if possible. Remember also that not all viewers need to have full access to your entire site. Certain areas may be reserved for your clients only. You could, for example, have a secure area for each client where the current status of their project is displayed.

Security is a crucial topic. It is best to choose an experienced Internet service provider who understands security and on-line commerce. Another option is to set up your own web server, but if you are contemplating this, you probably know more than I am trying to cover here! Unless you are computer savvy or else your business is intimately tied to the Internet, I would recommend having a professional Internet service provider host your site. It's not that it's difficult. It's just that you probably have other things you need to be doing. You don't want to bother with extra network administration tasks. Do have someone *inside* your organization be responsible for development of content for your site.

Working closely with your Internet service provider is the best way to learn what features are available to you. Don't just get every feature offered, but pick and choose what is useful to you. In dealing with technological areas, there is sometimes a tendency to assume you should give full control to the experts. That is not true. Many will try to sell you features you really don't need.

In addition to changing the way many sales are made, the Internet will change how people work. Telecommuting will become more and more of a reality. Many companies are already doing this. There is a tremendous untapped potential in helping companies use the Internet as a tool within their organization to get work done in ways that were not possible in the past.

When I talk to computer programmers, and especially Internet programmers, who are happy as employees and wish to remain so, I sometimes mention to them that I think, someday, most programmers will rue the day the Internet became popular. Absolutely despise it. They look at me like I'm nuts. "I'm making $90,000 a year right now due to the Internet! I love the Internet." Right now, that's true. But the area the Internet will most affect, regarding employment demographics, is computer programming, itself.

I know of at least two companies started in the U.S. by people born and raised as children in India. When starting their programming or multimedia company, the tight labor market was a bit of a limitation. They could not hire as many people as they would have liked in the U.S., so they started employing people in their home country. And, at the time, programmers in India were much cheaper than programmers residing in the U.S. You could literally hire five programmers for the cost of one here. That means their companies could program software for only about one-fifth the cost of companies using employees based entirely in the U.S. Equivalently, for the same cost, they could be five times more productive. Needless to say, these companies have tended to favor hiring more people where the labor is cheap.

At present, skilled computer programmers mostly compete only with other programmers who are locally based. Soon they will regularly need to compete with the entire world! I recall Ross Perot running for President on the agenda that free trade policies with Mexico were fundamentally bad for workers in the U.S. He said there would be a huge sucking sound of manufacturing jobs going across the border and out of the U.S. Maybe, I'm a little Internet-Perot, because I think we will hear that sucking sound over the Internet. Apparel and other goods won't flow over the Internet, but programming code will. This will bring great opportunities to intelligent people living outside the U.S., but it will cost jobs here. Programmers don't believe this, but I bet the day will come when experienced programmers in difficult computer languages like C++ will only earn $15 per hour.

As long as I am making bold (and, maybe, foolish!) predictions, I will also note that the Internet indirectly will present one of the greatest challenges to Microsoft. Microsoft is, without doubt, the biggest entrepreneurial success story ever. It commands a proprietary product required on all PC's (no, it's not Word, but Windows 98 or Windows 95 or Windows NT, the operating system that is necessary to run other programs on your computer). Many investors feel Microsoft has an unshakable position in the software industry, due to controlling this needed and proprietary product. If you wanted to use a PC, you would need to buy Windows in one flavor or another. Until recently, I would have agreed.

But, programs that need to run over the Internet had to work on many different computer systems, especially Unix-based systems, which are the large company and university standard. This has, in part, led to the popularity of a new computer programming language called JAVA (like the coffee). What is special about JAVA is that it is designed to run on *any* operating system at all. JAVA programs will run on a Windows PC, a Macintosh, a Unix box, whatever. It does this by allowing the makers of the operating systems to support what is called the Java Virtual Machine. Any operating system can support this Java Virtual Machine. And, if it does, then, any program written in JAVA can run on that operating system.

Most people buy Windows, as their operating system, because there is a good selection of software which runs on Windows. The same software would not run, for example, on a Macintosh or on any operating systems created by a new start-up company. Because Windows is the standard, most programmers spend their time creating Windows software. That's where the sales are. It's a case of the strong getting stronger in a chicken-and-the-egg sort of way! Because Windows is the standard, that is where programmers will put their development time. This leads to a large selection of Windows software, which reinforces Microsoft's dominance in the market and keeps Windows the standard!

Further, computer programming is difficult enough that programmers usually can only focus on one type of development. It is not easy to transfer a serious program written for one operating system so that it runs on another. This is why, for example, programs written for Windows may or may not have a Macintosh version. If it were trivial to convert the PC version to a Mac version, the software companies would do it and try to pick up the extra 2% or so more sales that would result. So, companies focus on only PC versions.

This is why I always say you have to have about a hundred pounds of brain damage to try to build a software company whose main product is an operating system. Until there is an abundance of software for your operating system, people won't buy it. And, developers aren't going to write any software for your operating system, until there is a market demand for it! And, yet, highly intelligent programmers try to build companies whose main product is… an operating system. Oprah could have a show, "Why Smart Programmers Do Stupid

Things." Several companies have actually written *superior* operating systems to Windows, but that just didn't matter.

However, JAVA could change all this. If JAVA becomes the development language of choice down the road, then any company can write an operating system that runs nearly all software! No longer will Microsoft have a proprietary product that is required on a PC to run "Windows" software. Software will run on *any operating system*—including some that are free over the Internet, such as Linux. How many people will continue to pay Microsoft $200 for an operating system then? Operating systems will still be classified as proprietary products from a legal standpoint, but from a consumer standpoint they will become commodities, as one is fully interchangeable with the others!

So technology advancement can overturn the current powerhouse companies. I have just shown one way the most powerful of all software companies, Microsoft, could be clobbered by the Internet. Further, Microsoft's own actions could hasten the result that they dread the most—being jarred out of the position of *the* most powerful software company. It seems Microsoft has done everything it can think of to hobble JAVA. Most compilers (these are the software programs that allow programmers to write code and turn it into a form that a computer can understand) tend to stay true to the JAVA specifications. But, Microsoft has tried to make its version of JAVA (via Visual J++) nonstandard. If programmers mainly used J++, Microsoft would be able to say what goes in JAVA world. But, that isn't happening. JAVA programmers are using other programming tools like Metrowerks CodeWarrior. Classes that teach JAVA programming are also shying away from J++. So, when Microsoft says, "My way or the highway," the programmers are taking to the information superhighway—without Microsoft. I guess the lesson is that you must go with the technological flow, so to speak.

The biggest factor limiting the Internet today as a means of commerce is fear. People fear using their credit card numbers over the Internet. That the major sites are very secure doesn't matter. Yet, most people have no fear of ordering with a credit card over the phone, when talking to a person they do not know, as long as the company at the other end is known to be reputable. In time, as consumers become more and more conditioned to ordering on-line with safe experiences, this fear will evaporate, and nearly every consumer will buy goods via the Internet from companies they know to be reputable, of course.

Direct mail will most surely be affected, catalog companies, in particular. To print and mail out catalogs can cost a tremendous amount, especially if the catalog is large and in full color. Due to this cost, catalog companies that try to retain the direct-mail model via snail mail (that's the good old United States Postal Service) simply will fail. The consumer will find the same product on-line. And, because the Internet marketer will not have to amortize the catalog mailing costs, the product will be cheaper over the Internet. Where do you think the customer will buy?

Essentially, the Internet provides full niche marketing power without the mailing costs. The Internet has full advantage in product selection and description, also. If the company desired, it could put the full technical specifications of its product on-line. A company could have links to the best reviews of its products. It could have graphics or schematics of the product, audio, video demonstrations, you name it. That will blow away what a catalog can do. And, people love their specialized catalogs. The Internet is a great tool for the niche marketer. Yet, there will be a slew of companies trying to sell to any given niche, so you will need to give some real thought as to how you will make potential customers aware of your site. Don't count on a listing with Internet search engines doing it for you, when there are thousands of other companies trying to do exactly what you are doing.

Chapter 8.
Expectation Values and Decision Making

I feel that this is, maybe, the most valuable chapter of the book. It introduces a way of making business decisions with which many people are unfamiliar. Yet, almost instinctively, many successful entrepreneurs have adopted this basic approach, regardless of what they call it or regardless of whether they even have a name for the method. The basic idea is that we want to evaluate a potential idea to see if it is really a feasible opportunity. We are interested in some measure of what will be the outcome of an endeavor (or a product choice), if it is deemed successful or if it is an outright failure. This is, by nature, speculative. Not all estimates going into our evaluations are going to be correct. In particular, estimates of sales are always difficult. You can easily be off by factors of ten or even more! Nevertheless, the method will allow you to know how many sales you need to break-even. And, it gives you a relative measure of potential upswing and potential downswing. It will also help you weed out undesirable ideas and concentrate your effort into profitable channels. It is a method implicitly used by many of the best investors.

So, just what are expectation values? They are the values you expect. Expectation values are your best and most realistic guess as to the outcome of a given endeavor. They try to account for the most likely outcomes and make a rough estimate of what effect extreme success or extreme failure has upon the financial success of the endeavor. In a way, they are the "average" outcome. By comparing the average outcomes of two different product ideas, you can then choose the idea with the greatest potential return on your investment. Do not be intimidated by the mathematics that follows. I tried to pre-expose you to some of this earlier to make absorbing it a bit easier. It is not really all that difficult, and, I think, you will be glad you learned it.

In a way, what we are doing is generalizing something that many people are already familiar with. That is the fact that we can multiply a probability of an occurrence by the value of the occurrence. We know a coin toss can come up heads or tails, and that, on average, it will turn up heads one-half of the time. There is a 50% chance that it will come up heads and a 50% chance it will turn up tails. However, now we wish to associate a value with heads and another value with tails. We want to give each side of the coin a weight representing the value of the outcome. We are interested in dollar values. Now, most people just associate unity with each outcome. By this, I mean a simple boolean value of win or lose. Or, equivalently, it is assumed the cost of a loss is the same as the amount made on a win. Assume you are betting $1. Then the following expression states you expect to break-even:

Expectation Value (outcome value) = +$1(0.5) + -$1(0.5) = $0.0

This equation says that the expectation involves two possible outcomes. Each possible outcome is represented as another term to be added to the right-hand side of the equation (if, for example, we were tossing six-sided dice, there would be six terms added together when calculating the expectation value). For our coin toss, there are only two possibilities, heads or tails. One of the outcomes involves winning $1. This is the $1 amount in the first term on the right-hand side. Because this outcome has a 50% chance of occurring, the $1 outcome is weighted by the factor of 50% (0.5 as a decimal). The sign of this first term is plus (+) because it involves getting a positive dollar amount. The second term is negative because it involves losing your dollar. This possibility also happens with a 50% probability. Notice that the sum of the terms in parentheses must equal 1—i.e., the total of all the possible outcomes must sum to 100%. This says that we, in our simple model, have accounted for all possible outcomes. This does not mean we actually need to include all possible outcomes in our model, but that we must make certain guesses and lump possibilities together, somewhat appropriately, so that the total of all anticipated outcomes is 100%.

Because the expectation value in the above equation is zero, it means that, overall, the "opportunity" of tossing the coin has no real merit. It has no real downside cost either. But, yet, you either win or lose a buck depending upon the outcome. How can that be? Well, as you probably have guessed, expectation values do not tell you about any particular outcome. Rather, they tell you about the outcome of a whole bunch of tries of the endeavor. What leads to one toss winning and another losing is volatility of the outcome. Even though the outcome of very many tosses can be predicted with great certainty, you only know each particular throw has a 50% chance of heads and a 50% chance of tails. You have no way of knowing which will come up on any given throw.

I find that some people believe that they can profit from volatility alone. They figure, "Well, I'll hit a streak of heads and then I'll be ahead and quit and I'll make money." Needless to say, they never do make money. And, even if they do have a lucky streak, they cannot go back and do it again! Remember, part of their plan is that they would quit when they were ahead! But they always want to get just a little further ahead! Or, they think they can do it again and go back. After all, the plan worked the first time! But that means the results will, as they say, regress to the mean. When they go back, the volatility will take away what they had gained earlier. The long-term result will be…the expectation value.

Casinos make good use of this principle. I don't really like the casino industry, as I see it as an attempt to exploit slightly ignorant people. It teases them with the chance of winning on volatility but, at the same time, keeps the expectation value solidly in the casino's favor. Suppose that a casino has a slot machine. The machine takes dollar bills (to keep things simple). About every twenty times the person pulling the lever wins, and the machine spits out $18 in winnings ($19 total). The person feels good and is happy to have made $18 with only one dollar. The person feels, if they play enough, they are bound to win. And, they do! But, in the end, they still lose money. Every twenty times they play, they will lose about $1. By looking at the outcomes of twenty throws, you will see this clearly:

Overall Outcome = (19)(-$1) + (1)(+$18) = -$1

The first term in the above sum represents 19 losses of $1. On the twentieth pull, they win $18 plus their dollar back. Overall, they expect to lose $1 every twenty times they play. If they play 100 times, they can expect to lose $5. Let's express the same result by looking at what we expect for one play. First, we can notice that the odds of winning are 1/20 while the odds of losing are 19/20. On a losing pull, you lose $1. A winning pull gives you $18 so we get:

Overall Outcome (one pull) = (1/20)($18) + (19/20)(-$1) = - $.05

What this expression says is that 1/20 of the time you win $18, and 19/20 of the time you lose a buck. So, the overall result is that you expect to lose five cents on one pull of the slot machine lever. You can see this is correct by noticing that by losing $1 every 20 pulls that you are losing $1/20 per pull. You should try to think in terms of doing this the second way, however. Think, "I need to multiply probabilities by the dollar outcomes and then sum over the possible outcomes."

So, if the casino has a total of 1 million people pulling this silly little lever every year, they expect to make $50,000. (You could also calculate that 1 million pulls a year amount to about 2,739 pulls every day of a 365 day year. That's probably a bit high for a reasonable number of lever pulls. Right? I mean 2,739 a day is a lot. So it looks like 1 million pulls a year might be a high estimate for the number of pulls. But, if we consider that the casino is open 24 hours a day, this amounts to only 114 pulls an hour or about two pulls a minute. That doesn't seem like so much anymore! Have you ever seen somebody at a casino pull the lever, then wait about half a minute before pulling it again? As you break numbers down like this, for any business estimate, be careful of thinking the number is too large or too small. You might well be correct, but sometimes a change of scale shows that the number is reasonable.)

The above is a very concrete use of expectation values. The casino can set the amount the machine pays out, and it can set the frequency so that the calculated expectation value will agree very closely with the actual outcome. In most business decisions, you will have difficulty knowing the probabilities of the outcomes. You will need to make reasoned guesses and be aware that you might be off significantly. If you are highly astute, you probably are asking, "Hey, if I'm going to be off by so much, why calculate the damn things in the first place?"

The answer is, in some situations, you will be comparing an Opportunity A to an Opportunity B. You can calculate expectation values for both endeavors. However, you will be off in both calculations, as you need to make reasoned estimates for both endeavors. "Great," you say, "I'm off, and I'll be getting more off!" Surprisingly, the calculation can still aid you. Consider the situation where you can produce one of two products, say A and B. A costs $100 to produce while B costs $500. These numbers are your expenses, and you have little excuse to be off on calculation of expenses. Usually, it is a matter of doing some research to learn the costs of the time and the material that go into producing the products. In some cases, especially when product research and development is required (R&D to sound more professional), you may not really know your expenses.

You will try to market Product A at $150 and Product B at $750. Now, which product is potentially a more profitable endeavor is impossible to answer, unless you can come up with some estimate of sales at the target prices. Let's assume that the products will demand about the same personnel and resources to develop. Now, obviously, if you can make a decent estimate of sales for each product, you will be able to multiply sales by estimated profits of $50 and $250 respectively. The bigger total wins and is the better product. Usually.

Let's assume you feel that you can sell approximately 1,000 of either product in the product's first year. That puts Product A at a total profit of $50,000 and B at $250,000. The estimated profitability is just the estimated profit per sale multiplied by the estimated number of sales. Recall, it is the sales that you will have the most difficulty estimating in most cases. If you were to write out simplified expectation expressions, they would be:

A Estimated profits = ($50)(1,000) = $50,000
B Estimated profits = ($250)(1,000) = $250,000

Now, this looks trivially simple. Why bother to call such calculation results expectation values and make such a big deal over them? Let's assume that the lower cost Product A has the potential to generate sales of a higher-end Product C, which you are already selling. This is because Product A and Product C are strongly related. This is a form of relationship marketing. B, on the other hand, is unrelated to your current products and customers. Now, if Product C sells for a net profit of $100 per unit, and we estimate that 20% of the purchasers of A will also buy one C, this means the values of estimated profits become:

A Estimated profits = ($50)(1,000) + (0.20)(1,000)($100)= $70,000
B Estimated profits = ($250)(1,000) = $250,000

The second term in A's expression represents the added sales of C because of the existence of A. Be very careful not to over count C's profitability! In particular, the 200 sales of C above should not be repeated in the calculation for C's expectation values. If you were currently selling 500 C's a year, it would be incorrect to write:

C Estimated profits = ($100)(500) + ($100)(200) = $70,000

The above is incorrect because the expression for A already measured the added profitability of more C sales *due to A*. If you added the second term to the C Estimated profits, then you would be double counting the profits. The correct expression for C would remain:

C Estimated profits = ($100)(500) = $50,000

It is precisely because of the existence of A that we are able to sell the extra 200 C's. This is why it is correct to put the added profitability in the expression for A. If the added sales of C had nothing to do with Product A, then it would not make sense to put the added profitability in the expression for A.

The modified calculation made no change in what product you would go with. B is still the better product. This is often true. High-profitability-per-each-sale products are hard to beat. But, if Product A and B had about the same profitability per sale, then the result would be that it now looks like A would be the better choice. Expectation expressions give you a simple way to add incremental factors affecting a product's profitability. Rather than just keep in your memory the fact that A could result in more sales of C and that the number would be about 200, you have a way to quantify this in one expression for Product A. Further, if after a few sales of A, it became clear that every two sales of an A would lead to a sale of one C, then twenty percent would have been a low estimate, and you could go back and put 0.50 in place of 0.20. The result is:

$$\text{A Estimated profits} = (\$50)(1,000) + (0.50)(1,000)(\$100)$$
$$= \$100,000$$

Usually, you won't know one precise value for the incremental sales of C due to A's existence. But, you can say that the added sales of C will almost certainly be somewhere *between* .20 and .50 times the number of sales of A. What this means is that you can calculate two expectation values for A to put the estimated profitability between $70,000 and $100,000. Now, if you feel that either possibility has about an equal chance of materializing, then as a simple estimate, you might guess the average profitability to be about the average of the two outcomes:

$$\text{Estimate of A profits} = (\$50)(1,000) + (0.50)(0.50)(1,000)(\$100)$$
$$+ (0.50)(0.20)(1,000)(\$100) = \$85,000$$

Be sure you understand the terms in the above expression. The first term represents the estimated sales of A. The second and third terms represent the incremental added sales of Product C due to Product A being produced. This second term assumes that there is a fifty percent probability (the first 0.50 factor in the second term) of generating 0.50 times 1,000 or 500 more sales. The third term represents a fifty percent chance (the first 0.50 factor in the third term) that the incremental sales of C will be (0.20)(1,000) or 200. The underlying assumption is that the two possible values of incremental sales of C each have a fifty percent chance of occurring. Notice that the value calculated, via the long expression, is the same as if you just averaged the two profit possibilities of $70,000 and $100,000. The value of writing the expectation expression (versus working the cases one at a time and then trying to average them at a later step) is that one single expectation expression is a clear way to see all of the assumptions you are inputting into your estimate of what will happen.

If you figured that the sales of every A would almost certainly generate closer to 0.50 sales of C than 0.20 sales of C, then, you might use an expression like:

$$\text{Estimate of A profits} = (\$50)(1,000) + (0.90)(0.50)(1,000)(\$100) \\ + (0.10)(0.20)(1,000)(\$100) = \$97,000$$

The above expression represents a 90% chance of generating 500 sales and a 10% chance of generating only 200 sales. In this case, the third term contributes only $2,000 to profits, while the first terms are on the order of $50,000. This is only about a 4% correction to the value, and, so, you can neglect the third term if you want. Expectation expressions let you see the dominant factors in a product's estimated profitability. In particular, it is clear that the added sales of C's are significant in the calculation of A's profitability. Writing out the expression helps prevent you from missing something significant. You can look at each term, see what it accounts for, and then add in any missing factors.

Like computer spread sheets used to make predictions, expectation values are only a tool. You don't want to spend too much time making calculations representing every possible outcome. All you want is a quick estimate. You want to focus upon the important terms in such an expression and neglect everything else.

Sometimes, the added terms will not represent more profits, but something that potentially could detract from profitability. For example, maybe, the sales of a new product will cut into the sales of an existing product. This would be represented as a negative term in the expectation value expression. As another example, consider the case where you know that Product B is very close to one of your competitor's products, dangerously close. Even though you will design and develop the product entirely on your own, maybe, there is a good chance the other company will sue you for patent infringement. You know this company is sue happy. You feel very certain that you would win in a court decision. But, then again, even if you are fully in the right, you might still lose. Further, some legal costs probably would be incurred.

Assume that there is a 5% chance that you will lose a lawsuit and owe $100,000. You are guessing here. But it is better to think about the issue and make the estimates, rather than ignore a possibility of which you are aware and just hope for the best. In this case, the expectation value expression for Product B becomes:

B Estimated profits = ($250)(1,000) – (0.05)($100,000) = $245,000

The second term represents the five percent chance of losing the lawsuit. Notice that the second term only minimally affects the overall expectation value. It is only 2% of the initial value ($250,000) calculated. Should you feel free to ignore this small term as you did with the small third term of the previous calculation? The answer is "It depends." It can be ignored in the calculated expectation value, as it makes little difference; however, you may want to leave it in, as it makes you aware of the probability of a significant loss. Notice, as with insurance, either this second term will or will not occur in reality. If you win the lawsuit (and, there are no lawyer costs to you), then the second term will be zero. You won't lose anything in profitability. However, if the long-shot happens and you lose the lawsuit, you will lose the full amount of the lawsuit or $100,000. It is good to be aware of issues of volatility like this. Sometimes, a product's overall expected profits are good, but there is some possible outcome that makes you really queasy. You can't absorb the *possible* negative outcome. Maybe a 5% chance of losing a lawsuit is too much.

Notice, even if you lose the lawsuit, you still come out ahead according to the expression. You replace the probability of 0.05 by 1, which represents 100% certainty, in the above expression, to see the result of this actual outcome:

B Actual profits = ($250)(1,000) − (1)($100,000) = $150,000

So, in this case, if you are really allowed to keep the profits of the sales of the B's, you still come out well, even if you lose the lawsuit! Getting $250,000 and a lawsuit that costs you $100,000 from B's still is a better deal than selling Product A's! However, you must ask yourself, "Is this reasonable? Is it possible for a company to profit despite infringing on someone else's patent?" The answer is that because the patent for B's is not held by you and because all your $250,000 in profits come directly from the sale of B's that likely any real lawsuit will demand that you remit the $250,000 in profits to the company holding the patent. Hence, the real outcome is that you lose $100,000 and make no money at all from the sales of B's. In this scenario, the correct expectation expression takes into account that on the 5% chance that you lose the lawsuit, you also forfeit the sales:

B Estimated profits = (0.95)($250)(1,000) − (0.05)($100,000)
                     = $232,000

The factor of 0.95 represents that there is now only a 95% chance you will keep the sales profits at all. Still, the expectation value is very large! What do you do? Now that you are aware of this unpleasant 5% outcome, you must ask yourself is the project still worth it? Could you afford to pay the $100,000 lawsuit? Would it affect your business adversely in any other way beyond the $100,000 loss? If your company can easily pay the lawsuit and if you feel that there are no other negative effects of this lawsuit, the best financial decision is to go with Product B. Product B still blows away Product A in desirability.

Notice, I'm not saying you should intentionally try to steal someone's patent rights. That is morally and legally wrong. But, there are companies that feel their patent or copyright should prevent anyone else from doing anything at all similar in concept. What these companies really want is a monopoly on the *idea*. Often, these companies understand copyright or patent protection can't stop other people from having ideas similar to their own, which aren't protected by the patent or copyright. Nonetheless, they use the threat of lawsuit to try to intimidate other companies to abandon the idea. Legal counsel, combined with expectation values, give you a handle in deciding what to do in such a situation.

Working through expectation values for your products forces you to think about the reasonableness of your assumptions. It encourages you to consider all significant factors affecting the profitability of the product. Unless you have a way to express all of these factors, you will likely just neglect them. You might be neglecting something important. The greatest entrepreneurs don't actually do these calculations. Rather, they have somehow developed a sense of what the most significant, contributing factors affecting profitability of the product are. Inside the gray matter, they make a decision. That decision, I would bet, almost always agrees with the results that would be obtained from reasonable estimates into expectation value calculations with an awareness of the potential volatility in the outcome. I make this assertion only upon knowing how successful entrepreneurs have talked about their reasoning process, about which of two directions was better for their company. They try to see the most important factors, the likelihood of those factors materializing, and then they base the basic go or no-go decision on this.

Another way you can use simplified expectation values is to ask, "What must happen for what I'm thinking to work?" Work backward and check if what must happen is reasonable. Ask yourself, "How much do I hope to make in this business?" From this, try to get a feeling as to whether the overall endeavor is feasible.

Suppose, you are a watchmaker. You get the great idea of making a pendant that hangs from a chain around a person's neck. It looks like a jackhammer and is cute. But best of all, it can start jumping up and down as if it were at work. You think it's a great gift idea. You wife thinks you're nuts. Well, each one is meticulously made by hand. It took you an hour to make the first one. You feel that with practice you could make ten an hour. So could other skilled craftspersons. Well, your wife is right. The idea sucks (sorry, if you tried this. No offense. It does sound cute). First, this is a product, not a business. It would be difficult to extend this business. What would be your future direction? A whole set of pendant tools?

Why does this idea suck, scientifically speaking? Suppose, you hope to make $1 million dollars selling these things. Let's assume you feel you can price them for $5 apiece. If you hope to make the $1 million in one year, this means you must sell at least 200,000. That assumes all $5 of the sales price is profit! But that certainly is not correct. The pendants take painstaking craftsmanship. So, maybe, they cost $4.50 to make. This means you only make a gross profit of $0.50 per unit. Now, to make your $1 million, you would need to sell 2 million of these.

Is this reasonable? Who knows? Someone did invent and sell the pet rock. By working backwards, starting from your costs and a reasonable sales price, you can get an estimate of the sales needed to generate any given level of profits. Smart entrepreneurs think this way all the time. They want to know if their idea is reasonable. All they have to go on is what they feel would be a reasonable selling price for the product and an accurate estimate of the costs to produce and market the product. Working backward, they estimate how many sales they would need before they were satisfied with the product's profitability. This gives them the number of estimated sales needed. They ask themselves, "Is it reasonable to expect this level of sales?"

Learn how to calculate basic expectation values. They help you see the most profitable undertakings, and they force you to become aware of what *must happen* for what you *want to happen* to become a reality.

Chapter 9.
Personality and Business Choice

Although certain ways of thinking and certain personal characteristics aid an entrepreneur, not all entrepreneurs have the same personality type. Not all successful entrepreneurs share the common stereotype of a Type A, ultra-driven-must-win-must-destroy-the-competition mentality. No doubt there are many of these people out there. But there are more reserved and less aggressive entrepreneurs who are equally successful.

Why does thinking about who you are and your personality have anything to do with building a business? I think it is essential. Not all businesses are alike. Different businesses favor different personality types. By giving some thought to who you are and what you want to do, I think you will be able to make a better choice in the type of business you want to build. This is the same sort of thinking you need to do when making career choices.

Consider the real estate business. From what I know, real estate involves much negotiation. You must push for the best price possible, when buying properties. You cannot pay too much for commercial properties and expect them to be a good investment. If you are selling, you must get as much as you can. In a way, real estate seems the business of one-time sales. You will probably never again interact with the person you bought a property from or sold a property to. You really want to get the best deal you can, and you don't care about the happiness of the other party. Long-term relationships mean little.

However, you will not let your properties sit idle, hoping for them to appreciate. Likely, you will rent them out. People in real estate tell me real estate is a great business because of two factors. First, while the properties typically appreciate in value, they can be depreciated from a tax standpoint. So, you are essentially writing off as an expense something that is increasing in value for you! Because of this rents generated turn into good cash flow to reinvest in more properties. Secondly, real estate allows the use of considerable leverage. Because the assets you are purchasing, properties, have good collateral value, you can control properties worth several times the amount you could finance from your own cash.

These are very good aspects of why real estate can make people rich. It is solid entrepreneurial thinking. Yet, real estate isn't for me. I hate personal negotiations. I know that I could hire people to do the negotiations for me, but that wouldn't be very good. Negotiating is too much a part of real estate. It's one of those crucial skills for people in this area. As you are getting started, without a doubt, you would need to do most of your own negotiations. It is just not the sort of role you can delegate. This is not to say I'm a weak negotiator. I'm not. It's just not something I enjoy.

Worse, yet, are the tenant problems. Renting to businesses is better in this regard than renting to individuals, but in either case this is a big part of where real estate gets its high PITA (pain in the ass) factor. There are people who will not pay their rent. You must evict them. There are some people, who before evicted, will destroy what they can of your property. It can be an unpleasant experience and just not the sort of thing I would enjoy. Between dealing with one-time negotiations and dealing with renters, I have no doubt that to be successful in real estate you need to be a bit aggressive. It seems helpful if real estate people actually enjoy a little confrontation.

Now, as I have already said, real estate is not a bad business from a financial perspective. It is a very viable way to make money. But, I really have a problem with people who promote real estate as the best business for everyone. It wouldn't be the right business for me. Not for any guy or gal who is slightly shy. Not for people who are a bit timid or for anyone who internally has a difficult time dealing with the hassles, like destructive tenants. It's not just what you show on the outside, but rather what you feel on the inside. Believe me, if

I owned properties that someone was intentionally ruining, I'd be the first to call the cops and chuck them out onto their asses. And, it's not that I'd give a damn about what happened to them. I wouldn't. They chose their fate. But, internally, this experience would be very upsetting to me. Repeated experiences like this would just make the whole business unpleasant. Others might really get off on the power trip of asserting themselves, "I chucked their asses out..."

If you are in the wrong business, you start to try to avoid the business. You really don't want to confront the bad tenant, so you let it pass. You aren't collecting the rent you should. They, maybe, destroy more property. And, it becomes harder to assert yourself. You really don't like the negotiations, and even if you got a good deal, you'd be thinking, "If I buy the property, maybe, the renters will be a real problem just like the ones I'm dealing with now." So, you stop seeking properties to buy. The result is that you are struggling with a small, non-growing enterprise that makes you unhappy, but not any richer. At the same time you are unhappy, someone else is doing the exact same thing and loving it! You fail and decide you are just not a business person. You simply chose the wrong business, not a bad business from a financial standpoint, but a business that just was not compatible with who you are as a person.

Maybe, you find a workaround to your unhappiness. If you are someone who enjoys fixing up older houses, maybe you team up with someone who likes negotiating the purchases and sales. As a team, you do great. You are doing the carpentry you love, and you aren't negotiating anymore. Further, you fix-up and then sell the places, and hence there are no tenant problems. You and your partner are doing great. You have complementary skills, synergistic skills. But, then, your partner is able to negotiate the purchase of several properties. "I can't fix all those up," you say. Your partner says, "No problem. We can hire some guys to help you out." Internally, you feel like, "I really don't want to." But, you say, "Yes." Maybe, it all goes well and you love it. You find you aren't doing much carpentry anymore. Rather, you become more of a supervisor of other carpenters. You are a bit surprised to find how much you enjoy your new role. That's great. But, the opposite can also happen. Maybe, you find you really don't like being a supervisor. It really doesn't matter why. It's just not fun for you.

A big part of being in business is being free to do what you want to do. If you're not having fun, that's not a bad statement about you. It doesn't mean you are not a "natural" entrepreneur. It might just be you are in the wrong role inside your organization. Or, it might mean you should be with a different type of organization altogether. This happens to design people all the time. The person is great as an engineer or a programmer, but just doesn't seem to do well as a supervisor or team lead. Often, others say, the person "just couldn't cut it." That really is an unfair statement. The person just wasn't in a role he enjoyed. When starting a business with a team of entrepreneurs, it is crucial you all agree to and feel comfortable with your mutual roles. Sometimes, the people who pair up to build the next "killer" company are very similar.

"John's a great guy. We should build a business together," you say. Of course, you think John's a great guy. He's exactly like you! You're birds of a feather. You start the enterprise. Suddenly, there are roles within the company neither of you wants. It was never discussed. Too often, each person is implicitly assuming the other will do the undesired roles. If your undesired list corresponds to the other person's "This is what I want to do" list, there is no problem. But, with you and John, you might have a problem. One reason that you should write out a detailed plan for your business is just to be sure everybody knows what everybody else is expecting of him. You want a team where everyone is working in his desired area.

Did you ever know someone who just wasn't frugal? Someone who rather than finding the best deal somehow always managed to find the worst one? Some people are naturally tight with money. They tend to get good deals. It is natural to them. Others, almost from a spiritual standpoint, seem to repel the best deals. It works almost at a metaphysical level. They aren't cost-conscious. Now, all business people need to be aware of costs and not allow costs to spiral out of control, but the frugal person would have a chance running a grocery store, where profit margins are razor-thin. The non-frugal person would almost certainly fail. People who aren't good at hound-dogging-out the best deals should especially avoid low-profit-margin businesses. Many ye-old-time entrepreneurs, those building businesses before the 1980's, might tend to associate cost control as *the* driving characteristic of successful entrepreneurs.

But, let's take our ideal industrial entrepreneur. He loves negotiating. He's tough and downright authoritarian. He's frugal. This person thinks, "I'm it, the businessman for all businesses." What happens if he would try to build an informational-programming company? I know what happens. He tries to be a bit too authoritarian. He doesn't allow the programmers he hires much flexibility. He fights their requests for wage increases. Soon, he has lost several of his best programmers. He can't seem to find anyone to hire. Customers' programs are getting behind. He goes out of business and complains, "There just aren't enough good programmers out there." Meanwhile, competing companies are growing rapidly and adding clients and staff. What is a strength in one business can become a weakness in another business. Early industrial companies, beginning with the railroads, were based upon the hierarchical, military organizational model. That model doesn't work well for most modern enterprises.

Enter an industry you enjoy. I am amazed when I see a company hire someone for its marketing department who has several years of experience in marketing, but who has no experience within the particular industry. For example, someone might have five years experience in direct mail within the automotive industry. Then, the person takes a position with a women's apparel company. Granted, both positions involve direct mail, but it seems unlikely someone very interested in apparel would have stayed with an auto parts company so long. Usually, the person is just looking for a job and doesn't feel any real affinity for either industry. This is how most marketing people get into their present positions.

The company that first hires them sets the industry in which they become experienced. It has always seemed to me that someone who has a real affinity for the industry is the best choice. Given the choice between two candidates, one of whom has the direct-mail experience and the other whose strength lies in really caring about and understanding the industry, I'd usually choose the person who cares about the industry. Tools can be taught, but a passion for an industry either exists or it does not. Many people do grow a passion for the industry they work in, but this usually takes a long time. When starting a company, it is always important to ask yourself, "Would I like this industry? What do I see my day-to-day role being?"

If you have zero interest in cigars, don't start a cigar shop. If the industry you contemplate entering is within a lifelong hobby area of yours, you are probably on the right track. You really need to learn what day-to-day operations are like for the business you contemplate. It's difficult to know an industry if you haven't worked closely with it. Liking cigars doesn't mean you'll like running a cigar shop or for that matter doing database analysis of cigar smokers. The more overlap between the business and your personal proclivities the better.

Any entrepreneur should have one of two basic characteristics to be successful. One was alluded to above. That's a passion for doing what it is you are trying to do. The other is the willingness to work really hard. It is true that you can achieve a level of success in business that allows you to kick back and relax. You've built your company. You've arrived. You have financial security. You have a great management team that can function without you. But this doesn't happen immediately! If kicking back is your goal, then you should sell your company. Often a business flounders when the principal owner decides he has succeeded. The drive is gone. What took years to create as enterprise value can be quickly lost. But, what if your goal has always been only financial? You want the money so you can kick back?

That's an honest motivation, but not really the best one. I know a case where a husband was really excited about building a business, but his wife was skeptical. She knew he was the "kick-back-relax" type. The company started strong, but then the relax mentality started becoming a barrier. Eventually, the business was little more than a hobby or even a theoretical concept. The family lost wage-income, while the guy played entrepreneur without having a real shot-on-goal of building a successful company. He probably still doesn't see the problem. I'm sure his wife dreads his next great business idea. She would do better to be the founder of the next "family" business.

It didn't help much that the business was very physically intensive either and that the guy planned to do a lot of the work himself! Sometimes, others see our weaknesses more clearly than we do. It pays to know an honest and good-willed person who can give us an accurate reflection of ourselves. The more we know ourselves, the better and more appropriate choices we can make for our lives.

For those of you reading this, whose real goal is just to get enough money to kick back and relax, there is nothing wrong with this. But, if you are to succeed, you must change, at least for a period of several years. You must develop the ambition to really bring your idea to fruition. Find something you really do feel passionate about. Be honest with yourself. While it is possible for an ultra-driven person to build a company in an area they are not passionate about, for you it would be nearly impossible. Find something you really enjoy, and, hopefully, a bit of ambition and drive will follow! A scene from *Cool Hand Luke* comes to mind. Paul Newman is a chain-gang prisoner. One day, rather than go about his job of laying road tar slowly, he starts to really haul ass. This causes everyone else to start to work really hard (OK, unrealistic, but, hey, it's just a movie), and they finish the road early in the morning. What do they do for the rest of the day? Relax.

Ultimately, you can find many satisfactions in running and growing a business well beyond money. One personal area I will mention that often holds people back from being all they can be in their lives and in business is a lack of chutzpa. That's a willingness to take a risk and be a bit bold. Step a bit out of line and be a bit more seeking in what they want. Social phobias can really hold you back in most businesses. There is nothing wrong with being shy. Many people are. It says something positive about the person, actually. It shows that the shy person really cares, that the person wants to make a very good impression and do a good job. Do you remember dating in high school? Or later in life? Being a bit apprehensive at a job interview? That bit of tension shows you care about the outcome. Those who are totally calm inside often don't really care. They have the attitude, "Well, if she won't go out with me, someone else will, so it really doesn't matter." It's a shame if you are so concerned with how you will be appraised by other people that you actually appear awkward and make a bad impression. You make a bad impression because you are tense. Others interpret this to mean you do not like them, when, in fact, the exact opposite is true. This has always seemed a horrible irony to me.

In business and in life, you will often get what you ask for, but it is nearly impossible to get what you want if no one else knows what you want. Especially in business, you must be willing to reach out and bring other people on board to share in your ideas. Many good things that happen to entrepreneurs happen because they took action. They took a risk while others sat by. That risk was simply the risk of looking like a fool as they sought out other people to help them. They made it happen because they brought together the team of people that could make it happen. And, yet, doing so certainly opens up the possibility of rejection, ridicule, or failure. It is easier to just sit on the sidelines. I write about this because I know what it feels like. I'm painfully shy. But, at a certain point, I think I just realized that this was a serious hindrance to my life. After all, we only have one life. Everything that you want to do must be achieved in a limited time. So while you might feel a bit tense inside, say to yourself, "Chutzpa," take a deep breath, and do whatever it is you fear. With repeated exposure to what you fear, the fear invariably lessens.

Chapter 10.
Long Shots and Diversification

You might come across a decision like this, "If we can do this and succeed at it, we will have phenomenal success. Yet, it is a bit of a long shot and trying to pursue this opportunity will take considerable company resources. Should we try it?" This is not an easy call. The nicest business decisions are the "no-brainers." These are situations where your costs to develop the idea are relatively small and the possible upswing is huge. It is not a major commitment of personnel time or financial resources. It can happen quickly. The endeavor can be abandoned rapidly with no or little clean-up cost if the idea appears unworkable. You do not need to retrofit the factory. Yet, it seems relatively certain that you will get a decent return on your investment. Tossed in for good measure is the possibility of phenomenal success! This is a situation where everything is in your favor. This situation is three or four kids getting together to build a software company. If it fails, oh, well, but if it succeeds, it can really succeed.

Sometimes long-shot opportunities appear and not everything is in your favor. Your company has $10 million in capital. Trying the new idea will take nearly all of it. If you lose, most of this money will bid you adieu. You choose to pursue the opportunity, even though the potential losses could be relatively staggering to your company. Now, what if your company has a few resources left over to pursue other ideas simultaneously? The fundamental question is: Should you use the remaining resources to pursue a sure thing so that you have something if your long shot (and first priority goal) fails? Or, should you shoot the works again and be thinking about another long shot? Many very knowledgeable entrepreneurs disagree with me on this one.

Those who say go with the sure thing tend to say, "Just because you are making one stupid decision is no reason to make another." This tends to show they would not pursue the first long shot. They think long shots are fundamentally bad. But, for those who shoot the works on one idea, or hopefully *opportunity*, I will say this, if the failure of the idea will greatly cost your company to the extent it will probably lead to bankruptcy, then, any conservative idea your company is pursuing, simultaneously, will probably not save your company. However, if the first long shot fails, it is just possible a second long shot will pay off and save your butt. Or, maybe, throwing all your company's resources into the long shot might be just what is required for it to succeed.

Fundamentally, you can't escape that you are betting your company on this one idea. I like to use an investment analogy to think about this. Suppose you purchase an aggressively-chosen stock. A turnaround company. You figure the chances are 50-50 that the company survives. If it survives, you feel the stock will probably go up by five or, maybe, even eight times in four years or so. If your estimates are at all close, this investment has an excellent expectation value. Let's assume you only have $10,000 to invest and you like this opportunity so much you put $5,000 into it. That leaves you $5,000 to invest elsewhere.

Now, I know there are already two camps forming as this book is being read. The first camp is saying, "Hey, if you like the first stock so much, why not put all $10,000 into it. That's the bold and gutsy move." The other camp is saying, "You'd be an idiot to invest like this. You have almost no diversification. You should, maybe, put $2,000 into your favorite stock and then pick at least four other stocks in which to invest the other $8,000." Each individual is expressing his own feelings and attitudes toward risk. Some people are more cautious than others. Some people take bigger risks. But, I am putting $5,000 into the first stock. Now, where do *you* put the second $5,000? Do you invest it aggressively, also? Or, do you invest it conservatively? For example, one choice is investing in a solid, electric utility company, paying a 5% dividend yield and trading at a reasonable valuation. The other choice is investing in another turnaround company, which also has, say, a 50 percent chance of biting the dust. But, if this company does turn around, the stock will go up, hopefully, three or four times.

Suppose you do invest in the conservative choice. Sure, you will have half of your capital intact if the long shot fails. But, it is a huge mistake to believe that you have any *diversification* at all. The performance of your two-stock portfolio will depend almost exclusively upon the aggressive stock. If it succeeds, your overall portfolio will go way up. If it fails, your overall portfolio will go way down. The conservative stock will probably not be capable of offsetting losses from the aggressive stock. On the other hand, a second, aggressive stock might just go up three or more times. This could offset the total loss of the first investment and lead to an overall decent return. Obviously, a collection of such aggressive stocks could give excellent results. But, one wild stock, flying around in an otherwise conservative portfolio, will have its way with the portfolio. Unless, of course, the wild stock represents only a very small percentage of the overall portfolio.

Similarly, a long-shot idea, taking massive company resources, can sink the company. A few sure bets will probably not be enough to offset the large losses. So, what do you do? Find another long shot to try? That way, if the first long shot doesn't pan out, there is at least a chance the second will save your company? Well, pursuing another long shot at this point probably enhances the likelihood of your company's survival relative to doing something which is much surer, but which doesn't have a large, potential payoff.

Using a hockey analogy, I call this the "shot-on-goal approach to success." You fire off two or three shots, knowing that, probably, at least one or two will get repelled by the goalie, but you only need one shot to get through to succeed overall.

However, business differs in one crucial regard from investment. As an investor, you can easily diversify among ten or a dozen aggressively-chosen stocks, for example, turnaround companies. If it goes at all well, one or two of these companies will manage to regain operational success and, hence, offset multiple companies that fail completely. It is precisely the large gains made on the successes that can nullify the entire loss of several of the companies in the portfolio. Overall, you wind up with a portfolio that has less risk and great potential. Given this, would it not be even better to have your company undertake several diversified long shots? The answer is a definitive, "No." Your company cannot do a dozen different things at one time. You only have so much effort, so many resources, so many people hours at your company's disposal. You only have so many areas of expertise within your company.

Running a business differs significantly from making passive investments in that you can make several passive investments. You can diversify. When you try to diversify *within* a business, you divide resources. This means each endeavor has fewer resources to make the potential, long-shot success happen. When you invest passively in a stock, the company is going to do what it will do, regardless of your holding the stock. I'm assuming you are not a Carl Icahn or someone who buys a controlling, or even significant, interest in the company. The potential success of any given endeavor, when looked at from the perspective of *inside* the company, is affected by trying to diversify. The more you try to do, the more difficult it is to achieve anything.

Because of this, if you decide to make a "bet-your-company" long shot, you should devote full effort to that *one* long shot. Do everything you can to make it happen. Trying to diversify your business is a pretty good indicator that what you are currently doing is not working as well as you had hoped. If this is so, a full change of direction is called for. Why continue what you started with, if it isn't working? There is no dishonor in admitting failure of a given direction.

All you really need is one good direction. Once you have found it, concentrate your resources in that direction. If you concentrate your force into one fundamentally-sound channel, you are more likely to succeed. Avoid "bet-your-company" long shots, whenever possible, by trying to measure the idea's viability before becoming fully engaged. Long shots with big potential payoffs are the ideal "opportunity" to risk-shift away. Risk-shifting is covered in the next chapter.

Chapter 11.
Risk-Shifting and Pursuing
Larger Opportunities

What do you do when your idea is bigger than your britches? What if your idea is something you aren't quite up to financially? You could start smaller and work your way up. That's called bootstrapping and is discussed elsewhere. Sometimes, however, there just isn't a good bootstrapping path to your goal. Your idea simply must start big. You could begin somewhere else entirely, build a different kind of business. Then, as you build wealth, at some point, you will have enough to pursue your initial idea. Both of these directions have merit and should be considered. But, maybe, you don't want to do anything else. You want to try the big idea that you are not financially capable of backing yourself. Then, you raise equity investment capital. You use other people's money to get your start.

Remember, an entrepreneur is a person who brings together the resources to make something happen. One of these resources is capital. Many of the greatest entrepreneurs lacked sufficient capital to achieve their dream alone. Any successful, publicly traded company is a good example. Microsoft, Dell Computer, etc., all raised external capital at some point. That is why they are publicly traded today. To raise capital for any large speculative idea, you invariably will need to give away a percentage of the profits from the endeavor. People who back larger ideas, as a rule, will not do so for only a fixed rate of return in the form of interest and repayment of principal on a bond. They want a percentage of the company. That is the compensation they demand for the large risk they are taking.

Just how much ownership you will need to give up depends upon several factors. The first factor will be the source of the funding. If you borrow from your mother, the percentage ownership demanded will probably be small. In fact, in rare cases like this, because of the relationship to you, the person might well give you the start-up capital as a straight interest-bearing loan. If you try to get your mother-in-law to back your idea, you will most likely need to give up a bigger percentage ownership! Hmm… This brings up a point: Do you really want your mother-in-law as a co-owner of your business? Some entrepreneurs are so quick to jump at the opportunity to get funding that they forget to ask this question: Do I really want this person owning part of my company?

I don't know of any specific cases where a company has raised funding and down the road there were serious conflicts between the funder and the fundee, but I have no doubt these cases are common. There could be a conflict between the goals of the investor and the founder. It might be that the investor sees himself as someone who will be actively involved in the company whereas the founder sees the person as only a source of capital. Maybe the investor is a venture capital firm, which wants to see the company go public, but the founder wants to keep the company private. The possible conflicts are endless.

Most entrepreneurs are very conscious of losing control of their company. They don't like giving a venture capital firm a controlling interest. They tend to feel, "I'd rather just build my company up a bit less rapidly and keep control." Nonetheless, some ideas are not suitable to bootstrapping, and some of the fastest wealth has been built up by people who shared the ownership and risk of their businesses.

Risk-shifting refers to basically retaining the upswing financially, but, at the same time, lowering your personal risk in the endeavor. Whenever you sell a percentage ownership of your company, in addition to losing some of the gain, a huge benefit has been obtained. That benefit is the drawing of cash into the company. The overall risk of the idea failing is the same. This doesn't really change. Many people don't understand this.

Although some will hoot and haw, as a firm backed by investors, your chances of success are now greater. I disagree. Usually, knowledgeable, long-term investors in risky ventures will only back viable ideas. This means that, if your idea gets such backing, it is probably a good idea from the beginning. It does not become a better idea because someone else is willing to back it.

Without argument, capital is a resource and lacking it your idea may never have the chance to be tried. In this sense, the ability to draw upon external financing gives you more options and makes bringing your idea to fruition more likely. However, this is not the result of the idea being any better. It is the simple result of having capital. Money gives a company options. This is a key factor in risk-shifting, and it benefits the entrepreneur, not the investor.

Suppose you want to start a company and need to invest $1 million of your own money, so that you could keep full ownership. With your $1 million, you do not need to seek investors. Let's suppose that you do have the $1 million to invest in your own idea. But $1 million is not a trivial amount to you. Maybe, it is the majority of your wealth. Just to have some numbers to make the discussion concrete, let's assume that your idea has a 50-50 chance of success. We have no way to know what these odds really are, but using some numbers will help you understand how risk-shifting works. Let's also assume that your idea, if successful, will earn $10 million within a few years.

Now, volatility here can really hurt you. If your idea fails, you lose nearly everything you have. You would be basically starting over financially. We assumed the chances of this happening are a huge 50 percent. That's not a fun position in which to put yourself. So, rather than using your own money, you use other people's money, sometimes referred to as OPM (Be wary of people who use the acronym OPM. Many of these people never had one good idea in their lives, other than the realization that selling some glitzy idea of building wealth to others is profitable. That is, they sell investors *the idea of building a company and getting rich*, rather than actually building one and making it profitable).

Let us assume that you can find an investor who will back you to the tune of $1 million dollars. He wants 45% ownership. We will not split ownership 50-50 as this can lead to a stalemate situation.

Although an acceptable way to end a chess game, a stalemate in business translates into a lack of decision making, which invariably leads to failure. You agree to give up 45% ownership and put the $1 million dollars in your business account. It is now called equity. Sometimes, you will hear terms, like paid-in-capital or contributed capital, but, at this point, you need lawyers anyway and the attorneys, together with lots of documents, will help you learn all these new and wonderful terms. The point is you have your money. Now, what happens if your idea fails?

It still fails. Having investors didn't change this. It still has a 50% chance of failing. But, if it does fail, you do not bear the full brunt of the financial pain. In fact, you bear none. You, as the president of the company, will collect a reasonable wage for your services, and, if the idea fails, you still have *your* $1 million that you did not need to invest in the company. Yet, if the idea succeeds, you come out way ahead. Sure, you don't own 100% of the profits anymore. But, you do own 55% of them. That amounts to $5.5 million. Not bad, given that you have taken *no real risk*!

You have shifted the burden of risk to the investor. You contribute the idea; they contribute the capital. You cannot lose! I have seen this happen repeatedly, even to the extent that the founding entrepreneur wins, even if the company does poorly. Suppose you raise $10 million from investors to create a manufacturing company, and you retain a portion of the ownership, say 55%. As pointed out, the capital within the company has value. This capital can be utilized to try to make more money. Your percentage ownership of that capital means that you own $5.5 million dollars. *Not bad for contributing only an idea*! Hopefully, the idea is a good one, so that your investors will also be pleased.

Unfortunately, in some cases, the idea is transient. In the late 1990's, this is especially true for companies having the word "Internet" in their name. Investors are paying tremendous amounts for such companies. I often joke to friends that, if they wish to start a company, they should put the word "Internet" somewhere in the name, or better yet, just "net." That makes you sound more trendy. Never mind that your business has nothing to do with the Internet! Of course, in several years, the reverse may be true. "Internet" might well be a dirty word in investment discussions. As in, "Damn, I lost $&%$%^& dollars in that &%$# Internet company." You may have a viable idea with real profit potential involving the Internet. You might even be generating significant profits, but you will need to downplay the Internet aspect of it! Such is life.

Anyway, you have just boosted your wealth by $5.5 million dollars without doing anything. OK. You wrote a business plan. You are willing to share a percentage of anything you make. You sought out and found investors to back your idea. But that's not really a great achievement! Not that it's easy, but it's not like you invented the telegraph or something. Further, in a major bull stock market, like we experienced in the 1990's, such a company might go public soon and be valued at some ungodly sum, like $200 million dollars. By the time this happens, you only own 25% percent of your company, but that's still $50 million dollars. Notice how you have shifted your thinking from how much the company is worth in terms of wealth within the company to your company's wealth as measured externally by the stock market. This is an extreme case of risk-shifting. Even if your stock drops to only one-quarter its present value, you are still very well off. And, operationally, the business could be doing horribly!

This is a huge advantage to being an entrepreneur over an investor. It is possible to retain the reward and shed a large measure of the risk. Rather than trying to own 100% of a smaller pie, you go after a smaller percentage of a bigger pie.

While many entrepreneurs immediately grasp the truth of the above, they often miss that you can shift risk and, at the same time, enhance the endeavor's chance of success. Suppose you have an excellent idea. You feel the odds are strongly in your favor. You have just enough to capitalize the project or are only slightly undercapitalized. As I discuss elsewhere, sole entrepreneurs are the fodder of buzzards. They don't do nearly as well as teams. Why not raise capital and bring some experience on board at the same time? What is far better than someone who only brings money to the table (not to discount such people. I like them a lot!) is someone who also brings some much needed skill to the company. Maybe it takes three or four of you together before you can fund the project. That's OK. In what areas does your company need strength? Maybe you lack marketing skills but know someone who has these skills. Maybe that person would like to join your ragtag group of entrepreneurs ready to take on the world. If the person is ready to invest a chuck of his own personal capital, you can believe he is sincere.

Finally, there is one last topic about selling equity to investors that should be addressed. That is answering the question, "What do I owe the investors?" I don't mean formally, as a percentage of your company. Rather, I mean this on a more moral-philosophical level. These people have put their faith in you as an entrepreneur. You owe them your best shot at building a profitable company. Sometimes, a person will feel, "Hey, I've arrived. It doesn't really matter now. I'm rich anyway." If you take this attitude, you are not only letting your investors down, but you are also letting yourself down. Don't you really believe you can achieve what you have claimed? And, what does it make you, if you knew what you were claiming was unlikely to succeed, but you promoted it as a great growth idea anyway?

This does not mean you should try to satisfy every little demand of all those who have invested in your business. Sometimes, that is neither possible nor desirable. Always try to maximize the long-term value of your company. What if the venture capital firm that provided you with start-up capital wants you to take steps to maximize the current value of your company's stock? (Usually, so it can sell out! In this case, they won't even be shareholders in your company anymore.) If you know the steps will not help your company in the long run, but might actually hurt your company, then there is only one answer you can tell them, "No." They have gotten a fair return from their investment. You are in no way obligated to serve their special interests above and beyond any other investors in your company. The greatest entrepreneurs and business people are not slaves to the stock market. They focus upon building the business. If you do your best at this, you are serving your investors well.

Chapter 12.
Cash Flow Versus Earnings
and Working Capital

Most people who work as employees for a living treat earnings and cash flow as the same thing. Here's what typically happens. These people know how much they will earn in the year. They know what their wages will be. Further, they usually have a pretty good idea of how much money they will earn in any given two-week period. Payday arrives. They deposit their paycheck in their checking account. They credit the checking account, and then they go shopping. They buy groceries. They buy household products. Maybe, a treat or two for having worked so hard during the week. Each time they write a check, they deduct the amount the check was written for from the remaining balance. Hopefully, they don't run out of money before the next payday!

Every time they receive their earnings, they are receiving cash. By and large, every time they buy something and absorb an expense they are paying cash. Their earnings and expenditures will match up nicely with their cash inflows and cash outflows. Because of this, they seldom give any thought to the fact that cash flow and earnings are different. Many business books belabor this point in painful detail. I don't want to do that, but I do want to be sure all readers understand that cash flow and earnings are not the same thing.

Cash flow refers to what you might think it should. It represents the flow of cash into or out of an organization. Every time you receive a check, it represents a cash inflow—assuming it doesn't bounce, of course! Every time you write a check for an expense, it represents a cash outflow. Cash flow represents actual cash availability, entering or leaving the company. This is not the same as earnings. Suppose you manufacture boats. A customer sends you a check for $100,000. This is payment in full for a boat you will build. Your company has just experienced a cash inflow. That's a good thing! But this in no way means your company has earned $100,000. In addition to getting the check, you have a liability. You must provide the boat! If you do not, you will need to refund the $100,000.

The boat has some cost to produce. Until you have actually delivered the boat and incurred all the costs associated with this job, you don't really know what your expenses are and, hence, your profits. You had better have good estimates of what it costs to produce the boat you have just promised! You might estimate your net profit at $10,000. This means that you have $90,000 in cash that, somehow, does not belong to you. There will be cash outflows to relieve you of that money.

The above scenario is the best of all possible worlds. You have cash coming into your company before you need to produce the product and deliver it. This means the cash can be used to build the product—to finance its construction. Unfortunately, for most businesses, the exact opposite is more likely to occur. The customer wants to buy a *finished* boat. You will still sell it for $100,000, incur the same costs, and make a profit of $10,000.

But, now, you must come up with the $90,000 cost to build the boat *before* you can try to sell it. You must pay $90,000 in material and wages before you receive the $100,000. This can lead to problems. At the very least, if you do not have the cash to build the boat, you will need to borrow. This means you will be paying interest expense, so your profits will be less than $10,000. At the worst, you simply cannot produce the boat.

Your cash flow position can get worse. Maybe, you do not collect the full payment immediately. Maybe, you allow the buyer to finance the boat. This means there is even more of a time delay before you are paid in full for the product you have created. Just for simplicity, let's assume the buyer pays you the $100,000 one year after you have produced the boat and the buyer has taken possession. It would be silly to allow this particular financing example, but let's use it, anyway.

When did you make the profits on selling the boat? If you can be reasonably sure that the buyer will not default on the payment, you have earned the payment of $100,000 when you deliver the boat to the buyer. Because you have also incurred the $90,000 in costs, and I am assuming you have already paid out this $90,000, you have earned $10,000 profit. Nevertheless, you won't collect a dime for one year.

So, your books show a sale in the current year and profits of $10,000. Those are your earnings. But, SHOW ME THE MONEY! Where is the money? There isn't any. There have only been cash outflows of $90,000. Even though you are doing well from a profitability standpoint, from a cash flow standpoint, you are hurting. You are out $90,000 in cash. This is the problem of cash inflow not being exactly correlated with sales and profits. Nor is cash outflow correlated exactly with expenses incurred. If you still hadn't paid your suppliers, you would owe them money, but have slightly more cash within your company at present.

So, when you earn money is not necessarily when you collect it. Yet, you have bills to pay. When they are due, they are due. You need cash to pay them. Suppose your boat building company had a rent due. You started the year with $90,000, we are assuming, and you could have paid the rent. But, now, you have no cash at all! And, you have made profits of $10,000! When running a business, you must be aware of the difference between profits and cash flow. You should seek to keep both high profitability and a strong cash flow into your organization at the same time.

Just as you can predict your profits on the boat from predicting your sale price and knowing your expenses, you can also predict your cash flow position. You know the expenses you will incur, and you can also estimate *when* they will be paid out. On what dates will the money actually be paid from your checkbook to the supplier? This tells you when your cash outflows occur. Similarly, you can predict when you will receive payment for your products. Here, it is one year down the road. Based upon this, you could easily draw up a monthly list of all estimated cash inflows into your organization and a list of all monthly cash outflows.

Estimated Monthly Cash Flow Statement (January)
Starting Cash = $90,000

Item	Date	Cash Outflow	Cash Inflow	Cash
Steel	Jan 1	$20,000		$70,000
Rudder	Jan 1	$2,000		$68,000
Wages	Jan 15	$5,000		$63,000
Interested Earned	Jan 31		$500	$63,500
Wages	Jan 31	$5,000		$58,500

Ending Cash = $58,500 which equals starting cash for February. We could then compare the above monthly *estimated* cash flow statement to the *actual* monthly cash flow statement.

If you find that more money will be flowing out of the company than flowing into it in any given month, you have a problem. You must plan ahead to cover the shortfall. Sometimes, trying to do too much too quickly, such as growing your company too fast, can lead to this sort of problem. If you *can* borrow money and the interest expense isn't a big deal, relative to how much you are making, then, you can cover the cash shortfall.

This is a very safe form of borrowing. You are only borrowing to cover a short-term cash flow shortage that you know, with a high certainty, will lead to cash inflows relatively soon. It is not as if there is a great chance of not being able to pay back the initial principal. Assuming you know you will be paid for your boat, you could borrow $90,000 at the start of the year, then, use the $90,000 to build the boat. In a way, it would be just like borrowing the money and putting it into a savings account. Now, people don't ever do this, because the bank will charge them, say, 10% as an interest rate, but only pay them 5% on the money in their savings account. But, in business, you might be earning much higher rates than 10%. Whether or not a bank will give you the money is a different issue entirely!

Later, we will look in detail at the effect such borrowing will have upon your company's profitability and the importance of the time value of money. But, for now, notice that if you took out a loan of $90,000 at 10% then, at the end of the year, you would pay the bank $9,000. Because you earn $10,000 from the boat buyer, you now only make $1,000 on the sale of a $100,000 boat! Financing costs have killed your company's profitability. And, the reason you needed to borrow was that your business was cash strapped.

The solution to this silliness is to avoid businesses that will have bad cash flow projections. Remember that you can estimate your cash flows just like you do your expenses. If you find the business you contemplate will be constantly pressured by cash flow problems, think seriously about entering a different business! Maybe, you can find some way to improve your cash flow position. For example, don't finance the boat buyer for a full year, but demand a certain up-front payment. That will help you pay the costs of manufacturing the boat.

There are two flavors of cash flow. "Good" cash flows represent money coming into your company. "Bad" cash flows represent cash leaving your company. We, sometimes, call money coming into your company positive cash flow and money leaving your company negative cash flow. In any given month, you will have either a positive or a negative number associated with your monthly cash flow total. This is your net cash flow for the month.

Just subtract cash leaving the company from cash entering the company for the month. This number is your net cash flow into or out of the company, or, sometimes, this is also just called cash flow. If the number is positive, you have more cash than you did a month earlier. If your monthly cash flow is negative, you will have less money at the end of the month than you had at the beginning of the month.

When you contemplate a business venture, estimate not only your expenses and profits, but also estimate the timing of those expenses and the timing of the revenue streams coming into your company. Companies with strong cash flow have a much easier time growing, so take every reasonable step to assure your business has strong cash flow.

Cash, or something that can quickly be converted into cash, is important. Further, this something must not be overly volatile in value so that its sale produces the anticipated cash. If the cash you receive for its sale is considerably less than anticipated, you might have trouble paying your bills. Some inventories would not make our cut and would not be considered working capital, while other inventories would be allowed in our definition of working capital. If we want to be really conservative, we would just call cash equivalents our working capital and neglect inventories and receivables entirely. You might wonder why I don't just use the formal definition of working capital and let it go at that. The reason is that we wish to focus, not on accounting definitions, but rather upon the details that are most important to effective decision making. When we think, "Working capital," we want to be thinking, "Cash." You can learn the formal definitions in any good book on accounting.

While most accountants lump anything that can be converted into cash within one year into the category of short-term assets, for us, one year is way too long. If what you are including in working capital cannot be converted into cash in at most one month (and, preferably, two weeks) that is too long. A key goal for any business is being able to pay its bills—rent, suppliers, employee wages, etc.—which usually need to be paid on a regular basis. Because of this, you can predict when you will need to have various amounts of cash on hand (so that you can turn around immediately and write a check to someone else! That doesn't seem fair, does it?). But, the unexpected does occur. A machine breaks and needs to be replaced. Other unforeseen expenses arise. An expense that was anticipated arrives early. Maybe, an opportunity presents itself, and you can only pursue the opportunity, if you can raise some cash right then and there.

The biggest source of stress in business is having bills due and not having the money to pay them. People who have struggled financially at any time know this. It is a horrible feeling. In some ways, if you have struggled with this as an individual, you are better prepared psychologically to run a business than if you have always had money.

Having bills due and not being able to pay them puts your company in a compromising position. If you don't pay the rent, maybe, you will be evicted. Not exactly the image you want for a growing and thriving company! Worse, maybe you won't be able to produce more products. It's difficult to produce products, if your machines are locked up inside, and you are locked outside! Maybe, you have contracted to produce products for a given client. You are not only legally obliged to produce, but if you fail to do so, at the very least, you will lose future business from that client. Without the cash to pay your suppliers, maybe, you will lose bargaining power with the supplier. In the worst case, the supplier will fear you are going belly up and will want prepayment for your next shipment.

Let's look at the other side. If your company is cash rich and a supplier sends you a shipment and offers a 2% discount for immediate payment, then you can pay the bill immediately and save 2%. It doesn't sound like a lot, but remember, for some industries a change in costs by 2% might translate into double the profitability on the sales! Maybe, you will see an opportunity to pick up some inventory your company needs at fire-sale prices. With cash available, you can do so. Instead of being stressed out about not being able to pay your bills, you are excited to pick up extra opportunities. Being cash rich is also desirable because, as your sales grow, you will need higher levels of working capital to sustain the higher level of sales.

How do you stay cash rich? It's not always easy. Maybe, it's even impossible in some industries. When you contemplate starting a business, give some serious study to how cash flows within that industry. Are all the businesses cash starved? That probably means your company will be also. After all, what is there you can do that the others cannot? Often, the answer is "nothing." But, if the industry tends to throw off a lot of cash flow, then, there will probably be several cash-rich companies in the industry. Just by knowing your expenses to produce your product, knowing what payment policies you will be giving your customers, and knowing how fast you anticipate growing, you can get a feeling as to whether your company will be cash-strapped. Growth is a key ingredient here. Many companies have adequate cash to support the current level of sales, but then, as sales grow by 25% or more, the company finds itself unable to produce the extra product. The company lacks the cash to do so.

Trying to grow in an industry that has difficulty holding cash is really difficult. If you desire to grow, choose a business that tends to throw off a lot of cash. By this, I mean the business has high margins; the customers tend to pay rapidly after the sale or even before the sale; suppliers don't demand large up-front payments. Companies that create services and intellectual capital products tend to be cash rich. High net margin businesses tend to be cash rich. Choosing a good business to enter is probably the most significant thing you can do to help you stay cash rich. It will be easier for your company to grow, and you will have far less daily stress in running the business.

Holding cash reserves is also good. It's the age-old idea of saving (cash) for a rainy day. I know several people out there are thinking this is a mistake. They would say, "Get the money invested and keep it working to grow." Yet, some of the fastest growth companies, such as Microsoft, have tended to keep high levels of cash. Many of the savviest investors tend to hold a lot of cash at times. Sometimes, the opportunity to put the cash to work just isn't really there. It would be silly to toss money into a bad investment, just to keep it "working." It would be far better to wait until a real opportunity appears.

Running low on cash can endanger the entire business. Every time you need to borrow short-term funds to grow, you pay interest. Keeping the profits your business has earned in the form of cash is often the best growth strategy for the money. Hold cash in a money market fund until you see how to utilize it effectively within your business.

Chapter 13.
Knowing Where The Value Is Created. A Comparison of Programming To CBT

This chapter will give a little insight into one of the industries with which I am most familiar. That is the field of computer programming and the closely-related field of multimedia development. For those not interested in these areas, I suggest you read this chapter anyway, as it will help you identify the most important aspects of your own industry.

Custom software development has grown explosively over the last decade and will probably continue to do so for awhile at least. The field is so hot that many computer programming companies, focusing on the newest area of Internet programming, have been able to go public almost immediately after being formed. Many of these companies have valuations way above what I feel is justified. Looking beyond this, a far greater number of computer programming, consulting, and development companies have achieved sales and profitability to justify valuations measured in the several hundreds of millions of dollars. And, all of this has happened within three to five years in many cases. Spectacular as this sounds, there are fundamental reasons why such explosive growth is possible.

Programming and software development is probably the ideal example of a good entrepreneurial business. This is because all aspects of the industry are in favor of the entrepreneur. This is why so many computer-oriented companies have grown so rapidly and so profitable. First, this is an area with almost no up-front capital costs. There are no huge machines to buy. There is no large investment in plant and equipment. Two or three people working on PC's, no different from those you find in many homes, have started such companies. Add to the cost of the PC's an equivalent cost in software, and many of these entrepreneurs were ready to go.

Nor is there any huge capital cost as the company grows. These companies still don't need any big, expensive machines. What they typically do need are more programmers. In fact, several companies claim the only limit to their growth is a lack of programmers. Whether or not this is fully true, I cannot really say. I think it is also, partly, the result of not being willing to take a chance and hire entry-level people and an unwillingness to pay the going rates in salaries to experienced people.

The other day, for example, someone showed me something quite amusing. It was an employment listing from a newspaper. The employer wanted a Visual Basic Programmer with two years of experience. In addition, the person was to have significant experience with Microsoft Access, Microsoft's database product, and data modeling skills. So far, so good. This is a common combination of desired skills. The funny part was the company advertised the starting salary at about $13.00 per hour. To anyone with any knowledge of this field, this was simply a ludicrous offer. The going rate for such a person would be at least half again this amount. For this wage, the company will get someone straight out of a technical college who has, maybe, two classes in Visual Basic. To people with the desired qualifications, the ad was more of a joke than anything else.

Fortunately, the company posting the ad was not a programming-oriented business. But, it goes to show you can ask for anything in the classifieds, no matter how ridiculous. Who knows, maybe some gullible fool will fit the qualifications and take the job, not knowing how underpaid he is relative to his peers. Businesses can be out of touch with reality. There is no other way to state it. Businesses can fail to understand the world around them and how it affects their business. This can only lead to bad decision making by the business.

Every business has a sphere of reality which must be mastered and about which the business must be aware. Because the above company was not intimately involved in the programming industry, it can survive, despite being totally clueless about current wages in the area.

But what if the business above were a computer consulting company? Would placing such an ad lead to new employees to grow the business? I'm thinking not. And, yet, the business might whine, "But, we can't find any people!" Always ask yourself if there is something you are missing before you start whining. Sometimes, everyone else is also whining, and you figure, "What the hell, I may as well whine too." But, if you come to understand what others are missing, you will be positioned to exploit your unique insight into the business. Success is better than whining. When you look at the fastest growing computer consulting companies, you will see they are very employee-focused. They pay and treat their employees very well.

The nice thing about a company which adds only personnel and not large plant and machines as it grows is that you can add people as needed. They are paid as they work. When interviewing a new employee, he doesn't say to you, "Well, I plan to work for you for the next ten years. And, because we've agreed I should be earning $50,000 annually, you'll need to pay me $500,000 up-front." You won't even be paying this person $50,000 a year at the beginning of the year. This person will be getting a check at the end of every two weeks or so. Further, he will have worked the two weeks before being paid for them! This is very much like receiving full supplier financing. You have the product before you need to pay for it.

Suppose your programming company is a consulting company. What does this person you have just hired do? Hint: Consult. He goes out to companies that need whatever it is that he can do—juggle, dance, write PL/SQL for Oracle, whatever. Suppose he stays at this company a week, and, then, the company is billed. The money owed the consulting company quickly finds its way to the consulting company. There is usually no large delay in payment. And, of course, a portion of this money will be used to hire more consultants. What are the other expenses of this consulting company? There aren't a heck of a lot of other expenses. And, so, a big chunk of the money remains as profit to the company. This translates into higher profit margins than most companies have. And, remember, the more revenue a company retains as profit, the more flexibility the company has, the faster it can reinvest and grow the business, and the faster the company founders can compound their wealth.

You might ask, "What is the compounding interval for a consulting company like this?" For all practical purposes, it is zero. There is no limit to how quickly earnings can be deployed to do more of what it is that the company does. If you can find the clients and hire the programmers, there is no fundamental reason you can't work on 100 projects your company's first year. Or 1,000 projects. Or a million. Industrial companies are limited to some finite compounding cycle. This cycle represents how long it takes for money invested in the company to make more money.

Even if the profit margins are high and the compounding cycles small, as discussed previously, it is no bloody good if you are selling a $1 product. You want large revenue per sale. That way your company doesn't wind up working really hard to sell a billion of some widget. Processing a billion of any physical product one at a time is a pain in the butt. It simply will tax the company's resources. Companies are willing to pay computer consultants a great deal of money for their services. Custom software, which is prewritten and slightly modified for the particular company, can fetch a custom solutions provider several tens of thousands of dollars per sale.

You can see computer programming or custom software development has a great business model. But, that never answers the fundamental question: Why are client companies willing to pay consultants and custom solution providers so much money?

Well, one guess would be, "Everyone else is paying them so much, so I guess we should too." That's a horrible answer. If the client doesn't know why it's paying someone a lot of money to do something, maybe, it should contemplate why. Maybe, you don't want to pay them a lot of money after all!

How do you market your services if you really don't know why companies contract with you? How do you know which companies to market to and what approach to use when trying to sell to them? The best way to market your consulting company is to explain *what you can do for the client*. You don't do this by explaining in your technical language, "Well, I can write some Java code that will allow a web browser visiting your HTML page to access an Oracle database. Data transfer will be fully encrypted, of course." Who the hell cares? That's not what the client wants to hear.

The technical explanation misses the big picture. Why is the client willing to pay for a database hooked up to the web? What value do you provide the client? The obvious answer is that it allows the client to make sales over the Internet. And, there are a lot of people on the Internet, which means, maybe, a lot of sales. The client understands this. This is why the client wants a web page and is willing to pay you to create it.

The fundamental reason programming is valuable to clients is because it helps them solve very technical problems, which allows the client to save a tremendous amount of money or make a tremendous amount of money. Or, as the client grows, things once done manually are not feasible without computerization. Computers allow a company to achieve things it needs to achieve to remain in business and stay competitive. Some of these things cannot be achieved in any other way. It all rests on problem-solving. That is why programmers are hired. Programmers are problem-solvers.

Not long ago, I was at the local post office where they sort mail. To sort regular letters, machines using optical character recognition software (OCR) read the address. A bar code was put on the letter, and the letter sent on its way into a tub destined for, say, Des Moines, Iowa. This all happened fast—10 to 15 letters per second. Given the tremendous amount of mail the USPS moves, it would be nearly impossible to sort the mail by hand. Certainly, the labor cost to do so would be prohibitive.

At the time, the Post Office still sorted larger pieces, such as magazines and 8½ by 11 envelopes, with machines where a person sat on a stool and keyed in a particular code for each piece of mail on a ten-key pad. Not only does this lead to employee carpal tunnel, but it requires the employees to memorize up to thousands of address ranges. This is exactly the sort of thing computers were designed to do. Yet, here were people, plugging away, doing the job in a very manual-intensive fashion.

The Post Office had a new machine, which was being tested to sort these larger pieces. The machine was a collaboration between IBM and some European company (whose name escapes me). They had people sitting at computer terminals typing the codes in! I asked the representative from IBM why they didn't just use OCR technology to read the addresses. I mean it's not like they didn't know the technology existed. They were using it for sorting letters! He gave me some song and dance about this not being a trivial thing to do. "With letters you always know the address is somewhere near the center of the envelope as it goes by. There is, maybe, a return address, but not a lot of other writing on the envelope to confuse the machine. With these magazines and larger envelopes, first, you have to find the address before you can read it. It might be in the center or one of the corners, and there is, often, a lot of other text on magazines to confuse the automated reader. But we're working on it."

Yeah, yeah. I'll tell you what is not a trivial thing to do. That's reading my handwriting. If they can figure that one out (and they did), then, they certainly can find the address on a magazine. Most people find the address so quickly that they never give any thought to the intellectual steps they use to locate it. To solve this problem, or one like it, you must fundamentally think about how you as a human solve the problem. Then you need to put together some code that has this limited ability. This would be a great problem to give a moderately-advanced class of computer science students. I'd bet most could solve it. Maybe, it would take all semester, but they'd get it. But, then again, this was IBM, not a bunch of enthusiastic kids with dreams of being the next Bill Gates!

I estimated, if the Post Office replaced the quasi-manual method with OCR, they could cut back on labor costs to the extent of about $1 billion dollars every five years. And, that estimate probably was low. Granted the Post Office is a huge organization, and this is partially why the savings are so immense. But, these savings clearly show the value of problem-solving. Find the address on a magazine; save a billion dollars in five years. Of course, the person or group solving this problem won't be very well-liked by the Postal Worker's Union! (Just as an aside: I was in no way involved with IBM or this project. I was just an observer.)

So, if you are starting a company to create custom software, what is the key ingredient you want your employees to have? Problem-solving skills. Yet, some company recruiters just don't get the picture. They ask, "Do you have any experience in Java?" The candidate says, "No." The recruiter says, "That's too bad. We really need somebody with at least two years of Java experience." The potential hire walks away, and the recruiter never learns the candidate has a 150 IQ and has solved problems that would blow away anything the candidate would be called upon to do within the company. Then, typically, this kid is picked up by some upstart company, and the company that didn't hire him keeps whining, "We can't find anybody."

Once you know the value in programming lies in problem-solving, you are far more able to see opportunities where some particular problem is costing a company a tremendous amount of money. If you see such huge, potential savings for a business, it is very easy to sell them on the idea. Show them how short the payback period is for their investment in software. After that, all those savings turn into profit for the company. Once you've found one area of savings, it is likely the same savings can be obtained in a similar way at different companies. You don't even need to solve another problem! Just reapply the same solution to a different company. Huge wealth has been created this way.

It should be clear the best market for a computer-programming entrepreneur to target is not the individual consumer, but rather companies. Preferably, sufficiently large companies that will reap great savings from your effort. That translates into high income for your company. Just as an aside, I do not know of one computer consultant who markets to individuals. They all market to businesses. Businesses are better able to pay for the problems you can solve.

Apply the same type of understanding to whatever business you are in or contemplate entering. Ultimately, what is the business about? Why is what you do of value? If you can answer this, you will be better than your competition. If you can't answer this, it probably means you lack conviction in the value of your own business. Maybe, there is no value created for the customer. Maybe, the idea was just a gimmick. Move on to a better business.

Until a few years ago, I had no knowledge of computer based training (CBT) as an industry. That, in retrospect, was quite amazing, given that I had such a solid foundation in programming and had also studied several closely-related areas of business. CBT is a subfield of multimedia design, which, usually, means CDs that are interactive with the user. Multimedia utilizes graphics, sound, video, and text to communicate something to the person sitting in front of the PC. At present, there is what is referred to as DVD, which will probably replace CDs as the "sophisticated" way of transferring such multimedia. It doesn't really matter. The exact format and the computer programs used to create the multimedia are just details. What is the larger picture? Where in multimedia does the value lie?

Problem-solving? No. But, good guess. Multimedia, like programming, is a very easy industry to enter. No backhoes required. Client companies are willing to pay a good chunk of money to other companies to create multimedia. As with programming, personnel is the big cost. But, where is the value created? If you are familiar with many of the CDs created for consumers, you might argue that there is no value. There is just a bunch of junky CDs pretending to be worth purchasing. If you have seen good CDs of this sort, you might think the value lies in entertainment to the purchaser. But, comparing even the better CDs to entertainment media, like movies or audio CDs, shows that interactive CDs aren't as good as entertainment. At least, not yet.

The value of multimedia lies within its subcategory of computer based training (CBT). The key word is *training*. Companies have a constant need to train their employees. Training can come in many forms. Some things are still best learned through books. For example, for the ideas I am trying to convey in this book, I believe a pure text is the very best format. What would I add to an interactive CD? A naked, dancing picture of Bill Gates? Glad you bought the book and not the CD, huh?

Other areas are really best taught by a person, especially things that demand demonstrations, followed by student attempts to achieve the result. Trades, such as welding, auto repair, etc., really demand a good instructor. A good teacher still is the very best method of training you can obtain for any purpose. I place the emphasis on "good." But, sometimes teachers are overkill. Maybe, a simple demonstration from which the student can watch and learn is more than adequate. In this case, a video serves well, providing the employees don't fall asleep during it!

Other examples of CBT are simulations of various processes employees must master. Some of these simulations are ideally suited for putting on a CD. A nice thing about a simulation is that the trainee can get "almost" hands-on experience, without actually doing the thing. Flight simulators are an example. The simulator gives the person an idea of what they will need to do without the possible loss of life and an expensive aircraft!

In all these forms, companies pay to create training for their employees. It makes the employees more capable of doing whatever they were hired to do. This translates into more employee productivity. If it doesn't, then, the training is worthless. So if you were producing flashy multimedia, and your business was not doing well, it would behoove you to consider creating training for clients. Focus upon conveying important information that is best conveyed through interactive media. Create something that has a clear value to the client. Try to know where the wealth within your industry is created and focus your attention there.

Depending upon the type of CBT you were creating, more advanced programming and problem-solving skills may or may not be crucial. A flight simulator that must respond as an airplane would is really more of a programming problem than a multimedia design project. On the other hand, many CBTs involve nothing more than a video demonstration and answering some questions about it. You don't need any super-programmers to do this. But, a good understanding of instructional design and how people learn best would be valuable. Seeing what skills you need is crucial when hiring employees.

It is not always obvious what skills are really needed by your employees. Often, as a company learns more about what it is really trying to do (or should be trying to do), it finds it has been hiring programmers, when it really needs instructional designers, or visa versa. So, first, focus upon understanding where you can create the most value for your clients. What is it you are trying to do? What is it your clients need you to do? Then, hire the people who have the skills to do this.

Chapter 14.
You Know Enough, But Keep Learning Anyway

One thing that often separates people who grow as individuals from those who tend to stagnate in life is that the growers tend to keep learning new things. What you know, sometimes, can be translated into what you can do within your business. You will not know how to profit from an area, unless you are aware of it. You will not see the opportunities. If you are always trying to grow as a person, by learning more and new things, then you will see combinations others overlook. Or, maybe, the others haven't overlooked them. That's not entirely bad either. There are many areas, like computer consulting, in which many people are building businesses. Often, these areas are in fields that have tremendous and growing demand. There is always room for one more company to muscle its way in!

But, how do you learn about the explosive growth possibilities? Luck plays as big a part as does trying to be a soothsayer. Many people believed, with companies like Microsoft in the software industry, the window of opportunity for new software companies was rapidly closing by the early 1990's. Yet, many of the most profitable programming companies weren't even started until the early 1990's. The growers were the custom software solutions providers that catered to businesses. Often, these providers used Microsoft products almost exclusively! Then, came the Internet, or, at least, common awareness of the Internet, and POW, a whole new area of computer-based entrepreneurship, building web sites or getting companies on the Internet, evolved.

It would have paid for someone working within the computer-programming field to keep up with developments! But whether or not you were a programmer when the Internet became popular was largely a matter of luck. The most innovative and best Internet companies, like Net Perceptions, were built upon a foundation of understanding and knowledge that *preceded* the advent of the popularity of the Internet. It was a matter of having technology or ideas that had application to the Internet. A person's positioning to seize an opportunity will vary, but learning never hurts!

To survive in many areas, you must constantly be learning new things. If you don't enjoy learning new software programs, for example, then becoming a computer consultant just won't work for you. If you really don't like learning new things, in general, then you are, probably, in trouble. For you will need to learn a whole lot of new stuff if you hope to build a business. I have always looked at this as a challenge and an opportunity rather than an unpleasant need. The key thing is that learning should be fun. Many people forget this.

School has brutalized them. They just never felt they did well and just wanted to avoid it. Whenever they hear the word "learning," it conjures up a whole range of past images, usually negative. Being berated by a teacher, for example. Many of the greatest entrepreneurs never really liked school. In fact, many of the largest information-oriented companies built were founded by those who never attended college or who dropped out. This does not mean that these people are not constant learners. It's just that they learn on their own.

The one huge advantage to taking classes, rather than self-directed learning, is that you meet people interested in a similar area. Whenever someone drops out of a school like Stanford to begin a business with several classmates, I usually assume they will succeed. That they have teamed up with many other bright people gives them a powerful advantage. Teamwork. Further, despite all I said about college not being important, I have found there is a great deal to learn from professors in academia. Often, they are at the forefront of knowledge. They will point you in directions you might not otherwise pursue, so you will not have to rediscover the wheel. "Gee, the square one didn't work so well." They can lead you to the round wheel without the intermediate steps!

For example, despite self-study of database design and querying, one class, at the University of Minnesota, showed me my methods were worlds behind how people truly knowledgeable proceeded. I had always thought the goal of relational database design to be the creation of tables, so that's where I started. It seemed to work well enough—that's all I knew. But, the class showed me, by focusing upon the logical structure of the data, I could do a far better job. I could see relationships that I wouldn't have been aware of before, and I could ask questions that would lead to a far better understanding of the data. If it hadn't been for being shown this direction, I might never have discovered it on my own. Learning this "new" method of modeling data made the class very valuable to me.

I remember watching a great TV show. This elementary school teacher was talking to a little girl, asking her why she wasn't studying and doing well. The little girl responded. "My brother says it's not what you know, but who you know that matters."

The teacher asked, "And, who does your brother know?"

"No one. That's why he's unemployed," answered the little girl.

This is cute because the little girl's brother has a consistent philosophy of life, so you can't really argue with him. But, he is missing a part of the picture. While the lesson of the show was, probably, what you know *is* important, I would emphasize *what* you know and *who* you know are intimately connected. If you know Java programming, you probably hang out with other Java programmers, and you will learn…more JAVA programming.

This is why there are families where the members all tend to be in the same occupation, lawyer families, police officer families, etc. Whom they know tends to influence what they are exposed to and what they will learn, a particular way of looking at life. It is difficult for a kid who is never exposed to an area to really get a feel for the area. He simply has no exposure to it. Entrepreneurial families are the same. Studies have shown, if you are the son or daughter of an entrepreneur or a business person, you are more likely to start your own company. You see it as an option. Working for others is not a given.

Anything you learn can change your perspective of life, not always for the better, unfortunately, but this is a risk you must take. One horrible danger of learning more is becoming disillusioned with what you see. Many people who know an awful lot about an industry are so aware of the pitfalls that they just don't feel they are likely to succeed in building their own company. I don't mean to sound trite, but never let the little facts interfere with your plans! Focus upon the biggest facts only. Toss aside the pesky little concerns. Often, you can work around them, one at a time, as they appear. But, taken together, all those little, lurking dangers become a quagmire dooming you to failure. There is no way to untangle yourself from their weighted sum. People who build businesses tend to move forward as they can. And, that is usually one step at a time. When a problem comes up, then, it is an issue to be dealt with. But never sweat the small stuff before you need to. And, yes, you will need to *sweat* the small stuff at some point!

One academic study asked the question, "What is it that most separates successful entrepreneurs from the average person?" The study found that successful entrepreneurs are far more likely to overestimate the control they have over any given situation. They tend to overestimate their own abilities more than the average person does. The key word is overestimate. Successful entrepreneurs tend to overestimate what they are capable of. No matter what their actual level of capability, they are more likely to *overestimate* their skills.

Many people who have the ability to build a business will never do so, not because they don't want to, but rather, because, at heart, they just don't believe in themselves. They will never take a sincere first step. To try any idea, you must be optimistic that it can succeed. Else, you will only give a halfhearted effort. This lack of dedication to your dream will lead to failure.

In another and unrelated study (I just find this sort of stuff fascinating), another group of researchers posed the question, "What is the thing that most distinguishes depressed people from the average, psychologically-healthy person?" The result was that depressed people tend to have a *more accurate perception* of their skills and abilities and what level of control they have over their own lives.

For example, if you were to ask a person suffering from depression, "What are the chances that you will be killed in a car accident? What could you do about this chance?," most depressed people would give an answer more nearly correct than a non-depressed person would. Further, the non-depressed person would probably tend to believe there was more they could do to avoid the accident, for example, defensive driving through the accident.

When I first read the summary of these two studies, I must admit I was a bit shocked. For this says a more accurate perception of reality will not lead to living a more successful or happier life. It can have the opposite result entirely! That just somehow doesn't seem fair, now does it? You have a more realistic understanding of things, and, for it, you are rewarded with less success! So, when I write it is possible to learn so much that you abandon the idea, this might mean one of two things.

One, the idea really sucks. This means the underlying business model is bad (margins are low, etc.). There are fundamental weaknesses in the endeavor that make failure likely. But, the second possibility is that you know so much now that you see many of the pitfalls. Seeing the pitfalls does not mean they will do you in. It seems, in a rational world, seeing these pitfalls should prepare you somewhat to deal with them. But, I guess is doesn't work that way. Oh, well, who said we lived in a fully rational world?

So when you reach the point of being able to say to yourself, "I think I know enough that I could do this now. I don't know *everything*. But, I think I'd have a *chance*," it is probably a good time to act. Jump in and get started. Learn as you go from that point on. Then, you will be able to focus your learning more appropriately to what is really needed at the time. Never let your perception of reality interfere with your vision of what can be.

Chapter 15.
The Role of Luck In Business.
The Importance of Getting Started Now

One thing successful entrepreneurs tend to share in common is not only the initiative to get started, but also the tendency to follow through and bring the project to completion. They tend to act fast on ideas and initiate their plans as soon as possible. In particular, they bring the project to fruition. Often, their success is attributed to having taken action while others sat by. Many contemplated starting a similar business, but never got it off the ground. In technology fields, business students sometimes talk about "windows of opportunity." This means there is an optimal time to start an enterprise. If you start too early, the resources may not exist to bring your idea to completion. This is a limit of existing technology. Maybe the market has not really been exposed to the type of product you will be selling. The market does not yet exist.

Consider someone who decided to become a freelance, web page designer. Back in the early and mid 1990's this was a tremendously in-demand field. Few people had the knowledge to do it. People simply lacked the exposure to web design. Freelancers could easily make $60,000 or more a year. Yet, the basic skills demanded could be acquired in a weekend (HTML—hypertext mark-up language is really easy to learn. Anyone can create a simple web page). Now $60,000 a year for a weekend's worth of learning is not at all bad! Compare this to the many students who were completing four-year engineering degrees, many of whom would be happy to make $30,000 to start. (Today, starting salaries are about $40,000 per year for engineers. Engineering and computer programming are cyclical fields. Young engineers and programmers should chant this to themselves over and over.)

Today, nearly every college graduate—certainly, graduates of any computer science program and most graduates of technical college programs in graphic arts—know HTML and can design a basic web page. If you look in the newspaper, you will see some Internet service providers picking up entry-level web page designers for $9.00 per hour. And, they are finding candidates. This is because the skill is so simple that there is no barrier to entry. Why pay someone $60,000 annually when you can spend a few weekends training someone and pay the person $18,000 a year? The window of opportunity for freelancers, creating simple web pages with HTML alone, has closed. If you know Perl, Java, database design, and e-commerce, that's another story!

But, consider trying to be a web page designer before web pages were "cool." Back when they were still exclusively the province of academic and government institutions. During this time frame the window of opportunity was also closed. The people who created on-line content did so as graduate students or as members of the government institution that employed them. If you were to go to a typical business and offer to design a simple web page for them, they would have thought you were nuts. They would have asked, "What the hell's a web page?"

Now, in our example, the cost to you would just be embarrassment, but what if you had sunk all your savings into trying to build another technological company before the market existed? You have seen the future, and you got squat for it. It's like an army of soldiers trying to take a hill. Being first is not always the best! Most entrepreneurs need not worry about this. But if you are contemplating a high-tech business, it is something to be aware of.

Many people fail at entrepreneurship by not bringing the idea to completion. You need a marketable product ready for shipment before you can really earn money as a business. Many people have great ideas. Marketable ideas. Viable ideas. Yet, they never materialize as profitable products. The reason is that the product is never brought to completion. Often, the person or group gets another idea and then abandons the first endeavor to work on the second idea. But a third idea comes, and then number two is slowly relegated to the past. What happens is that the company runs out of money and, yet, isn't even close to having a marketable product. People with PhD's are notorious for this. They keep seeing improvements to the basic idea. They lose sight of the fact that the goal of business is to produce a product ready for shipment to the customer. Being reflective and pensive is a great strength in an investor, but it is a flaw in an entrepreneur. The best entrepreneurs tend to be rapid prototypers. Once they get an idea, they want a serviceable version as soon as possible. They don't stop to contemplate all the aspects of the greater theory of what they are doing. They'll, maybe, give that some thought later. But, for now, ACTION is the name of the game.

Getting started early is of value to any entrepreneurial endeavor for another good reason. Not only might the window of opportunity close, but also, often, the idea simply will not work. There is a tremendous value in knowing this. You could contemplate an untenable idea for years! Where would you be when you initiated it? If the idea isn't workable, you want to be free to move on to another idea. By just being in the game of business, you are far better positioned to take advantage of any opportunity that comes your way than those people who are merely contemplating.

Most successful entrepreneurs don't like to admit it, but luck does play a role in the success of a business. Often, rather than determining the downright success or failure of an enterprise, it will determine the overall level of success the enterprise experiences. Consider the most successful entrepreneurial company of all, Microsoft. Started and built from the ground up by its founder, Bill Gates, Microsoft is, without a doubt, the biggest computer "success story."

Why is Microsoft the most successful company? Is it because Bill Gates is the best entrepreneur? The most brilliant businessman? The smartest of the computer nerds who built a business? Hardly. Bill

Gates is typical of entrepreneurs. He knows business and makes fundamentally good decisions. Of this, there is no doubt. He saw that programming software would be a great growth industry and jumped to begin a company. In fact, he dropped out of Harvard to begin Microsoft. He feared the window of opportunity to build *the* dominant software company would close, if he waited until after he completed his degree. Yeah, sure, Bill.

There is one reason, and only one reason, Bill Gates is the richest man in the world today and Microsoft is such a success. Nearly everyone in the computer industry knows it. It has to do with a decision. A decision made by IBM. IBM decided to outsource the creation of the operating system for the first personal computer they would market. In other words, they chose a company that would eventually have a proprietary product that would be required on nearly every PC made. In short, IBM contacted Microsoft and Microsoft ran with it. As an aside, IBM actually tried to get another company to write the operating system, and it was Bill Gates, himself, who had referred IBM to this company! This company sent IBM packing! I guess they just weren't interested! IBM came back to Gates and said, "They don't want to." And, Gates said, "No problem. We'll get you one." I'm just paraphrasing here. If IBM had contacted some other company (and they agreed!) to write the operating system, there is no way Bill Gates would be the richest man today. He would not have a proprietary product, which is required on nearly every IBM-compatible personal computer sold. Some other company would control this product.

The point is not that Bill Gates owes all his success to luck. I have no doubt that, if IBM had never approached Microsoft, Microsoft would still have grown into a substantial company. Maybe, Gates would be worth a few hundred million dollars, something more comparable to the score of other software companies built in the 1980's. Solid business skills and good decision making will lead to success. Most of the time at least! What skills and good decision making will not do is guarantee phenomenal success. Whether a company succeeds in becoming a billion-dollar enterprise is dependent upon a host of factors simply beyond anyone's control.

Luck does play a role in business. Business is a "positive sum" game, if you will. By this, I mean your chances of winning are quite good. Because of this reality, getting started early is a huge advantage. Let's use an analogy to understand why. Consider three different games: chess, backgammon, and a simple coin-toss. Each game's outcome is influenced by several factors, but we are only interested in the role of luck and skill. Chess, obviously, is a game that favors either a natural talent for it or, else, a dedicated study to it. I won't get into whether it is inherent ability or training which improves a chess player's ability. It doesn't matter. What does matter is that the more chess skills a person acquires the better player he will be. The chances of an average player lucking out and beating Gary Kasparov are very, very slim. For all practical purposes, Kasparov will win. Luck has almost no bearing upon the outcome. Because of this, dedicated study of chess should pay off. It should lead to the development of skills that will enable better play. Contemplation and speculation will lead to being a better chess player. Natural talent at seeing the possibilities on the chessboard will lead to more successful play. Business is not like chess, where skill and skill alone determines the outcome. The "best" entrepreneur will not be the most successful.

Now what about the coin-toss? Heads you win, tails you lose. What benefit does contemplation and study before the match gain you? Will hours of pregame preparation lead to better play on your behalf? Certainly not! The outcome is determined by luck and luck alone. A huge investment of time in an attempt to improve your play is simply wasted time. This must be seen. There are some people who never make this crucial connection. They feel they can "outsmart" the lottery. They can find a way to pick the numbers that will come up in the draw. They feel they can mastermind games that cannot be affected at all through their study. I might add, while some people would immediately scoff at such individuals, these scoffers would immediately turn around and believe they can mastermind the futures market or time the stock market. The ability to see where your efforts are not having any effect is crucial to success as an entrepreneur. At the least, you can ask, "Is it, at least, even theoretically possible for my efforts to have an effect?" If it looks like nobody has had any lasting ability to master the field, be very doubtful that you would achieve such mastery.

It's amazing how tenaciously some people stick to their "plans," despite all of reason going against them. I know moderately intelligent people (and, the only reason I can't call them very intelligent is precisely because of this tendency I am about to describe!) who feel they can mastermind the futures market. They are smart and hard-working, so they figure they should be able to succeed at this endeavor. They believe other people fail at futures, "because they didn't stick to the plan or because they didn't study enough."

I ask such people if they feel they could mastermind the coin-toss. Heads you win, tails you lose. They say, "No, obviously not."

I say, "Ah ha, and what is different about the futures market?" Usually, they want to rattle off a list of reasons, "Well, you can predict…"

I say, "No, you can't. The futures market was started precisely because no one could predict prices of volatile commodities. Suppose you build steel boats. You have a certain number of orders lined up. You don't want to warehouse all the steel. Yet, you know prices could go up. And, if you agreed to sell the craft for so much money, you will need to build and sell it, even if you lose money in the process. You are legally bound. You can't just change your mind when you are contracted. Because your profit margin could be eroded if prices went up, you want some form of *insurance* to protect you against an unpleasant rise in the cost of your crucial supply. Someone else is willing to sell you a futures contract. They will guarantee to deliver to you the steel you need at some fixed price, say, the current market price. They are hoping to profit as they feel the cost of steel will go down, and, hence, they are selling you a right that will expire worthless. You accept the deal and increase the price of your boats slightly to absorb the cost of this futures contract. You don't look at it as an investment, nor even a speculation, but as insurance against the unpleasant change in prices. Is this reasonable?"

Typically, they agree it sounds like good business practice. I go on to look at the situation from the steel mill's perspective. "They are afraid that prices will *drop* and their profit margins will erode. They will gladly forego the extra earnings they could obtain, if prices were to increase, in order to lock in some sales at the current market price. It allows them to know how much they will receive for their product and, hence, make reasonable business decisions. If they have no reasonable estimate of how much they will be paid, how can they know if they are covering their production costs? Because of this, they are willing to sell futures that lock them into producing the steel and selling it at the current market rate. They will not be able to sell it for a higher rate if such a better rate can be obtained. But, they are insured if prices plummet. The cost of the futures contract becomes just another expense of doing business to the steel company. Does that sound like reasonable business practice?"

Invariably, they agree the steel mill is making good business decisions. I finally ask them, again, if they feel they can predict steel prices. "Yes," they enthusiastically reply. This always kills me. I go on to say, "Now, you've just agreed that people who use steel every day, people like boat builders, people who know steel *intimately*, cannot predict steel prices. The people who produce it, the mills, can't predict its price. These are the people who read magazines like *Metals Today* and *Alloy Monthly*. Despite this intimate knowledge, they are willing to absorb an insurance expense, the cost of futures contracts, to protect them from volatile price fluctuations *they cannot predict*. Now, why again do *you* feel you can predict steel prices?"

The sad fact is that they go on believing they can mastermind steel prices. Or wheat or soybeans or whatever. Entrepreneurs must know when to give up. You cannot expect to succeed if you are playing a game that is stacked against you. This is not to say you should run from adversity or rejection of your ideas or that you should run from market competition. Many valid ideas were scoffed at and rejected time and time again. No one seemed to be interested. Yet, the entrepreneurs kept on, believing in their dream. And, eventually, they succeeded! But, their idea was *fundamentally workable*, and they saw this. They knew the idea could work mathematically. They knew there was a need in the marketplace for their product, even if the market didn't yet recognize the need! They were not like the compulsive gambler who keeps going back to the tables to lose. The gambler has no valid reason to believe he will succeed. The house stacks the odds against him. And, the house controls the gaming rules! The more you play, the more you will lose.

Business, however, is not a losing game. If anything, your chances of success are quite good, assuming you work hard at a *tenable* business idea. It is reasonable to assume you can succeed. Imagine a casino, where rather than setting the odds against you, the odds are set in your favor. Heads, you win $5. Tails, you lose $1. The usual 50-50 chance as to the outcome. The more you play the better. Contemplation of the endeavor will not aid you in making more money, but more play time will. You would want to get to the gaming tables early. Yet, no one is going to offer you such a deal. No one will show you such a casino. If there were such a place, it would go bankrupt or change its ways. You must unearth the opportunities. You must see them. You must work hard to realize them and bring them to fruition with a marketable product. You will be responsible to see that the plans you pursue are at least viable. That is the way you will find a casino with the odds in your favor.

Yet, luck alone will never get you there. Life is more like backgammon than either chess or a coin toss. You throw the dice. Then, you make a move. The numbers that come up may be good or bad for you, but you always have a best move, or, at least, equally good moves. You can hope for the lucky throw, but how you play whatever throw materializes is all you can really control. You can study backgammon intensively, yet be beaten by a less skilled player. A combination of luck and skill determines the outcome. Your goal should be to be a good player, to see and appreciate the difference between good and bad moves. This calls for some study, but, then, get out there and play! If you are at all good, you will win your share of hands. That is really all you need to succeed, to become financially secure or even rich. More contemplation can never overcome the luck element of business, nor can thinking about an idea prove its viability in the market place.

In life, maybe, you have time for three or four "hands" of business. Each one might take anywhere from only a year to, maybe, ten years, before you really know if you are winning. Three or four years should give you a pretty good idea of how well your idea is doing. One thing that is not well-known about many entrepreneurs, who have achieved phenomenal success, is that the business in which they achieved their success was not their first, or, in many cases, even second or third business. In some cases, they failed repeatedly. I remember reading about Charles Schwab. Apparently, before succeeding with his discount brokerage firm, he tried to start some sort of animal amusement park he named "Congo Land." Think Jurassic Park without the attitude. No, really. I'm not making this up! I guess the short story is that it didn't work. Oh well, we all have our Congo Lands, although most of us don't have anything named nearly as creatively! Doesn't it sound like the beginning of a great story of early business ambitions? Congo Land. It's the sort of thing you can look back on and laugh, but no doubt, while you are struggling with your own "Congo Land," it will not feel as pleasant. Only you can decide whether or not to stay with your original idea or to move on to another.

Many informational companies and manufacturing companies do succeed but not with the first product they envisioned. Rather, it was the third or fourth or even tenth product idea, within some larger category, which led to their success. Which way do you take your company? Which products do you go with and which do you abandon? These are some of the most difficult decisions an entrepreneur is forced to make. In a way, it would be nice if a product-idea either just succeeded or failed outright, rather than just drag on without really telling you. Your estimates are always the start, your first guess at expenses and sales. But the numbers that matter are the ones that are actualized—the ones that happen in reality and not just inside your head. The only way to get even the slightest handle on those numbers is to get your business started, get the product out, and try to market it.

Chapter 16.
An Introduction To the Nature of Compounding and the Time Value of Money

More and more people are becoming aware of the role compounded earnings or reinvested stock dividends play in building wealth. The idea is simple. Once you are making money, rather than taking the money out of the project and spending it, you reinvest the money. This reinvested money is used to support a higher level of sales, which grows the company. By reinvesting the money, you let the nature of compounding work for you. Compounding, by its very nature, is exponential growth. This means huge gains can result from modest initial investments. Further, time is a powerful ally. Most people, if asked to calculate how much money they would have after investing a given sum for 10 years at a return of 10%, would significantly underestimate the amount. If they were asked to do the calculation for 30 years at 12%, they would be off by even more.

Many people would do the calculation correctly. Almost all of these people have taken a math class or read a book that taught them how to do compounding calculations. So, if other people seem to understand this, and you feel you do not, don't fret. It doesn't mean they are more intelligent than you. It means they have studied the material before. By the end of this chapter, you will have a thorough understanding of compounding. Plus, you will really understand how larger levels of wealth are created. This chapter is a basic introduction to understanding compounding and the time value of money, which is a related concept. Both of these subjects are crucial for the entrepreneur and investor to understand. If you feel you already understand these calculations, read this chapter, anyway. The goal is to internalize and own the understanding of compounding. Ask yourself, "If I had not been shown how to do these calculations, would I have been able to derive the methods of doing these calculations on my own?" Usually, the answer is "No."

Let's begin with what would be most natural but incorrect. You want to know how much $10,000 grows to if invested at 10% annually and left alone for 10 years. Well, in one year, we would reason that we would get back the original $10,000 amount plus one year's interest at ten percent of the $10,000 which is $1,000. Expressed as a multiplier expression, on the original amount, this is $1.00 + 0.10 = 1.10$ where the 1.00 just says we get our money back at the end of the year. The second term of 0.10 is just the ten percent interest we are given at the end of the year, expressed as a decimal, rather than as a percentage. So, at the end of the first year, you would have $11,000. This part of the calculation is correct. Further, it can be arrived at in either of two ways. The first and most obvious way is to just add the initial $10,000 to the $1,000 interest you collect. The other way is to first calculate the multiplier expression of 1.1 and then multiply it by the original $10,000.

While the method of adding the sums seems most natural, try to get into the habit of calculating the multiplier expression and doing it that way. You can always check your answers one against the other. They should approximately match. If they do not, then go back and seek a mathematical error. I say "approximately" because there will always be some small round-off error. But, the difference should be very small when compared to the other dollar amounts involved. Always use a calculator to do these calculations. Working it out the old-fashioned way—pencil and paper—is just too tedious.

To be sure you are comfortable with the basic method, let's do another calculation. Suppose you want to invest $10,000 at 12% for one year. At the end of the year, you would have 1.12 times the original amount or $11,200. Similarly, you could add twelve percent of $10,000 back to the original amount of $10,000.

Now, here is where the common misunderstanding occurs. Suppose rather than investing the $10,000 for one year at 10% that you let it sit compounding at 10% for, say, 5 years. How would you calculate the resulting amount? What most people want to do is to say, "Well, the first year I got $1,000 in interest, so, as my money is sitting for 5 years, I will get five times $1,000 in interest or $5,000. This means I will have the original $10,000 plus $5,000 or $15,000." For short periods of investment, this method is good enough. But, the method always misses the interest earned on interest. Over longer periods of time, the method will yield values that are way too low. You must calculate interest-on-interest to be correct.

You might have known that you were neglecting interest on the interest, believing it to be insignificant. For example, at the start of the second year, you know you have $11,000. So, compounding this amount over the second year at 10%, you would get $11,000 plus ten percent of $11,000 or $1,100 for a total of $12,100. The naive way would have given you $10,000 plus twice the $1,000 interest earned the first year or $12,000. So it would seem that the difference is rather small, and it is. This is because the time interval of compounding is so small.

You might reason that the added interest the third year on the difference of $100 is only $10 crummy dollars and, so, conclude that worrying about interest on interest is even more insignificant. Over a long time period, however, there are many of these interest-on-interest terms, so that, even though none of them is big, the sum of them is significant. In fact, eventually, the sum of all these smaller interest-on-interest terms will exceed the original amount in significance. Further, these individual terms, themselves, are growing. In time, the later of these "insignificant" interest-on-interest terms will be larger than the $10,000 principal. So, you would be making a major error in believing that interest-on-interest terms are negligible.

Let's do the calculation for 5 years the long way. At the start of the first year, we have $10,000. At the end of the first year, we have $11,000. This is just the original amount and the 10% interest on the original amount. But, the end of the first year is also the start of the second year, and we know how to accurately calculate the interest earned over one year. We just need to take 10% times the starting amount at the beginning of that year. So, at the end of the second year, we will get 0.10 times $11,000 or $1,100 in interest. Thus, at the end of the second year, we have a total of the amount that we started with at the start of the second year, plus the interest over the second year. This is $11,000 plus $1,100 or $12,100. Hence, as the start of the third year is also the end of the second year, we have $12,100 to invest in the beginning of year three. But, we know how to calculate the interest earned over year three. It is just 10% times the initial amount that we have at the start of year three. This interest amount is 0.10 times $12,100 or $1,210. This is the interest earned over the third year. At the end of the third year, we have a total of the interest earned over the year and the amount that we had at the beginning of the year or a total of $13,310. Hence we have $13,310 to invest at the start of the fourth year. Over the fourth year, we do what we have been doing before to accurately calculate the amount of interest earned over any given year. We simply multiply the starting amount by the interest rate. That gives us the interest earned over the fourth year. Added to that is the amount we invested at the start of the fourth year. So, we start year four with $13,310. We earn interest of 0.10 times $13,310 or $1,331. By the end of the fourth year, we have a total of $14,641. We have just gotten to the beginning of the fifth and final year the money will be invested. Over this last year, we will earn $14,641 times 0.10 or $1,464.10 in interest. At the end of the fifth year, we will have a total of $16,105.10.

All we did above was calculate the interest earned over one year for a given initial amount and then take that as the next year's starting amount. This method is accurate. It is fully correct. If we had used our naive method, we would have just added 5 times the first year's interest of $1,000 to the principal of $10,000 for a total of $15,000. Even after only five years, we are off by over a thousand dollars. The difference of $1,105.10 between the correct method and the naive method represents interest on interest. Now, you could continue the above calculation for more years. Or, you could choose a different interest rate. Or, you could choose a different starting amount rather than $10,000. However, if you did the calculation in the above way for, say, compounding $10,000 at 10% over 35 years, you might go batty.[1] The method of doing the calculation is too long and involved. We want to use the multiplier method to do such calculations much more quickly. Let's just write down the amounts that we have at the start of each year.

Amount	At Start of Year	Interest Earned Over the Year
$10,000	1	$1,000
$11,000	2	$1,100
$12,100	3	$1,210
$13,310	4	$1,331
$14,641	5	$1,464.10
$16,105.10	6	The money is taken out at the start of year 6

Just writing down the terms in a table, like the above, makes doing the calculation much easier. You simply multiply the starting "Amount" for the year by the interest rate (here 10%) and that number becomes the "Interest Earned Over the Year." You then add that calculated "Interest Earned Over the Year" to the last term listed in "Amount." The new total is entered into the "Amount" column below the last existing term. Even though the calculation is the same, organization has made things easier for us. Still, for 35 years, the above method is tedious.

The multiplier method will be much simpler. Notice that the "Amount" term in the second row ($11,000) is just 1.10 times the amount right above it ($10,000). The $12,100 term is just 1.10 times

---

[1] In fact, if you were able to read the entire previous paragraph from start to finish, my hat is off to you! If you felt a bit irritated as you read it, that's a good sign. You sensed that describing several years of compounding in a written paragraph is not the easiest to follow. How you organize information can facilitate (or hinder) your analysis of the data.

the amount right above it ($11,000). Every term in the "Amount" column is just 1.10 times the amount above it (Recall that this multiplier is just one plus the interest rate expressed as a decimal. The one just says you get your money back, and the decimal part expresses the interest rate). Each succeeding term in the "Amount" column is simply picking up another factor of 1.10. We could modify the table as follows:

Amount	At Start of Year	Overall Multiplier Expression Applied to Initial Amount
$10,000	1	(1.10)
$11,000	2	(1.10)(1.10)
$12,100	3	(1.10)(1.10) (1.10)
$13,310	4	(1.10)(1.10) (1.10) (1.10)
$14,641	5	(1.10)(1.10) (1.10) (1.10) (1.10)
$16,105.10	6	The money is taken out at the start of year 6

Starting from the initial $10,000 we can calculate any term in the amount column simply by multiplying the initial starting amount (here $10,000) by the overall multiplier expression, where each multiplying factor of (1.10) represents one more year of compounding. So, to get the total amount at the start of year six, for example, we would compute $10,000 times (1.10)(1.10)(1.10)(1.10)(1.10). A shorthand way of writing some number multiplied by itself a given number, n, times, is using power notation. So (1.10)(1.10)(1.10)(1.10)(1.10) = (1.10) to the fifth power = $(1.10)^5$. Here n is 5. Your calculator can do these power calculations easily.

If you wanted to know what $10,000 compounded at 10% would become in 10 years, you would just calculate $(1.10)^{10}$ times $10,000 which is $25,937. We will neglect change. If you wanted to compute what the $10,000 would compound to in 35 years, it would be $10,000$(1.10)^{35}$ = $10,000 (28.1024) = $281,024. You should do several of these calculations, until they become second nature to you. Don't feel bad if it seems a bit difficult at first or you make errors. That's only natural. In time, you will be able to do this sort of compounding calculation quickly. Notice what 35 years of compounding will do to an initial investment of $10,000. It will turn it into $281,024. The naive method would only have given $10,000 + 35($1,000) = $45,000. So, multiplying the first year's interest by the number of years the money was left invested would be horribly wrong. The true value, the one which will materialize, if your money gets an annual rate of return of 10% over 35 years, is the larger value of $281,024. These results seem amazing. I vaguely remember something written by Warren Buffett (or about him) that said he was flabbergasted by compounding calculations. It just seemed such an incredible thing to him. The results are incredible. The above shows how people can build large wealth via investing over long periods of time, even without ever building a company.

The results are even more impressive as the compounding rates are increased or as the length of the compounding time interval is increased. For example, at 12%, an initial investment of $10,000 becomes $527,996 in 35 years. At 15% it becomes $1,331,755 in 35 years. If we extend the compounding time interval, the results are also dramatic. $10,000 invested at 10% over 45 years becomes $728,904. The results are the most dramatic when the compounding rates are high and the time interval is long. For example, $10,000 compounding at 15% for 45 years becomes $5,387,692. Not bad for a $10,000 investment. You should verify all these calculations for yourself. You now understand what compounding is all about.

You might be thinking, "I understand why compounding is important to investments, where I invest so much for so many years and it grows at some rate of return. I can use the above methods to estimate how much I will have after so many years if my money compounds at some estimated rate of return. Further, I don't even need to understand the mathematics of compounding to benefit from it. All I need to do is invest in a good rate of return investment, such as a diversified portfolio of well-chosen common stocks, and then hold the stocks for a very long time. But, why is understanding compounding important to the entrepreneur?"

The answer is the stock market's growth is intimately tied to business. The overall stock market tends to grow exponentially precisely because that is how business growth occurs. A growing business will generate profits. These profits are reinvested to make more profits. The calculations expressing a business's growth are essentially just like the above calculations. Businesses can calculate growth in revenue and profits for a given product.

Often, entrepreneurs are most concerned with growth in revenue. Even if the market exists, the company must have sufficient working capital to produce the amount of product it believes it can sell. Once you can write down an expression that shows how *your* business compounds money, you can analyze your business more thoroughly, just like you learned to do in Chapter 8 using expectation values. You can better see how your business is strong and where it is weak. You will have insight into what can make your business more profitable and where the bottlenecks to your business's growth occur. You will be able to estimate the overall effect operational changes have upon your business's growth.

Intimately related to compounding is the time value of money. The idea behind the time value of money is that a dollar now will have more value than a dollar down the road. This is not one of those birds-in-the-hand versus birds-in-the-bush situations. Be sure you understand that. If I offer to give you a dollar right now or I promise to give you a dollar in one year, both offers have complete certainty. I always keep my word. (No, you can't have a dollar. This is just an example). The risk of default is another issue entirely. Suppose you know that you can invest in a conservative money market fund and get an interest rate of 5%. If I give you a dollar right now, you can put it in the money market fund, and at the end of the year, you will have $1.05. OK, maybe the money market fund won't be too happy about your only investing a buck, and, maybe, five cents more or less doesn't make you feel like Bill Gates, but the fact remains, at the end of the year, you are five cents richer than if you had received my payment at the end of the year. The reason you are richer is because you have been able *to grow the money through compounding*. If you are given the money at the end of the year, you are denied the opportunity of compounding the amount over the year.

When we are dealing with a buck over one year, at a rate of 5%, it might seem a moot point, but, in business, the magnitude of the money involved alone can have a tremendous impact. Suppose, you sell a custom machine to another business for $1,000,000. If the business pays you right away, and you put the million dollars in the money market fund at the crummy 5%, in one year this amounts to $50,000 in interest. Now, $50,000 is still "small," when compared to $1,000,000 but, remember, the $1,000,000 represents, not profit to the company, but only revenue. Suppose that your company has 10% net profit margins. That's not bad, remember. That means of the $1,000,000 revenue the sale of the machine brings your company, only $100,000 is earned as profit. Collecting payment now, versus the end of the year, amounts to 50% more profits on the sale! Such is the power of the time value of money! Companies that understand the time value of money and the power of compounding tend to make intelligent financial management decisions. People who start businesses unaware of general financial management issues are often played for the fool. By this, I mean they accept payment terms that could actually endanger the company's survival. The people the company is doing business with are not trying to hurt the company, just to get as good a deal as they can. Getting a good deal involves not only the price at which a product is bought or sold, but also the financing terms of the deal.

Suppose you find some gullible fool to give you $1,000,000. You promise to give it back in one year. You don't mention interest. The fool agrees. At the end of the year, you return the $1,000,000. In the meantime you have made a decent living just from the interest on the $1,000,000! (No. You can't have a million dollars. It's just an example.)

Some companies make great use of the time value of money. Insurance companies, in particular, collect premiums before any claims are filed. This means even if the total paid out in claims equaled the amount collected in premiums (How'd that happen? They'd better raise their insurance rates or do a better job of selecting whom they insure!), the insurance company would still have the time value of the money during the delay between the time when the premium is collected and when the claim is paid out. And, the time value of money on a few hundred million dollars is nothing to sneeze at! People like Warren Buffett just love businesses where the time value of money works in their favor, for they know they can turn around and invest the money at rates better than the 5% we were toying with before.

Unfortunately, we are not all Warren Buffett, and many insurance companies have gotten themselves into deep doo-doo by trying to aggressively invest the money that they would only be holding for a short period of time. In other words, the premium is paid and a certain reserve should be set aside and conservatively invested to cover a possible claim, but Nooo, the wannabe-Buffett decides a hot Internet stock is a good holding place for the reserve set aside for claims. If the stock had gone up, this aggressive investor would have walked away richer, but the stock plummets, and the company no longer has sufficient funds to pay the claim. Bankruptcy or a government bailout follows. This is simply irresponsible business management.

If the government would not bailout the company, many individuals who paid premiums into the insurance company wouldn't really have insurance. The insurance company has failed its customers. It isn't protecting them from calamity. If the company expects a government bailout, it is taking a huge risk and expecting to receive all the benefits, if the risk turns out, and expecting somebody else to absorb all the costs, if the risk fails. That somebody else is us, the taxpayers. This amounts to nothing more than a potential transfer of wealth (unethically) from the taxpayer to the insurance company. There is a difference between making good use of your knowledge of the time value of money and trying to be too aggressive with the concept or using it unethically.

Working capital within your company that will be needed at some known date in the future should be invested so that it will be available. That it be *available* is most important. Often, there is a desire to maximize the time value of this capital, while it sits "idle." Because needing money, when you don't have it, is one of the most stressful aspects of entrepreneurship, always be especially conservative when trying to "keep your money working" for short periods of time. I am in favor of treasuries or a money market fund for money you know will be needed soon to pay some upcoming bill. Money, not needed soon, should be reinvested into *your* business, if it can be done so efficiently.

In the above example, I used a conservative rate of 5%, typical of a money market fund, yet most often the rate in which you will be interested is the rate at which *your* business can compound the money. Suppose you were able to collect payment for the $1,000,000 machine at the start of the year. What would you do with the money? You would probably not invest it in a money market fund. Nor would you take a trip to Jamaica! You would most likely invest it within your company to create and market more of your product, or, maybe, develop new products. When doing time value of money calculations, it is important to know what your company's internal rate of return is (or your business's ROI, Return On Investment). This rate of return corresponds to how the money will actually be used.

The question is, "If our business had $1,000,000, at what rate could we compound it?" Let's assume it took your company one year to build the machine. Further, we know that the cost to make this machine was $900,000 (as the profit margin was 10% of $1,000,000). Let's also assume the full amount of $900,000 had to be invested at the time construction of the machine began. So, you invested $900,000 and in one year generated $1,000,000 (remember, we have assumed payment for the machine just after it is completed and sold) for a profit of $100,000. This means your rate of return was (100)($100,000/$900,000) = 11% where the factor of 100 converts the decimal value to a percentage.

Some people might be wondering why the rate of return on the money wasn't equal to the net profit margin of 10%, but was higher. This is because, when you earn 10% on $1 million in revenue, the initial amount invested to create the product was lower than the full $1 million. It was only $900,000. So, you made $100,000 on an investment of only $900,000. This is an 11% rate of return. It is important not to see connections that do not exist! Working everything out from first principles prevents this.

The rate of return your business can generate is substantially higher than a conservative money market fund. This should be so, if only because your business involves higher risk than the money fund. If you find the rates of return you are able to get on your business are only comparable to a money fund, you should be thinking about taking your business in other directions. If you had another contract lined up to produce another machine, you could instantly put the $1,000,000 revenue collected to make another machine. This would mean that, rather than missing $50,000 in money fund interest, you would be missing out on more like $100,000 profits from the sale of another machine.

You might instantly say, "Hey, 11% of $1,000,000 is $110,000, so why are you only saying we get $100,000 in missed time value of the money?" This is because I am assuming the second machine will also cost $900,000 to create and can be sold for $1,000,000. The other $100,000 collected from the first sale could be, for example, placed into the money fund to earn $5,000 over the year, but, unless you had other funds available to start construction of a third machine, this $100,000 could not be invested at the higher rate. We could, for completeness, add the extra $5,000 in interest to the $100,000 to say that we are passing up $105,000 in wealth, if we were to grant a one-year's payment deferral to the buyer of the first machine. You can see just how important the time value of money is. It can significantly affect a business's rate of growth in sales and profits.

In one case, the business defers payment for one year and is not able to internally finance construction of a new machine to sell. This slows the business's potential growth. In the other case, money is collected right away, and the construction of a second machine can immediately begin. Ask: "How can *that* amount of money be invested?" In particular, the value of a small sum above $900,000 could not be invested at the higher rate, because the second construction involves a substantial initial amount. If, however, you were producing lower-priced widgets, you could manufacture so many more of these widgets for the $100,000 and all of your money would be invested at the higher rate. This is one of the reasons why businesses which must make large capital investments to grow tend to grow less rapidly than companies that can immediately put smaller received sums to work. The first type of company, by the nature of the business, can only grow in large steps with significant time between each step. The second type of business can grow in a more continuous fashion.

Crucial in calculating the rate to use in your time value calculations is whether the market exists for a second machine. Suppose you cannot seem to generate a sale of another machine at present. Then, the 5% money market rate is more appropriate than the 11% rate. You cannot put the money to work at the higher rate. Worse yet, suppose the company buying your first machine says, "Well, we can't pay you right away. I guess if you won't finance the machine for us, we cannot buy the machine." Unless you finance the machine, you won't generate a sale at all. So, your credit and financing policies are not only affecting how effectively you can use the time value of money, but are also affecting your level of sales.

Many businesses extend liberal credit and payment policies to generate more sales. "Buy now. No interest. No payments for One Year. If you're alive, you qualify!!" I'm sure you've seen this type of pitch. The company will give up the time value of revenues to generate more sales. I am not, personally, very fond of this approach from the perspective of running a business. Your business should be fundamentally strong enough to resist such policies. You really let the cat out of the bag, if you start to extend credit to dubious customers, if you allow payment way down the road, and you adopt other such liberal policies. You start to add uncertainty as to just how much revenue will be defaulted upon.

Further, giving up the time value of money often makes maintaining profitability more difficult, especially for competitive, lower-margin businesses. But, what is an entrepreneur to do, if the competition is extending such liberal sales policies? If you don't match them, you will lose sales. This is another reason to favor building a business that has proprietary products. When you are just one of the crowd, you will be forced into fundamentally unsound business practices or else you will lose sales. Losing sales often means you cannot effectively pay your overhead costs, such as retail rental space. You are thrown into a damned-if-you-do-damned-if-you-don't situation. All aspects of running a profitable business are intertwined. You want to enter a business that has a strong business model.

While most people will see the possibility of reinvesting in their company to do more of the same thing, make a second machine, for example, they will not always stop to consider what other projects the company might undertake. Whenever you choose to do one thing, this means some other things will not be done. Opportunities will be passed up. Some people are obsessed with this opportunity cost. Others neglect it entirely. Consider opportunity cost, but don't sweat it. Just ask yourself, when trying to come up with a measure of your company's internal rate of return, if there is some other area your business could enter if you had the dollar amount considered.

Maybe, your company is considering manufacturing an entirely different type of machine. You know that your company has the capability to manufacture it and feel reasonably assured you can sell the machine, once you can demonstrate a working prototype. This machine is sufficiently inventive, so you will be able to patent it. You believe this will give you a commanding position in your market. You reasonably believe you will be able to make the machine for $900,000 and sell it for $1,500,000. It probably will take one year to make it and generate the first sale. In this case, it is likely that giving up one-year's time value of money has a reasonable rate greater than the 11% rate calculated before. Using the above estimates, you would be getting a return rate of 66% on this new machine. It could be argued that there are uncertainties involved, so 66% is too high. On the other hand, what if the creation of this machine does give you command of the market, and, as a result, you are able to instantly line up a dozen more machine contracts? While you clearly should ignore long-shot opportunities when calculating the time value of money to your company, do not ignore possibilities that are very, very close to being doable.

In our above examples, we assumed that it would take one year to produce the machine. I did this for simplicity as most people are used to calculating rates of returns over one year. By making the assumption that $900,000 was invested at the start of the year and that it took exactly one year to produce the machine, I simplified the picture to the usual time frame of one year. Real business is not so simple in that all of the aspects conspire to make one year the natural time frame. There is nothing magical about a year, as far as business is concerned (with the exception that you must calculate annual results for investors and the IRS). Each business typically has its own compounding cycle that differs from one year. This compounding cycle is closely-related to what is sometimes called "inventory turnover."

Unlike inventory turnover, the compounding cycle must take into consideration when you actually receive payment for your products sold. The cycle is measured as the time it takes for an initial cash investment to come back into your company in the form of a cash payment. When you think in terms of compounding cycles for your business, think in terms of cash-flow cycle.

The bad news is the calculations will not immediately give you an annual rate of return. The good news is that a business's compounding cycle is often less than one year. So, while the mathematics is just a bit more involved, there is a real tangible benefit to this complication. It helps you get richer faster! This is very important to understand. It is one of the reasons some businesses can grow much more quickly than others. It relates to the ability to rapidly reinvest money to grow the business (review the chapter on bootstrapping). Remember, investing for the long-term and compounding over many, many years is a great way to build wealth. This is because, mathematically, you are raising the compounding rate to the number of years compounded. For example, compounding at 15% for 20 years gives $(1.15)^{20} = 16.36$ as the factor by which to multiply your initial amount. In forty years, the multiplying factor is $(1.15)^{40} = 267.86$. Increases in the exponent (or, the power 20 and 40 above, which represent the number of years) have a tremendous impact upon increasing the multiplier expression.

There is not much you can do to live significantly longer to benefit more from the longer investment periods. You could not double your life expectancy from 90 to 180. Yet, by careful selection of your business, you can effectively achieve the same result (higher numbers in the exponent of your money multiplier expression). Let's assume, in our above example, it does not take a full year to make one of our machines. Suppose it only takes six months. Then, within one year, we can build one machine and another in sequence. How much money did it take, as an up-front investment, to manufacture both of these machines? You might guess double the cost of making one machine, or $1,800,000. This amount, while correctly representing the total cost of manufacturing two machines, is not the same as the amount needed to manufacture two machines in one year. You only need $900,000. In the first six months, you manufacture the first machine. You collect payment for it immediately, and, then, turn around and manufacture a second machine. Because each machine earns you profits of $100,000, your total annual profit is $200,000. Notice what happens to your annual rate of return. It is now 22% or doubled.

Many people miss this aspect of business. They feel, to finance and manufacture a given amount of product, they must multiply the cost of one product by the number of products they hope to sell. They assume they will need this much money to invest at the beginning of the endeavor. That is not true if money can be reinvested from early sales to finance sales that occur later in the year. If you can turnover your product (and collect payment for it) n times within one year, you only need the total cost of goods sold throughout the year divided by n. In the above example, n is two. You can think of this as squeezing two compounding periods into one year!

Suppose, we were producing products that had smaller initial production costs. In the previous example, only $900,000 of the first $1,000,000 collected could be invested at the internal rate of return of the company. The other $100,000 could be invested in a money market fund. If you could produce more product for the extra $100,000, the rate of return is even higher than 22%. In fact, it is calculated as follows: First, raise the compounding rate for one cycle plus one to the number of compounding cycles there are in one year. Finally, subtract one. The result is $(1.11)^2 - 1 = 1.23 - 1 = 23\%$.

The factor of $(1.11)^2 = 1.23$ expresses the fact that an initial investment compounding at 11% every six months, in one year, will grow into 1.23 times the initial amount invested. This is a 23 percent annual return. Remember, the one in this expression is just saying you are getting your initial investment back. You get back $1 + 0.23$. The one follows along naturally in the calculation of multiplier expressions. When you get to the end result, you must subtract one, because you are not getting a rate of return of 123%, but only 23%.

As another example, suppose you can produce four machines within one year, one right after the other. As before, each machine costs $900,000 to build and is sold for $1,000,000. Within one compounding cycle, you are still getting an 11% return. But, now, there are four compounding cycles in one year, so your overall rate of return would be $(1.11)^4 - 1 = 1.52 - 1 = 0.52$ or 52%. But, we are neglecting that each machine requires a starting amount of $900,000, so in this case, a more correct expression is really just 4 times 11% or 44%. If you could put all of your capital to work at the quarterly rate of 11% then 52% is correct. It may seem I am belaboring a minor point, but many people miss this. Your particular business will compound money in a slightly different way from other businesses. Businesses requiring large up-front investments often have some "leftover money" that simply cannot be invested at the higher rate at which the business normally operates. So, you have $1,000,000. You still can only begin production of one machine. Left over is $100,000. Similarly, even after producing three machines, you only have enough to begin construction on one new machine. Only when your total profits plus initial capital invested becomes $1,800,000 will you be able to start construction of two machines simultaneously and be able to finance this construction entirely from within.

All of this assumed you are paid for the machine most recently made immediately after the construction is complete. What if you are only paid one year after making the machine? What is your compounding period? Although you are staffed to make up to four machines in one year, because you are waiting for payment for the first machine, you cannot begin construction of the second machine until one year later. So effectively, your compounding period is one full year rather than the more beneficial one-quarter of a year. In this case, your growth is limited by the rate at which you are collecting payment for your machines. It doesn't matter that you *could* make four machines in a year, you simply don't have the *capital*. If you have a growing a company, it is important to ask yourself, "What is limiting my growth?" Are you limited by plant manufacturing capacity (here, four machines per year) or are you limited by the cycle of cash flows coming back to your company from previous sales? Once you know where your growth bottleneck is, then you will be able to work to eliminate it. This is why you want to write an expression for how *your* business compounds money.

You have already learned a great deal about compounding and the related time value of money. However, there are two terms you will often hear among business people, so I will briefly mention them. You already understand them. It's just vocabulary to you at this point. The first term is the future value of a present sum. Or, sometimes, you will hear, "The future value of so many dollars." This just means that, because any amount now can be compounded to yield a larger amount in the future, you multiply the so-many-dollars-now by the multiplier factors you learned above to get its future worth. It is no more than compounding the money forward in time. So, if you know the going rate you could get on a given amount of money is 10% over 10 years, then $1,000 now is worth the future sum in 10 years of $1,000 times $(1.10)^{10}$ or $2,594.

Similarly, you can work backward, asking the question, "Suppose I had so much in ten years, how much is that worth today?" Just divide the future amount by the appropriate multiplier factor to get the present value. So, for example, $1,000 to be received in 10 years is worth only $1,000 *divided* by $(1.10)^{10}$ today or $386. The rate of return from which you are working backward is sometimes called the discount rate. The money must be discounted by so much. So, if we choose a discount rate of 12% rather than 10% over the ten years, the multiplying factor is $(1.12)^{10} = 3.10$. So $1,000 received in 10 years is now only valued at $1,000 divided by 3.10 or $323.

If you find this chapter confusing, reread it. And, then play around with some compounding examples on your calculator. After awhile a light bulb flashes, and you say, "Ah, now I get it." At that point, you will be able to translate a given dollar amount forward in time by compounding it at various rates. Or, if the situation demands, you will be able to discount any given future sum back to its present value.

Chapter 17.
To Incorporate Or Not To
Incorporate?
That Is the Question

The short answer is "Yes." You generally should incorporate your business. As an entrepreneur, one of your goals is to protect yourself and the money you have already earned. Entrepreneurs want to keep potential financial upswing intact, while minimizing the downside risk. Incorporation is one way to minimize your downside risk. Invariably, most of your wealth will be within your company. As you are growing your company, your personal funds outside the company will possibly be quite trivial. Many entrepreneurs sink nearly their entire wealth into their company when it starts. You could argue, "Hey, all my money is within the company. So what, if I don't incorporate? It's not like my personal assets amount to anything. And, I know being incorporated will only protect my personal assets outside the company. Incorporation, in no way, protects against the loss of assets *within* my company."

You would be overlooking the possibility of liability above and beyond the total value of everything you own. Take the case of a guy who sets his company up as a sole proprietorship. This means he and his business are considered legally inseparable. He is his business. He is *personally* responsible for all its debts. Usually, this doesn't matter. For if he wishes to borrow money from a bank and his company does not have sufficient cash flow and collateral to justify the loan, the bank will not loan him the money, anyway. If he has significant capital outside the business, like a house etc., the bank will loan him the money, contingent upon his signing personally for the loan. He will be held personally responsible for the loan if the business fails, whether or not he incorporated. So, why incorporate if you will be held responsible, anyway?

The answer is that, while he will be held personally responsible for this loan, he will not necessarily be held responsible for other debts the company incurs. Suppose our owner, Harvey, starts a restaurant and needs to borrow $50,000 from a bank. Because he is only renting the site for his restaurant and has few other assets within the restaurant, he needs to sign personally for the loan. He will need to repay the loan from his personal funds, if his restaurant fails.

One day a customer enters his restaurant and falls down a flight of stairs. Our owner believes he is protected because he has insurance. He is shocked to find his cousin, Terry, took Friday off and didn't pay the insurance premium due for the month. His insurance has lapsed. The owner has paid his premiums for two years on time, but guess what? The insurance company decides to drop him as a client. They can do this because there was a lapse in the premium payments. They choose to drop him because they know a claim is eminent.

The customer sues the restaurant and wins $1 million dollars. The restaurant now has a $1 million dollar liability. This liability is just as real as the bank loan. The restaurant owner talks to his attorney, and despite paying his insurance premiums like clockwork for two years, the attorney advises him that huge legal costs would be involved to sue the insurance company and the restaurant owner would probably lose anyway in the end. After all, the premium was not paid, and the contract clearly said that the insurance company could cancel the contract under this condition (note: some attorneys might be able to win this case. I am not an attorney and am not rendering legal advice. Whenever you have legal questions, consult an attorney. This chapter only describes some ways incorporation *might* come into play).

Well, Harvey doesn't have $1 million dollars within the business. He cannot pay the debt. This is almost certainly the end of Harvey's restaurant. I don't know, maybe, he can offer to give 90% of the restaurant ownership to the injured party and agree to stay on and run it or some such thing and, maybe, the injured guy will accept this as payment for the $1 million. Probably not. Deals like this often don't please either party. The guy wants his money, not a restaurant. So, the restaurant will need to be sold. But, its value is only $100,000. Obviously, the incoming new owner will not absorb the liability. (See the chapter on buying a business. You certainly would not want to buy this business from Harvey, if there was any doubt as to who "owns" the $1 million dollar liability. If the contract Harvey was waving under your nose said something like, "And the purchaser agrees to incur all existing and future liabilities of said restaurant," this obviously would be a horrible acquisition for you. Did you even know about the lawsuit? Always have your attorney research possibilities like this.)

Let's assume Harvey sells the restaurant for $100,000. He gives the money to the injured party. But, now, the injured party, Frank, just to have a better moniker than "injured party," says, "Hey, wait a minute. You owe me $1 million. You're $900,000 light. I want all of my money." That's not an unreasonable response, now, is it? Would you settle for a tenth of what you were owed? Harvey explains he has sold the entire restaurant. There is no money left. Frank says, "Hey, what about your other assets? Sell them." Harvey is starting to not like Frank as a customer! But, I guess it doesn't matter. Harvey is out of the restaurant business, now, anyway. Harvey doesn't feel he should need to sell his house. That'll make his wife mad at him. And, after all, Harvey's house really wasn't part of the business.

Whether or not Harvey had incorporated comes into play in a big way. If Harvey didn't incorporate, then the rest of the $900,000 debt is his. The consequences of the lawsuit will live on even after the business is gone. And, in one form or another, Harvey will bear the cost of the consequences *personally*. But, what if Harvey had incorporated? Harvey could tell Frank, "Hey, Frank, I'm sorry, guy, but I've sold the entire value of the business. You've gotten all the wealth there was in the business. There is no other choice but to default on the difference."

Frank says, "Sell your house." Harvey explains his restaurant was incorporated and his house is not a corporate asset. It is personal real estate. Frank doesn't quite like the sound of this, and he goes to his attorney, and the attorney explains that Harvey is correct. The judgement went against the corporation, not Harvey, personally. Frank says, "Well, sue Harvey, personally, then." And, they do. And so, Harvey and Frank find themselves in court again.

At the very least, Harvey has a fighting chance to keep his personal possessions and not need to declare personal bankruptcy. Harvey might still lose, but, then again, he might not. This is getting suspenseful, no? Frank and his attorney argue that Harvey is personally responsible for Frank's fall. After all, the business was responsible, so why wouldn't it follow, because Harvey owned the entire corporation, he is not really the corporation? The judge decides that, even though Harvey owned the entire corporation, Harvey has not done anything personally irresponsible to invalidate the corporate structure. Harvey had taken all responsible actions as a business owner. It was sufficiently clear the insurance's lapse was not an intentional attempt to cut corners by Harvey, but a bad oversight by someone Harvey trusted. That Harvey had paid the premiums so many years convinced the judge that Harvey and Frank (but not the insurance company) were the victims of Murphy's Law, what can go wrong will go wrong at the most inappropriate time. Had Frank not fallen when he did, Harvey probably would have kept his insurance or gotten another policy. If Frank had fallen a month earlier or a month later, Harvey would have been properly insured.

The $50,000 Harvey personally signed for with the bank is still owed, along with any other liabilities for which he personally signed that were not purchased, along with the restaurant, by the newest owner. But, that is a far better position than being held personally responsible for the remaining $900,000. This is why entrepreneurs incorporate, to protect against unforeseen liabilities that could wipe out the business and, then, invade personal wealth. The hope is that, even if the business goes under, at least the personal assets of the entrepreneur will be saved. The entrepreneur will not be forced into absorbing huge personal liabilities.

Yet, there are many cases where a person or a group of people incorporates, and, upon business failure, the owners are held personally responsible. It is important to be aware of why this happens. Simply put, some people abuse the protection of incorporation. Harvey really did try to run his business responsibly. He was not trying to escape the payment of debts he likely couldn't pay or to use the corporate structure to cut corners in terms of insurance expense. This is important. If your business is undercapitalized or improperly insured, it is clear the corporation would, upon such a lawsuit, collapse. The law looks very badly upon those who do this.

In this type of case, someone gets the brilliant idea, because he can form a corporation, he does not need to worry about insurance to protect the business from contingencies, such as the one we've discussed. So, the business will save a few bucks on premiums. The owner figures, if the company is sued, without insurance, it will surely fail. So, he keeps as little money in the corporation as he can. If there is a huge liability, he thinks he will minimize his personal loss *and the business loss*. He is trying to use the corporation as a pass-through device and funnel the profits to himself. His corporation is undercapitalized and not properly insured to do the kind of business it is doing. Some enterprising individuals set up several corporations which are really just the same business but broken into chunks. They feel any one part of the business being sued will not bring down the other parts. In these cases, it is clear that the protection of incorporation is being abused.

This is a difficult thing for some people to understand. They know the whole idea of incorporation is to protect personal assets. Then, I'm saying, if you don't insure the corporation or you have just a little money in the corporation, you will be held personally liable. Incorporation does protect personal assets upon the failure of the corporation, usually, but this does not mean you can run the business irresponsibly. You must take all reasonable precautions to see the company can function as an independent entity and survive as such.

If you have customers coming to your business, there is a chance they could be injured and the corporation held responsible. As a responsible business owner, you must anticipate reasonable possibilities like this and take reasonable steps to prevent such occurrences from destroying the business. In other words, incorporate, but treat the business as if it were a sole proprietorship from a responsibility standpoint. You should take every precaution to protect the corporation, itself.

Incorporation will not protect you from personal wrongdoing. If you make an irresponsible decision, you will be held personally responsible, whether or not you have incorporated your business. You don't use a corporate legal structure to cut corners in how your business is run. If you are an electrical contractor and hire people, not legally qualified to do that kind of work, you are responsible if they screw up and destroy something or kill someone through incompetence. You knew you should not be hiring such people, but to save costs, you sent unqualified people out on jobs. Even if you didn't know this, it is still your fault! Anyone can plead ignorance. But, as the owner of such a company, you are simply not allowed to be ignorant of laws so relevant to your company. So, be responsible and conscientious, as a business owner. Know the laws that directly apply to your company and follow them. I hate to say it, because it is so obvious, but use good judgement.

Mingling personal finances with corporate finances also screws up the protection incorporation would have otherwise offered you. Suppose you want to buy a new car. You don't have the money in your personal account, so you write a check from the business account. You treat the business account as though it were your personal account. You cannot do this. Well, you can, but if you are sued, you will likely be held personally responsible (there could also be criminal ramifications, but that is beyond the scope of this book). This also causes confusion. After all, what if you are the only business owner? In some metaphysical sense, you do own all the money in the business account! So, why can't you mix and match accounts? Maybe, this gets back to being undercapitalized. You are conveniently switching your money about as it suits you. It doesn't suit the government! The law expects to see two accounts, a corporate business account and your personal account. And the two should not mix!

From a management standpoint alone, you should keep your business account separate from your personal account, even if you are a sole proprietorship. Why should you need to wade through a bunch of irrelevant purchases, having nothing to do with your business, when you are trying to examine your business records? It's sometimes difficult enough to figure out what's going on with only business records present, let alone mixing in personal records.

Some new business people feel they have discovered the fountain of tax evasion upon starting a business. They write off everything as a business expense! Breakfast, lunch, dinner, the theater, etc.,—never mind these have absolutely nothing to do with running the business. They don't really care how the written off expense fits into the business. The IRS cares! Remember, expenses are those costs a business incurs to generate income. If the cost doesn't help to generate sales or produce product, it is not a proper expense. It is stupid to try to use corporate funds for personal uses or to write off personal expenditures as business expenses, hoping to save a few tax dollars. The "savings" just aren't worth the potential penalties involved. This is a case of taking a significant downside risk for a meager upside gain.

To remove money from the corporation, pay yourself a regular wage or dividends or both. Use money from your wages and dividends for personal purchases. This money is exactly the same as if you had earned it working for someone else or as if you had received dividends from the local power company stock. It's your money to do with as you please. You won't get into trouble with the IRS or anyone else. Wages and dividends create a clear way to record just how much money you are taking from the corporation.

"What about double taxation when a smaller company pays dividends to its shareholders?" you ask. There are two types of corporations, S corporations and C corporations. Both types offer incorporators the same legal protection of personal assets. However, they are taxed differently. The C-type corporation is the standard corporation and, yes, when it pays dividends, those dividends are taxed twice—once as income to the business and, secondly, as income to the person receiving the dividends. To afford smaller companies the legal protection of the corporate structure and to prevent smaller companies from suffering the burden of paying double taxes on dividends, the government invented the S-type corporation or the small business corporation. The S corporation is treated as a pass-through entity in regard to taxes. S corporations do not pay income taxes. Rather, the income is passed through to the shareholders, and they pay income tax on it, once.

So, S-type corporations avoid the much-worried-about-but-seldom-paid double taxation. (Larger, publicly-traded companies often do pay dividends that are taxed twice.) The curious thing about S corporations is that the shareholders need to pay taxes on profits earned, whether or not the S corporation actually pays these profits as dividends or whether it keeps the money to reinvest for more corporate growth. This leads to what is sometimes called "phantom income." You don't receive it, but owe income taxes on it, anyway! If you set up an S corporation and, especially, if you have capital investors, you need to look into this and understand it. You and your investors need to be in agreement as to what type of corporation is set up and how such taxation issues will be treated.

Often when a company is just starting, phantom income is not a problem, as the company is not generating significant profits yet. If there are corporate losses, these losses are passed through to the investor. The investor gets to write off the loss from a tax standpoint. This is why some investors will favor an S corporation type. They save money on taxes, while the company is getting off the ground! Going to one of these investors and saying, "We did better than expected this first year," is a bit of good news and bad news at the same time.

Usually, they say, "Great, keep up the good work." And, you say, "No, I mean we did much, *much* better than we predicted. You know we were predicting a loss of $200,000. Remember, we talked about the big tax break you'd get if we set ourselves up as an S-type corporation? In fact, we made $2 million dollars. Oh, by the way, that'll probably mean you'll owe about $300,000 more in taxes this year." And, of course, you weren't planning to pay out any dividends as profits are being reinvested for growth! The thing to do in this case is to keep explaining to the investor that the company's early profitability is really a good thing and not a bad thing. Stay focused on that message. Then, try to pay sufficient dividends to take some bite out of the tax liability. This is a great way to help the investor understand the difference between profits and cash flow!

Money can be withdrawn from a corporation as wages or salary. This avoids double income taxation, as the wages are treated as a business expense. You will only pay personal income taxes on your salary. Unfortunately, there is a whole swarm of smaller taxes that will hit any income you pay yourself as wages. First, you will pay Social Security taxes. This siphons off about 15% right there. There are unemployment taxes on the first few thousand of your earnings. This lobs off some more. It sometimes seems to me the tax system is stacked against the start-up entrepreneur who has small overall profitability. A new S corporation's paltry earnings of $10,000 could easily wind up in an overall incremental 55% tax bracket when all income taxes and employment taxes are allowed for!

You would still pay Social Security taxes, if you set your business up as a sole proprietorship. You really don't lose anything by incorporating. Many smaller businesses never make enough to be limited by having a C-type corporation. If you can only afford to take $30,000 from the business each year, it might as well come from a C corporation as wages. And, you will not pay double taxation. You will never pay dividends. This assumes you are not trying to pay yourself a huge salary. If the IRS feels you are paying yourself a wage, far in excess of what is "reasonable," it assumes you are trying to avoid double taxation. It will reallocate some of the money as dividends. The IRS is skeptical of high wages paid from a C corporation to the founder.

Some clever individuals reason, if you can pay dividends from an S corporation and have them taxed only once, as personal income, the best of all worlds is to have an S corporation and pay yourself no wages at all. Take all your money out in the form of S corporation dividends. After all, the IRS doesn't want you to pay yourself a huge unreasonable wage from a C corporation. Even if you did this, you are still hit with those silly Social Security taxes. So, let's do away with wages altogether! Well, the IRS doesn't like this, either. It feels you must pay yourself at least a reasonable wage. Otherwise, it figures you are trying to avoid Social Security taxes. So, if you have an S-type corporation and pay a lot in dividends, but no wages, the IRS will reallocate some of the dividends as wages.

The general rule is, while you can always just pay yourself a small wage from a C corporation and take the rest out as doubly-taxed dividends, with an S corporation, the situation is reversed. You can pay yourself all the wages you want, and the IRS will not have a problem with this. Take it all out as dividends and the IRS might not like it. As a rule, the IRS doesn't have a problem with your paying the largest tax bill possible!

The solution, of course, is that, if you want to take a good chunk of money out of your corporation, you should probably set it up as an S-type corporation. Pay yourself a reasonable wage for the kind of work you are doing, i.e., a salary comparable to what others in similar job roles are making. Then, pay out the rest in dividends. This should minimize the tax bite. But, first, ask yourself, "Do I really want to take a lot of money out of my company?"

Remember, the best way to grow a business is to keep reinvesting money earned within the business to make more money. If you keep drawing money from the business, you won't have internal funds to finance more growth. One of the best "harvest" strategies for a business is to grow the business until it is sufficiently large to interest investors or other businesses. Then, you can sell your business for a significant multiplier of your current earnings. If your company is earning $1 million per year, you might be offered a p/e (price-to-earnings) ratio of 8 or more for your company. If your business is growing fast or has something internal making it uniquely positioned, such as valuable proprietary products, you might be offered much greater p/e ratios. This means, when you leave your business, you will walk away with eight years of current earnings ($8 million in the current example) as your "gold watch" retirement present. This is your return for building your company. Plus, you are taxed at the more favorable capital gains tax rate, when you build a company and later sell it.

Many people who start a business aren't aware of this selling of the business as an exit strategy. They tend to think in terms of using the business to generate profits and, then, withdrawing the profits. Either way works. If you want to withdraw cash, an S corporation is best. If you are trying to grow your business and sell it down the road, then a C corporation is, probably, the better structure.

The biggest reason you need a corporate structure are those pesky, but lovable, entities, referred to as employees. Don't get me wrong, as you probably can tell, I like the concept of employees. But, the reality is they can and do make mistakes. As a sole proprietor, you are responsible for any liabilities incurred by your business, even if they are accidentally incurred by the actions of an employee. This means a poor judgement or misconduct of one of your employees can sink you financially, both as a company and personally. This is simply too great a risk. If you have employees, it is only prudent to incorporate. That way, at most, they can sink only your business!

I shouldn't even need to mention partnerships, but I will. There is no good reason to setup any business as a partnership. In a way, this is worse than a sole proprietorship. At least, with a sole proprietorship you have control over what is happening within your business. With a partnership, both you and your partner can make serious decisions affecting the business. If fact, your partner can make a decision and take an action with which you totally disagree. Suppose his decision puts the company at risk and doesn't work. That's bad enough, but even worse, you are personally liable for your company's debts. This means actions of your partner can adversely affect your personal worth. You are held accountable for debts incurred by your partner. Even if you trust your partner's judgement fully, there is no good reason *not* to form a corporation.

An alternative to a corporation is a limited liability company (LLC) which also provides liability protection to entrepreneurs. I discuss corporate business structure in more detail in my book *How To Start And Run Your Own Corporation: S-Corporations For Small Business Owners.*

Chapter 18.
The Definition of Entrepreneur:
Bringing Together the Resources

As previously mentioned, entrepreneurs don't need to do everything themselves. They can hire others. They can outsource. They do not need to know it all. In fact, we can define an entrepreneur as a person who undertakes action to bring together resources. Surprisingly, the entrepreneur might not even be one of the crucial resources, just the one who understands what resources must be acquired for the business to succeed and then sets about acquiring those resources. "Seek the needed resources and bring them together to do the project quickly," should be the entrepreneur's motto. Resources include people, financial capital, and the project idea. If you can pull together those three resources, the idea can happen. If you fail to bring together the needed resources, the idea won't happen. It's that simple.

Most entrepreneurs generate the idea themselves and, then, seek the other two resources. Consider the movie industry. Suppose you have written a movie script, and you want to see it made into a film. Obviously, you could submit it via the traditional channels. The most obvious place to send it would be to film production companies. They will send it back to you, and tell you to get an agent. You could, then, send it to an agent. Maybe, if you are lucky, an agent would take you as a client. You still haven't sold the script. Your script is still one of thousands trying to be made into a film. You have come a long way. You have an agent, but you still have a long way to go.

In order for your script to become a film, someone with the ability to put together the team and capital to film it must become interested. This can happen in roundabout ways. Quentin Tarantino's script, *Reservoir Dogs*, eventually found its way into the hands of Harvey

Keitel, via Keitel's wife, whose friend was teaching an acting class. Lawrence Bender, who knew Tarantino, was enrolled in the class. Keitel saw it was a good script and was willing to put money into it. It became a very successful film. Maybe, a director will see the script or a big name actor will read it and like it. Any of these has tremendous clout to get a script made into a film. But, most of these people don't really want to be responsible for the whole production. After all, these people want to direct or act, not run around doing non-creative, gopher work.

In movies, it is the much-maligned Producer, who is the entrepreneur. I write Producer with a capital P because Producers are very important. Without them, you wouldn't see very many films. Producers, typically, have no talent, not as directors or actors or otherwise. Yet, they are often the most successful members of the movie industry. There is a film-industry tidbit that actors and directors, even if wildly successful for a period, can still wind up broke, but producers always have money. Directors can become popular, have a bad film, and recede into obscurity. Actors do so even more readily. But, the lowly Producer seldom does. The Producer brings the team together to make the film—the camera person, the casting person, the director, and the rental equipment needed. The Producer acquires the permissions to film at various locations. The Producer often delegates through others. For example, the Producer, himself, will not necessarily hire each actor. That's what people, who specialize in casting actors in roles, do.

If the Producer knows how to raise funds to make the film, that Producer can become a full-fledged movie studio! Why would you do all this gophering around for a wage, when you could have a significant cut of the box-office gross and residual royalties? This is why movie studios go out of their way to isolate Producers into two camps—Producers who bring together the resources, other than capital, and Producers who raise capital. If the studio chooses moderately stupid people in each role, so much the better (Just kidding. Most Producers are actually bright. They just play dumb. As a group, they tend to watch too much *Columbo*). Then, they will never learn the secret that they don't really need the studio at all.

They can go it alone and make a hell of a lot more money. The value created in a movie studio is built around bringing together resources, nothing more and nothing less. It is the contacts that are crucial.

The movie studio is a fun example, but hardly the only industry where the value lies in bringing together the resources to complete a project. Consider the computer-consulting field. Do you remember old Henry from Chapter Three? Don't feel bad, no one else does either. But, Henry did go on to become a successful consultant, or, more correctly, he built a successful consulting company.

Here's what happened. Henry got in way over his head. His first project sucked, but a friend told a local company Henry was a talented guy. The company hired Henry to write some custom software. Henry figured, "No problem." He took the job. Quickly, he found himself in over his head. In fact, he didn't have a clue what he was doing. He even cried. He contemplated returning the several thousand dollars the company paid him in advance. He didn't really want to do this, but if he knew he couldn't complete the project, then, he would do this. After all, Henry was an honest guy. But, as luck would have it, Henry watched *The Magnificent Seven* and that key phrase, "Men are cheaper than guns," resonated in his mind. Henry was a likable guy. He had acquired many friends in the programming business. Certainly, one of them would help him. So, Henry went out and asked a knowledgeable friend to help. Henry made more and more progress, as he kept going back to his friend for help. Eventually, it was clear to Henry that his friend would be more efficient, if just left alone to finish the job. The job was completed, and Henry gave *most* of the money the company paid him to his friend. The company was very satisfied. Henry's friend was very satisfied.

Henry's reputation spread. Soon companies from all over the world wanted to hire him as a consultant! He already had two or three contracts in the works, when he accepted several others. "How can he do it all?" other consultants questioned. "Henry's a super-programmer. He's a genius. Didn't you know that?" Well, no, Henry wasn't a genius. Far from it. He was closer to being a Forrest Gump. In fact, Henry went by his middle name. His first name was Forrest and his last name was Gump. Why not? Henry doesn't exist, remember, so I can name him anything I like! Eventually, word got out that Henry didn't do all his own programming. Henry wanted the word out. He needed more programmers to keep up with the demand for his services. He founded F.H. Gump Computer Consultants.

Now, Henry had a difficult job. He had two lists. The first list was of companies that wanted Henry to come and do a project for them. If Henry, himself, couldn't make it, it was OK that he sent one of his "underlings," for Henry wouldn't hire someone who didn't know what he was doing. Companies knew this. F.H. Gump had a great reputation among businesses. The other list was of consultants who were now employed by Henry, either as independent consultants or as employees. Each of these people had certain skills. More people wanted to come and work for Henry every day. Henry treated his consultants well, paid them well, and was considered a brilliant guy. So, everyone wanted to work for him. Every night, Henry went home to work on his company. He began by writing the two lists onto one sheet of paper. More than one sheet of paper confused Henry. On the left hand side of the page was the list of companies that needed a programmer. On the right hand side of the paper was the list of available programmers. With his best effort, Henry considered which programmer was best for each company. He then drew a line between the company and the programmer. That programmer was to go to work for that company.

It was an arduous task. But, Henry was well-compensated. Each line he drew earned him several thousand dollars. Henry drew so many lines he got carpal tunnel! He became very wealthy. But, as fate would have it, F.H. Gump was not to have a happy ending. Henry purchased a new hibachi to roast hot dogs and stuff. While he was working one day, drawing his lines and roasting wieners at the same time, his lists caught fire. Henry didn't have a backup of his valuable lists. He didn't know which companies needed consultants. He wasn't even sure which consultants worked for him, anymore. Many companies, expecting Henry to send someone, were pissed, when he didn't. The ten-year-old boy next door tricked Henry into believing he was one of Henry's consultants. The kid flubbed up a couple of Unix projects. F.H. Gump's reputation went up in smoke.

I wonder how many companies derive their entire business worth from two lists. The goal of the business at heart is simply to match up items from each side of the list.

What made Henry successful was reputation, reputation with both the client companies, needing his services, and reputation with the knowledgeable employees, who went to work for him—reputation as being honest, concerned with the satisfaction of all stakeholders in the endeavor. Henry wanted to see clients' projects done well at a fair cost. He wanted to see his employees (technically, some were employees, and others were independent consultants) well-compensated for their work. If Henry had been only interested in making money and had tried to exploit either of the other stakeholders for his own benefit, he probably would have failed. To be considered as the person who can bring together the resources, you must be taken seriously. Your reputation is crucial. Never, never forget this.

Chapter 19.
A Lesson From Direct Mail:
Test First

Every area of business you learn a bit about tends to give you new ways of thinking about business in general. There is a good deal to be learned from the marketing area known as direct mail. Most new entrepreneurs are familiar with saturation advertising—display advertising, repeated over and over, until it sinks into the consumer's psyche. Over the radio, over the television, on billboards, in magazines, in newspapers, in…well, you get the picture.

When you find yourself singing the jingle of a common commercial, you've been hit with saturation advertising. When slogans become comic relief lines in major motion pictures, that represents the force of saturation advertising.

This method of advertising or marketing your services isn't appropriate for most new entrepreneurial companies. It costs too much, and too much of the message is delivered to the wrong consumers. So, while saturation marketing works for Pepsi, it probably won't work for you. At least, not yet! You need to target your marketing efforts to the likely buyers of your products.

Your buyers will not be equally spread out among the larger population, but will be grouped by common similarities. The grouping may be geographically-based. Usually, it is psycho-graphically-based. Use these known groupings to help locate potential customers. What you are selling will have a niche market, containing the likely buyers. Focus your marketing effort into that niche.

Your marketing effort will be easier, if you sell to companies, as you will know which industries are likely to buy your products or services. You will be able to get industry association lists, or, just look up companies in the Yellow Pages. If your product or service appeals to barbershops, you know how to find them. But, when you market to consumers, the phone book won't help you. Sure, there are a lot of names you could look up. But, by and large, all these people are very different.

Suppose you are opening a shop selling bicycles and related items. If you start to call people at random from the phone book or send fliers to all local addresses, you waste too much effort. Wasted effort means wasted money. Most of the people contacted just aren't into cycling. They won't buy your product. Doesn't matter how good it is. Doesn't matter what your prices are. They just aren't interested. Whenever you are trying to sell to people who just aren't interested, you are wasting your effort.

Rather than do this, seek to market your niche product intelligently. Market only to qualified buyers or people who are already predisposed to buy your product. One place to look for customers would be any magazines that cater to cyclists, *Cycling Today* or *Cycling Tomorrow* or *Cycle Rider* or *Cycle Whatever*. Now, at least, people subscribing to these magazines are interested in the sort of products you are trying to sell. But, there is still one problem. If you sell via a local retail shop only, then, probably, most of the magazine subscribers live nowhere near your store. That's easy to correct. You just intersect the subscribers with your home state or some zip code areas of your state. Magazines can sell you the names of only the subscribers in the zip codes you desire. There will still be some waste. But, it is far less waste than sending to all the subscribers within the U.S.A.

This illustrates the difficulty in starting a local specialty store. You are fighting geography and lack of interest. Both together are a powerful force. There simply aren't as many interested buyers within your area as you would like. If you were to do something everybody needs or wants, like selling doughnuts (who doesn't like doughnuts?), you would have much higher interest about your shop within any given geographical area. Unfortunately, something that appeals to everyone is often a commodity. Consumers buy it based upon price, or because they are very, very close to the store. These areas of business are, usually, well-served by existing businesses. This is a tough and undesirable area for an entrepreneur to enter.

If you cannot appeal to more customers living near your business, expand and serve a larger geographical area.

This is made much easier by direct mail and the Internet. Rather than sell your products only locally, you can market them to the world, or more appropriately, those members of the world who are interested. And, there are a damn lot of cyclists in the whole world, even within only the U.S.A. There are a whole lot of *any kind of people* in the *whole* world. The Internet has shown us, no matter how weird you are, there is a veritable army of like-minded people out there. You're not as unique as you thought!

Interested buyers will not view your catalog of cycling goods as junk mail. They will love it! It addresses their hobby. It excites them. Maybe, they'll even order! You already know how to reach these affinity groups, direct mail to targeted lists. These lists are commonly available. Go to your local library and ask the librarian for information on mailing lists available for rent. The librarian will point you to some resources. Else, look in the Yellow Pages. There are companies that specialize in providing mailing lists to businesses. Look at the United States Postal Service web site.

That brings up the question, "How do I know the list I am about to rent really has only cyclists on it? What if they just took names at random from the phone book? I already know what that gets me. Doodley." Boy, are you the skeptical sort! That's good. Well, you could ask around. Ask other companies, which rented lists from this company, what results they had. But what if the product really sucked? That might explain a lack of response to the mailing, also.

How can you protect yourself from mailing out 100,000 pieces (or, God forbid, 1,000,000) only to find your promotional mailing didn't work? Sending out catalogs, printed in full color, is quite a cost. Even if your mailing package is only a simple letter, you might be sending it at a cost of $0.50 apiece. Multiply that by 100,000 and you have spent $50,000. That's sort of a big investment in the mailing.

The answer is to test the mailing package on the list for a smaller number of subscribers. Don't try all 100,000 at once. Maybe, try

10,000. Or, maybe, only 5,000. That way your initial cost to find out is small. If the list doesn't work, you haven't spent $50,000 to learn this. And, there is nothing to say you must, on a second mailing, roll-out all the way to 100,000. Maybe, send out 20,000. Professionals in direct mail tend to call this decision to mail to a larger number of people on the list "rolling out."

The intelligent reader is probably already asking, "What if the first 5,000 aren't representative of the remaining 95,000? Maybe, the remaining 95,000 will buy far more as a percentage of mailing pieces sent out or far less." That is a great concern. After all, would it not be possible for the company selling you the list to have two lists, one of 5,000 cyclists and another of 5,000,000 claimed cyclists! That's a worrisome thought. After all, the person renting you the list will try to put the most likely buyers on your short list of 5,000. That way you will rent the larger list.

Well, in short, there are techniques you can use to protect yourself from outright fraud like this. For example, you can get a zip code distribution of the list and then demand that your 5,000 are drawn from only the zip code areas you specify and that you get all the addresses in these zip code areas. You will know there is a problem, if the list contains 1,000,000 people, but they only can give you two people from Minnesota for your test, for example. This introduces the possibility of geographical effects, but there are more sophisticated ways to get around this.

Let's neglect outright fraud in trying to sell you the list. If you roll-out in several steps, you will invariably see a big drop off, if the first part of the list you rented was not representative of the whole list. There is a broader question: why is a small sampling of the list representative of the whole list and just how large of a sampling do I need to be sure it is representative of the whole list? Obviously, mailing to five people on the list wouldn't be representative of the entire 100,000, so why should 5,000?

The answer to how much of the list you must sample is that it depends. The number you need is usually not as big as you might fear. Five or ten percent of the list should give you a pretty good idea, assuming the list is at least 100,000. Consumers, once grouped by affinity interests, tend to be very similar in their buying habits. People not experienced in the direct mail business tend to be amazed at how accurately direct mail gurus can predict the overall response of an entire list based upon only a small sampling. Going back to our simple letter mailing at $0.50 apiece, the guru spends $5,000 to mail to 10,000 and from this can predict, usually fairly well, how the entire list of 100,000 will perform.

This is the power and the secret of direct mail: testing. You spend $5,000 to find out. Not ten times that much. After all, maybe, the list doesn't work. You have just saved yourself $45,000 which would have been wasted! If the test of 10,000 does poorly, you don't mail to the remaining 90,000. You need to come up with another idea or find another list! Or, maybe, change your offer or some other aspect of what you are doing.

But, if the list works, you roll-out and mail, eventually, to all 100,000. Just to have some numbers to play with, let's assume you can make $100 on every sale you generate and that 1% of the people on the list buy your product.

This means that 1,000 people on the list make you $100,000. The other 99,000 don't buy. Oh, well, you will, probably, mail to them again! First, note, despite making a very nice $100 profit per sale, the profit, when expressed per all the individuals receiving the mailing, only represents $1 per package sent out. You made $100,000 and you mailed to 100,000 people. Remember, each piece cost you $0.50. So, you see that one-half of your profit is equal to your promotional costs!

This is a sad fact of direct mail. The overall promotional costs are high. This is because, despite good list selection and testing, most of the people receiving the mailing still aren't buying. Even when they are interested in the basic area of your product! You are failing to sell 99% of the time. It's amazing you can still make money, but you do.

It should be immediately clear that, if you are spending so much as a percentage of your profit on promotion *when you have a well-selected list* that has been tested and shown to be successful before you rolled-out, you could never succeed using direct marketing methods in mailing to individuals selected at random. You need a targeted list. Never assume you can succeed with any old names. You will fail.

The next most crucial thing to notice is that you really only risked about $5,000 to make $100,000. Sure, the larger mailings may have failed to do as well as predicted, and you could lose a bit more. But, by and large, your roll-out results should not be too far from your estimates. Assuming you do this all properly, of course. And, if you built in just a tad of conservatism, your results are just as likely to be off in the good direction of making you slightly more money than you had estimated.

This is an excellent position to be in. You only invest larger amounts of money in the promotion once you know with a high certainty that it will work. You do not have to shoot-the-works, having only little idea as to the outcome. You are only risking a little to potentially make a lot. Consider the analogy. You are a stock market investor. You can only invest in stocks and not sell stocks short (Short selling means you are betting they will go down. If you are not familiar with the term, that is OK. Selling stocks short is not a smart idea, anyway. So, it is not worth studying). You have $100 to invest in the stock market, if you choose. Wouldn't it be nice if, at the start of the year, you could spend $5 of the $100 to find out, with a very high certainty, which way the stock market will go? Suppose the market will go up either 10% or drop 10% and each occurs with equal probability.

If after spending the $5, you learn the market will go up, you commit your resources. You invest your remaining $95 in the market. At the end of the year, you get your 10% return, so you have $104.50. If you learn that the market will go down, you stay out of the market. At the end of the year, you have $95. You're still out the $5 for the information. Had you invested, you would be out 10% or $10 leaving you with only $90, assuming you didn't buy the information and just made a random guess to invest.

Without the information, you would have ended with $110 or $90 depending upon the outcome. The average of these numbers is $100 which says you expect to break even. With the information, your ending average is $99.75. Humpf. You lost $0.25! Oh, well, the best-laid plans of mice and men...The problem is that your information cost was too large, relative to what you learned. Suppose you had $500 to invest rather than $100, but the information cost ($5) remained the same. Without the information, you still break even. You expect to end the year with $500. But, now, with the information cost, if you know the market will go up, you invest and earn 10% on $495 for an ending amount of $554.50. If the market will go down, you don't invest the remaining $495, and that is your ending amount. The average of these amounts is $519.75. Here, the information cost is low enough, relative to what you learn, that you make money overall. You have turned a zero-sum game into a positive-sum game.

Basically, you come out ahead (in our second example!) because you have absorbed a small information cost to tell you the results ahead of time. Unfortunately, many investors try to do precisely this. They feel if they pay some stock market guru $100 per year for an investment newsletter, he will be able to be an oracle and predict what will happen. Then, they either commit funds or not, based upon the guru's advice. The problem is that it has never been shown that anyone can predict stock market behavior. In this regard, my example is not realistic. It is only an analogy. In business, however, there are many cases where you can absorb a small information cost to get an excellent idea of whether your endeavor is truly viable and just how much can be made in the endeavor. Direct mail does exactly this.

Extreme direct-mail pundits really get a kick out of testing. They not only test to see if a list will work, but they vary the mailing package used and the offer. They ask questions like, "What will happen if we raise the product's price by 50%? Will we make more money, overall, or less money? What if we write the promotional letter with a different slant? What if....?" They seek not to find *any* profitable offer, but to find *the most* profitable offer. While this level of testing is OK for a marketing-oriented company, it is often overkill for a true product-oriented company.

If you write and sell a semi-custom piece of software, for example, you probably do not want to vary the estimated-base price just to see how many more or how many less sales leads you get as a result. Often, direct-mail companies are willing to take a loss on an initial mailing to add to their customer list. They hope to recoup the loss and make more on sales that materialize down the road. While I am a big fan of entrepreneurs selling products to a market niche and targeting their marketing only to that niche, the purpose of this chapter is not to promote direct mail. Rather, it is to take the lesson learned above—test first to find out; then, if the test justifies, commit your funds to the larger project—and apply it to more general business problems.

Whenever you plan a new venture, ask yourself, "Is there some way I can start small and risk just a little of my capital to find out if the idea will work? How certain can I be of the results of the test in predicting the overall results?" Once you start thinking like this, you can become very powerful. You will be thinking in terms of absorbing small information expenses to learn about the overall feasibility of your idea. You will be minimizing your financial risk, while allowing for large (roll-out) possibilities. You will be aware of the uncertainties involved in your predictions.

Chapter 20.
Selling Benefits, Savings, "An Image"

The more personal psychology the entrepreneur understands the better. In fact, as Daniel Goleman's books (*Emotional Intelligence* and *Working with Emotional Intelligence*) show, the ability to work with, understand, and relate to people is the most crucial aspect to individual success in life. Work on your social skills, if they are weak! But, even if you are an emotional-intelligently-challenged individual, you can still succeed! You need to know one thing: Why will people buy your products?

You might be selling products to other businesses, which are interested in making more money. If you can clearly demonstrate to them that you can save them a great deal of money, your selling job should be easy. Especially, if you are one of the few who can render the service for them. Company owners want to save money because it makes them wealthier. Even mid-level, nonowner managers want to find ways to save their company money. It makes them look useful! But, what if you are selling products, not to businesses, but directly to consumers?

What makes consumers buy products? At one level, there is an obvious need. Consumers will buy food. They don't have much choice. They can choose what type and where they buy it, but that's about all. Unfortunately, businesses selling these much-needed items often have the most difficult time making money. Margins are low. Many other people are thinking, "People need to buy food, so I can't fail to sell it and, hence, make money." While the first part of the assumption is true, the conclusion is blatantly false. The more essential a product is the more likely moderately affluent and affluent consumers take it for granted.

What consumers don't neglect are the fun little products that add something to their lives. If you are trying to sell to consumers, you will probably do better if you sell a nonessential product with personal appeal. You want to sell your products to people who have purchased the necessities of life and are now asking, "Is this all there is? I want more!" Many marketing books tell you to sell the benefits of your product to the consumers, and I agree. If your product has a tangible benefit, for example, it saves the purchaser time, you can emphasize this feature.

But, ultimately, I don't believe people buy features. They buy toys, fun products. Even more, they buy products that support the image they have of themselves. A consumer wants to make a statement about the kind of person he is, or, at least, the kind of person he believes he is. If your product supports this self-image, the person will want to buy. If the product contradicts the person's self-image, he will never buy it.

Sometimes, products supporting an image are also necessities. People who buy houses are not only looking for shelter, but also a house that reflects the type of person they are. Usually, there is just one factor, size. And, comfort features, I guess. People want comfortable homes, yes, but just as much, they want status symbols to show how much they can afford. People want reliable transportation, but they also want cars reflecting their personalities. How many teenagers want to go out and buy a station wagon? Not many. They all want sports cars. Some macho, young men want pickup trucks or motorcycles. This is understandable. After all, they're only kids!

Some people see themselves as conservative and rational. They like getting a good deal and showing how financially savvy they are. They tend to favor more modest homes and cars. They claim their purchases are made to save money and, often, that is true. But, at a more fundamental level, they see themselves as intelligent because of their approach to products. They are not *naively* throwing away their money. Further, they see the amount they have managed to save as an indicator of their frugality and financial wisdom. To these people, saving and making money are very important. Other people see themselves as risk takers, adventurers. They go bungee jumping, kayaking down rivers, backpacking in the woods.

Usually, people go through a series of self-images. First, they want the sports car, when they are young. As they get older, they want the status of being frugal and smarter than the average consumer-bear. They want career status. By about the time they get into their forties or fifties, they revert. They are risk takers again! You can't sell them the wrong products at the wrong point in their life cycle. You can't sell a conservative guy a risk product or sell a person seeking risk a conservative product.

When you understand how an individual customer views himself, you will be better positioned to sell to that customer. If you have no real concept of the person's self-image, you will have trouble relating to him about what he truly feels passionate. Neglecting this, you cannot know how to sell to him, nor even if your product is appropriate to his interests. This doesn't apply only to person-to-person sales. Most products sold to consumers cannot justify the large marketing cost of personal selling. Many cannot even justify the marketing costs of direct mail. (This is a reason to avoid low-margin, low-contribution products. You cannot apply the most effective sales methods.)

Let's assume your product can justify a direct-mail promotion, or, at the very least, an inexpensive flier. What would you write to motivate a purchase? Remember, as mentioned in the chapter about direct mail and testing first, it was pointed out that response rates could be really low, measured on the order of one percent. This means for every one hundred pieces sent out, you generate about one buyer. If your promotional copy can sway just one more buyer in two or even three hundred, it can lead to a much more successful promotion!

Many new marketers make the mistake of thinking they must answer possible criticisms of their product. It's too highly priced. It lacks this or that, etc., Many recipients of your mailing will instantly grab onto one of these criticisms, but there is little you can do to sway their decision and get them to order your product. They are essentially looking for a reason *not to buy*. They will find one! You could send an encyclopedia of counters to their possible criticisms (at a substantial mailing expense), and you still would not get the sale.

Not all customers are created equally. Some are viable buyers. Others are not. Don't waste your time trying to sell to people who are not likely to buy. Focus your attention on those who are sincerely interested in making the purchase. Next, focus on those on the fringe of making the purchase. They haven't made up their mind yet. Some marketers refer to these possible buyers as qualified prospects. Whatever you call them, this is where your sales lie.

If you keep trying to sell to unqualified buyers, besides annoying them and wasting your effort and resources, you are overlooking that they are usually rationalizing the decision not to buy. It is not that they have serious questions about this or that aspect of the product. It's not that it's "too expensive." If the price were less, they would likely still think it too high, or, else, they might start to question the quality of such a cheap product! You can't win. They don't want it, and they will darn well think of a rational reason to support their decision. They just aren't interested. Let it go at that.

Conversely, buyers tend to rationalize making the purchases they desire to make. The fifty-year-old guy next door, who has just purchased a sports car, emphasizes that it gets excellent gas mileage. It is quality-made, so it will last longer, etc. It is likely another neighbor who points out that the guy looks great in the car, or, maybe, it makes him feel twenty years younger, or, maybe, the guy is flaunting his wealth. Often, observers have a better perception of why a person buys a particular product than the person.

Some people, specifically telemarketers, are encouraged to keep trying to sell the product, if it appears there is any chance that the person on the other end of the phone might just, possibly, say, "Yes." They know some people have a hard time saying, "No." They play on this. News Flash: Such marketers have inferior products. That's almost always a given. If these marginal or semi-satisfied sales are needed to succeed, get a new product. You must be able to succeed financially by selling to people who happily buy your product. If you need to sell to "dissatisfied" customers to generate enough sales to make money, you will fail. Your product is just not strong enough.

I recall a door-to-door salesman, who was selling some general-purpose cleaning product—and, I mean general purpose, as in "The only cleaning product you will ever need." It could rub out stains, do the laundry, wash walls, maybe, even, brush your teeth. I don't know. I never learned just how far the product would go. I told him, "I'm just not interested and won't buy, so you're wasting your time trying to sell it to me." He thanked me and moved on. He knew the futility of trying to sell to someone who wouldn't buy. He was a charismatic guy, and I wished him luck making sales. He smiled and said, "It's not a matter of luck." A few hours later, I needed to go to the store, and as I drove up the street, I saw this same guy, dressed in his suit, several blocks up, still going door-to-door. It was a hot day, and he was sweating. I contemplated stopping and asking him, "Why the hell are you selling this &*^^$ cleaning product. You're a good salesperson. Have you ever considered selling custom software?" Given a product he believed in and that was worth the cost of personal selling, he could be very successful. Ultimately, he was correct. Success in selling is not a matter of luck.

Let's suppose you have an excellent product. You will not waste time countering every possible objection by the people who are going to rationalize not buying, anyway. What do you say to those who might buy to generate the sale? It depends. What motivates *your* buyer? You need to understand the psychographics of your buyers. Psychographics is like demographics without the geography! Are they greedy? Are they afraid? Do they see themselves as self-reliant? Do they see themselves as intellectuals? As charitable people? Pinpoint this and appeal to that aspect of who they are.

Your promotion should appeal at two different levels. One should be the rational, "Yes, this is a good product. I like it." The other should appeal to the more sublime, a motivation probably not even clearly expressed by the customer. Maybe you, the marketer, cannot even express it! It's a sense of being happy. The product gives them warm fuzzies. It makes them feel more like themselves! It supports their self-concept, their self-image. When you understand this, you have become a master marketer in theory. Of course, execution of what you know is another thing entirely!

In *As Good As It Gets*, Jack Nicholson plays a talented writer who understands human behavior very well. He could give you a lecture all about it. Nonetheless, he has trouble applying what he knows. He is constantly saying the wrong thing or making the wrong impression. This is shown in a scene after he has just put his foot in his mouth and driven away the woman he loves. He is sitting at a bar and spilling his soul to the bartender in the stereotypical fashion. He is saying (I'm paraphrasing here... I don't remember the exact movie lines), "And...I said the wrong thing. I don't know why I did that. And, I mean this is the kind of lady who, if you make smile, you have a life...but, instead, I'm here talking to you, no offense, a moron, pushing the last legal drug."

We are not all naturally talented salespeople, nor copywriters. The most successful entrepreneurs fall into one of two camps. One is the hard-thinking number cruncher who understands the fundamentals of business or has a good command of the product area. This person tends to delegate marketing and, especially, selling. Second is the charismatic promoter who really enjoys and does well selling an idea, of reading people and responding. Now, there is nothing wrong with trying to do both, but if you are just not up to selling, you can hire others to do this. It's not like romantic life in a movie, where you must overcome your weakness. Hire those who complement your skills.

There are people to whom you should be able to sell—*your clones*, those in the population who think like you do! You understand them, because you are one of them. This is often neglected, when someone with industry experience builds a successful company. Everyone is quick to point out the person had experience and knew this and that about the industry. That the person saw a flaw in the way other companies were operating. Sometimes, the person's wide resource of contacts within the industry is played up. But, seldom is it mentioned that the person has had a lifelong interest in the area. That is usually reserved for articles about people who build successful businesses from a base of no experience! Being able to relate to your customer is one of the best reasons to enter a business you care about. This will help you immensely in your marketing efforts.

Chapter 21.
Relationship Marketing: The Cost of Losing Clients

It's difficult to get rich by selling to onetime clients. The best situation is creating something once and selling it forever, repeatedly, to the same people. If prices are high, so much the better. Usually, unless the thing is modified or improved in some way (or the old one wears out), the customer will not buy it again. Customers are funny in this way. This method of marketing is one of the reasons Bill Gates is so rich. How many times have you purchased the same Microsoft product, Word, for example? Doesn't it seem like an endless chain of upgrades? Bill Gates has turned you into an annuity! This is why many of Microsoft's customers aren't fond of Microsoft. They feel they are paying again and again for the same thing, like Bill Murray in *Groundhog Day*. But, in all fairness to Bill, sometimes, his upgrades really are an improvement.

In the software business, there are two reasons to sell an upgrade to a newer version of a product. One is to make improvements and eliminate bugs discovered in the current version. Two is to earn more profits. This is selling an upgrade for the sake of selling an upgrade. While you could argue this is morally dubious, you cannot deny it is profitable.

Software often has a definite cycle. The first version, say, 1.0 comes out. Despite tremendous effort to make it bug free, Version 1.0 is always flawed. No matter how well you tested your software in the lab, some twelve-year-old will find some way you completely missed to make it crash. It just won't play nicely with some other software the user has on his computer. You could not test your piece against every possible program with which it might try to interact. Because computer users know Version 1.0 is usually buggy beyond all get out and users will wait to purchase it until it's been upgraded, few companies have a Version 1.0. Instead, they start at Version 1.3.4 or some such number. That way, it's not buggy Version 1.0 the consumer is buying.

The software package sells, and people find the bugs and write the company nasty letters. The company keeps a list of these nasty letters. These are prime candidates to sell the upgrade to! Software is one of few businesses where sales can be made repeatedly to slightly dissatisfied customers. Usually, in other industries, dissatisfied customers never buy from the company again. Now that the company has a list of bugs, it can squash them (no offense meant to any animal rights people out there). Plus, the company probably thought of some good improvements to its software. So, the company sells an upgrade. It might be called Version 3.03. Sometimes, it is actually called Version 2.0. This is because software vendors know customers are expecting to see some serious improvements between Version 2.0 and 3.0. Bugs are not only minimized, but all those great features the $70,000 per year software engineers overlooked have been suggested by other twelve-year-olds and have been incorporated in the newest version.

Customers are happy now. They have a pretty much bug-free program with good features. Unfortunately, this means they don't need to send you any more money. So, you make the "killer feature list." Your word processor will not only process text fast and accurately, but, now, with full speech recognition, it will flirt with you, occasionally, throughout the day. Well, that's only one of twenty "must have" features. Version 4.0 comes out (actually 3, but who's counting?). Customers say, "Ick. It's slow, and it's using up my whole hard drive." Fortunately, the customer will not have to wait long before the whole cycle begins anew. And, so it goes. Some of the features will be removed or "streamlined" in the next upgrade. Version 5.0 will be the best ever.

In fairness to software companies, some ongoing effort goes into upgrades. It's not a trivial change, usually. The ideal, remember, is to create something only once. That way you can redeploy energy into other areas, while your first creation continues to sell. The thing you don't want to happen is to wind up exerting continuous effort, despite there being little financial return to you. An example would be a newsletter. If you get a few hundred plus renewing subscribers, paying you a hundred or more dollars annually, you are certainly getting at least a decent return on your time spent researching and writing the newsletter. But what happens if you only get four dedicated subscribers? You still must produce 12 monthly issues every year. If this is meant to be a serious financial endeavor, you are failing miserably. Worse, you can't get away from the damn thing, short of shutting it down completely. But, that's just like starting over.

The above is why I am so fond of projects. Most consultants share the same favoritism toward running their life in a project-oriented approach. They like to do one thing, hopefully well, and move on to another project. The last project is forgotten. It can be put behind you, and your mental and physical energy can be put into whatever interests you currently. What position are you in from a time-management, time-availability perspective, if the endeavor doesn't go well? Just as you can absorb financial liabilities, you can also incur time liabilities. The ideal business would have something which, once created, remains to generate sales. You can then focus on marketing. The bulk of the creation time is behind you.

A good example of the above would be a custom solutions provider who has developed an inventory management system. Once it is working well, more time could be spent marketing the program rather than in continuous development. This maximizes the payoff of what you have created. It is more difficult to do this, if you are still spending most of your time working to improve the product. Yet, many really are tinkerers at heart. For them, the great fun of a company is continually improving the product. Further, to keep up, especially in the programming field, you will need to modify your product constantly.

If you are not improving the product or, at least, changing it in some way, your sales will tend to taper off. Most things created once tend to be sold once to any given customer. So, to grow, you need to find new customers. But, finding new customers tends to be much more expensive than reselling to current customers.

It is a horrible loss if you sell to a customer who is satisfied and you have nothing more to sell him. This brings us to the area of relationship marketing. Whatever you sell will give you a customer list—people who have purchased from you. These people share certain similarities. In the above example, the customer list consists of companies that have purchased your inventory management system. These customers have other related needs your company can fulfill. By selling related services, you can work toward thinking of your company, not as a company producing a product, but as a company serving its client base. Rather than marketing a particular product, you are marketing to *a particular group of people*. This is relationship marketing. You are seeking to build a long-term relationship with your clients. To know and understand them, their needs and their concerns. Then, you can serve that market very effectively. You will sell related products. And, the huge cost of acquiring new clients becomes far less of a problem.

Despite the above spiel, I do not know of any custom software solutions providers who started with the idea of relationship marketing in mind! Rather, what they were selling was so high-end that the cost of finding new customers was relatively small. They could use salespeople to market the product. Because there was so much demand for what they did, finding new customers was never really an issue. They would read the above and say, "Hell, related products? We can't even keep up with selling the basic product we have now. New customers are abundant!"

In practice, past clients come back and ask if you can do some related service for them. If you can, this might be a good thing to remember. Maybe, you can offer a similar service to your other previous customers. The custom solutions provider generally says, "No. We only do such and such." But, what if you are not in the fortunate position of having plenty of new clients? Then, change your focus from thinking in terms of your basic product to thinking in terms of the basic market you serve. So, it would seem.

Guess what? Often sales to one type of client will plateau. Maybe, you have sold your inventory program to most of the retail companies in the country! You have a great working relationship with these retail companies. You could be thinking in terms of relationship marketing. But, you stay product focused. You see another industry that could benefit from an only slightly modified version of your product. You make the changes. You find you have a whole new market that was just as profitable as the first. This path seems to be taken in the area of custom solution providers. I should really say semi-custom, for they are modifying the same basic code over and over.

Despite my love of the idea of relationship marketing, all of the fast-growth companies I know have stayed product focused. Usually, it is the companies that see themselves as relationship marketers which have struggled to grow. Often, which way your company grows will happen organically. Either you will see new markets for your existing product, or you will see new products for your existing market. Do what you see, and you will grow naturally in the best direction for you.

It amazes me that one company, selling one slightly-customized product, would have such explosive growth in profits and sales, despite needing to find new customers for each sale, while companies that know their customers intimately don't do nearly as well. Yet, it happens. The basic product the first company is selling is so high-end (i.e., each sale generates excellent revenue and profits) and so in demand (because its value to the client is clear) that relationship marketing never comes into play, as a practical concept, for them.

Onetime buyers would kill companies selling lower-end products. They must do relationship marketing to survive. They must generate repeated sales to the same client base. In either case, clients must be satisfied. A big source of business to the custom solution, provider-programmer companies is word-of-mouth business. Reputation, if you will. So, even if you are selling only onetime to a client, it is still crucial to please the client—to do a great job in the customer's eyes.

The best way to satisfy a customer is to under promise and to over deliver. If customers get more than they expect, they tend to be satisfied. If what they get falls below their expectations, they are dissatisfied. Businesses that throw in something extra as a bonus to the customer understand this. Yet, some customers will not be satisfied, even with an excellent job. Usually, they feel your product costs too much. They are satisfied with the quality, but not fully satisfied with the price. If your prices are in-line with your industry, there is little you can do (or should want to do) about this. After all, you are in business to make money! It gets back to the old maxim of not being able to please all of the people. Even the best companies don't have 100% customer satisfaction.

If you seem to be generating nearly as many dissatisfied customers as satisfied customers, reevaluate what you are doing. Maybe, it's just not up to snuff. Have you ever received a small gift from a mail-order company as a thank you? But, the basic product you ordered was cheaply made and grossly overpriced? Those extra gifts don't quite work as well, I would imagine. Probably, the company wants to make you feel guilty about sending the product back! "Gosh, how could we return the $55 melted chocolate cheesecake that seems kind of old? After all, they sent us a free box of cookies."

Your basic product must be good. No knowledge of customer psychology will save your company and let it grow, if you are trying to sell subpar products. To become a relationship marketer, the most crucial goal is not to generate the first sale, but rather to generate the second and the third sale to a customer. With each succeeding purchase a customer makes, it becomes *more likely* that the customer will make future purchases. This represents your real customer base.

Suppose you are a mail-order retailer of PC software. You mail catalogs to prospective customers. You get two orders. You re-mail your catalog to both. You do not hear from the first customer. The second customer makes a second purchase. At this point, the second customer is, usually, much more valuable to your company than the first. That customer was satisfied enough to do business with you again. He had an interest in buying more of the sort of thing your company sells. Both of these points mean that the likelihood of making future sales to the customer is enhanced.

You can begin thinking in terms of your customer-relationship life expectancy. Many direct-mail companies find that a typical relationship lasts 2-5 years. Let's say 3 years, just to have a concrete number with which to work. This would be the average time you expect any given customer to buy products from your company. But, the average doesn't describe all of the customers individually. It only represents the aggregate. Suppose you have a customer who has been with you for four years. What is that customer's expectancy? Certainly it's not zero now that the customer has been with you for more than three years. It would be silly to say it was -1 year. That customer should have been gone a year ago! What's he doing still hanging around, messing up our mathematical analysis? This customer is a good customer, not a bad complication to your analysis! This customer will probably buy from your company for several more years! He contributes to an overall higher customer-relationship life expectancy average. These customers represent the profit center of your business. These are your above-average customers! This customer is part of your real customer base. Treat him well.

But don't believe it is always better to have a higher average customer-relationship life expectancy. Suppose you contemplate buying one of two businesses. By coincidence, both have tracked their average customer-relationship life expectancy. One claims one year, but the other claims four years. Which business is doing the better job? You don't have enough information to answer that question. You might think it is the one with the four-year average. But, what if that business has not been adding to its customer base? It has a high average, simply because it doesn't have any new customers! It isn't growing. Maybe, it has saturated its market. Maybe, a competitor is getting all the new business. In fact, maybe, it is the second business! The second company doesn't boast a long customer-relationship average, but the reason is that they are adding many new clients! This is a good example of needing to understand what the numbers really mean in business. Look beyond the numbers, and ask what they mean. Learn to ask, "What is it that's causing the numbers to be what they are?"

As you build a relationship business, don't worry about actually calculating your average customer-relationship life expectancy. Just focus upon maintaining satisfied customers, especially making the second and third sale. Do calculate what percentage of first-time customers you are able to convert into second-time buyers. Calculate what percentage of second-time buyers convert into third-time buyers. If industry-wide averages exist for these numbers, compare your success to other businesses. If you are below the industry average, you are not doing a good job. Unfortunately, this industry data is difficult to come by. Most companies that calculate these averages tend to be hush-hush on disclosing the numbers.

Try to understand what is important to your customers. If your customers are businesses, it helps to try to understand their business. What is important to *their success*? If you can help them in these key areas, your company will be able to build a long-lasting relationship with them. This would apply less to, say, a company selling office supplies than to a database-consulting firm. The more closely you *work with* a client company, the more valuable it is to understand their business. You don't need to understand a shipping company's business to sell them paper clips. But, if you are programming the company's database, the more you know about shipping businesses, in general, and their business, in specific, the better. The more you work with the business and know the business, the more you are able to help them.

Losing customers is expensive, compared to finding new customers. Ask yourself if your company is a product-based business or if it is a relationship-based business. Or, are you a bit of both? A bit of both is the strongest position.

Chapter 22.
Supplier Financing, Customer Financing

Raising money to sustain higher levels of sales is often difficult for companies. The problem lies in that, once a product is sold, there might well be a delay between the time the product is sold and the time that payment for the product is collected. Industrial companies and retailers of higher-end items suffer more from this than companies that are more service-oriented or create intellectual merchandise. While most entrepreneurs starting a company instantly see bank loans, equity sale of part of the company, and raiding the piggy bank, as possible financing options, two of the most valuable financing methods are often overlooked. Those sources of financing are supplier and customer financing.

Supplier financing is exactly what it sounds like. Many businesses buy products from suppliers and turn around and resell the products. Often, the raw material purchased from the supplier is not sold just as it is purchased, but is molded into something entirely different. A boat builder might buy steel, but the product sold is a boat, not the raw steel. A company programming computer software might not have any suppliers at all. We neglect suppliers of minor expenses, like a few office supplies, and are only interested in supplies purchased to be directly used to create product to sell.

Keep in mind that the supplier has a vested interest in seeing you sell more of your product. The more product you sell, the more you will buy from him! Because of this, suppliers can be a great source of financing. Not that they will loan you money. But, they might loan you material or whatever they supply. Then, you can use the material to produce your product. You can sell your product and pay the supplier for the material already received, when your customers pay you. You are able to produce and sell far more of your product than otherwise would have been possible, if you had had to finance the raw material cost yourself. You have shortened the compounding cycle.

Let's take a simple case of a retail liquor store. This store is a simple reseller. There is no product being created or modified. All the store does is sells individual bottles (cans, kegs, whatever) to customers who reside locally. The store has rent and personnel costs which must be covered, in addition to making a profit. So, the cost of the bottles is marked up above the purchase cost from the distributor. When the retail store runs low of a particular liquor, the store reorders from the distributor. Every sale by the retailer to a customer is also a sale of the distributor to the retailer.

Suppose you wish to start a liquor store. You need product on the shelves, so customers can see the product and purchase it. Much of your inventory sits on the shelves, and some might be stored in a back room. Retailers need to remember that, usually, it is only products on the shelves that can sell. Sure, a customer might ask if a given product is in stock in the back. Especially, if it's a specially-priced product on advertisement! But, most customers will just assume an empty space on the shelf means the store is out-of-stock. A favorite pastime of retail store managers is to walk the store looking for empty spaces where a given product usually sits. Then, they go in the back rooms and see if they can find the product. Sometimes, the product is simply not in the store. But, sometimes, it is somewhere back there. If they find it, someone is not getting the products to the shelves properly, and the store is probably losing sales.

The store must be able to quickly find where in the back room the product is stored. It's not like a person's garage where you can just toss things in there and then hope you can find them later. You need an effective method of storing the inventory so that you can rapidly know what you have in stock and where it is. This helps prevent your from running out of product. It also prevents customers from standing around, while you rummage around back there, looking for something they really want! Usually, this means shelves in the back room will be labeled. Every time a product is put back there (the technical term for this is back-stocking the product), you record that this particular product is now stored in that particular location. This is usually done by a star-wars-like pistol that shoots a red laser beam, first, at the location bar code and, then, at the product bar code. The data is immediately sent to a computer which keeps a database of what is stored where. All retail stores need some sort of effective, inventory-management system to see that their shelves are full of product.

But, what about when you first open your store? Suppose that to fill all the shelves would require $50,000 in merchandise, and you don't have $50,000. One solution would be to buy just the amount of inventory you can afford and not utilize the rest of the store floor space. This is a horrible solution. People don't like shopping in stores that are half-empty. Maybe, it makes them feel sorry for you. Maybe, they feel like they don't have a good selection. Suppose you had ten bottles sitting on your shelves and the rest of the shelves were empty. Many people, who might otherwise shop at your store, will just walk right by. Bulging shelves draw people into a store far better than empty shelves. So, instead of setting your ten bottles far apart to try to create the impression of a bountiful store, you go to various liquor distributors and see if you can get them to give you $50,000 in merchandise to fill your shelves. Then, you can work out some payment terms. Invite them to visit the location where you contemplate starting the store. Get them involved with the excitement of beginning a new store.

Now, the distributors have costs they must cover. But, like you, their cost of goods sold is less than the price they are charging when they sell the goods. So, maybe, you will need to give them $10,000 up-front for the inventory. That's understandable. That helps the distributor cover his costs. But, why should you need to pay the full $50,000 up-front? After all, if your store does well, you might be buying $250,000 or more in inventory from the distributor every year (this would amount to turning over your entire store inventory five times in one year. If you stocked $50,000 in inventory and sold $500,000 in liquor every year, you would be turning over your inventory ten times per year. Notice that $250,000 and $500,000 refer to the cogs of your liquor and not the total revenue your store generates). You are potentially a very valuable customer. If you open a second store, you will buy even more from the distributor. Suppose you eventually have five stores and each store buys $500,000 a year from the distributor. You are potentially a $2.5 million client to the distributor. Never forget this. Many people fail to negotiate good contracts, because they don't see the true value they offer the other party.

Mention your growth plans to the distributor. Ask if they could support such high levels of sales in a few short years. Ask if they will accept $10,000 in payment now for $50,000 in inventory. It doesn't hurt to ask, right? You want to be very diplomatic. You don't want to threaten, but you want the distributor to know that you know that there are other liquor-distributor-fish in the sea. You want the distributor to know you will be very grateful to the distributor who stands by you, when you are just getting started. Let them know you would be pleased, if they are the one to stand by and grow with you. And, as an aside, never forget this. There are people who will stand by you from early on. Never destroy those friendships. These people and companies are invaluable to you. Conversely, and, maybe, I shouldn't say this, but you will find many, who were not there for you when you started, who later are eager for your business. My attitude is to hell with these people. Don't get me wrong, if they are useful to you, don't hold a long-term grudge. But, if what they offer is only slightly better than the distribution deal you have now, it's just not worth a few pennies to make a switch. Stick with the people you know you have been able to count on. And, always give them the chance to counter any serious offer a competitor makes.

So, what happens? The salesperson from the distributorship says, "No." After all, he's only an employee who doesn't really benefit if you and the distributor grow. But, if he takes a chance and supplies your inventory, and your business goes bad, and you start drinking heavily, and you consume your entire inventory, then he has to explain to his boss, who yells at him, why he let you have so much inventory. Maybe, he is fired. From his perspective, the deal is a no-go. When you are certain that a given representative from a distributor will not help you, contact someone higher up in the food chain. Say nice things about the representative you are bypassing. He might well be the guy you will be dealing with down the road. Explain, preferably to the owner of the liquor distributor, you understand the concerns of the representative who you talked to. He's concerned about financing that level of inventory. But, maybe, the owner will see things differently. After all, he is the one, inside the distributorship, who benefits most if you succeed. Focus on the potential upswing. Show him your business plan demonstrating you have researched the industry and know what you are doing.

Maybe, you cannot even contact the owner of the distributorship. Maybe, the company is so large that your potential sales of $2.5 million are insignificant to them. The owner is always on his private jet, and they just won't put you through. They keep saying, "No." OK. That happens. Seek another distributor. Maybe, the ideal distributor for you is not some giant selling $1 billion a year. Maybe, you need some smaller distributor that is more growth-oriented. If you are too small, relative to your distributor, you might have trouble convincing them of your company's potential value as a customer. If you are too big, the distributor might not be able to keep up with *your* sales. It's like Goldilocks and the three bears; you need to find the right size distributor for you.

Eventually, you will be able to set yourself up with a pretty sweet deal. You rent the store, so you don't have a huge location cost. You pay your employees as they work for you, so there are no up-front costs here. Finally, you were able to secure a full $50,000 in inventory for about $10,000. As the inventory sells, you pay more and more to the distributor. You entered a business that demanded a significant inventory you could not finance via a bank or the piggy bank. When you open your second store, it will be easier in many respects. You now have a working relationship with the distributor. It will be easier to get the distributor to pre-finance inventory for the second store. The distributor is getting a solid level of sales from you now. The distributor doesn't want to lose your existing sales. The distributor doesn't want to lose you as a customer. So, they will probably give you the inventory. Rarely, will you have a distributor who doesn't want to grow with you.

Some industries are more favorable to supplier financing. It is important to keep in mind the potential value your business represents as a customer to the supplier and also that everything is negotiable. You can't get great deals, if you don't ask for them. Ask for the deal. And, don't fret, if you get rejected. There are other suppliers out there.

Customer financing is just using money, supplied by the customer, to fulfill that customer's order. This is a way of life for many businesses. This type of business can grow rapidly because, as you generate more business, you simultaneously generate the funding needed to produce the sales. Customer funding might pay for all or part of the cost you incur to produce the customer's product.

One example of customer funding is a custom boat-building company which custom designs and builds yachts. You talk to a potential customer. He specifies what he wants. You tell him he will need to pay so much up-front for you to undertake the design. He agrees. Further, the up-front fee for the design is nonrefundable. You make this very clear to him and put it in the contract. If he backs out later, he will lose this amount of money. You do this to prevent tire kickers (hull kickers?), who aren't really interested in going all the way through with the project. Especially on big projects, it's a good sign if the customer will put some money down up-front. In addition to generating the funding you need to build the product, it helps weed out uncommitted buyers. While some businesses like to keep trying to sell to people just on the edge of being interested (thigh-masters, "How to Win Lotto America in Five Easy Steps," etc.), such people can absolutely destroy other businesses. It's an issue of resources. You want to be working on projects that will be concluded. Beware of the free consultation in some businesses.

Freelance videographers find many smaller companies which really do want to make a promotional video for their companies. But, the companies will simply never pay what the videographer would charge. Sure, they will talk about it, but when push comes to shove, it just won't happen. If you are constantly talking to two or three such people a day, it prevents you from getting any real work done! It is not always easy to know which clients are serious and which ultimately will let you down. Payment up-front is as good a way as any to weed out nonserious prospects. Unfortunately, you will weed out some serious prospects, also. Sometimes, you just need to accept that.

But, back to our boat-building example. The customer agrees, and a design is created. The customer likes it and decides to undertake construction. If the client had decided not to follow through with the construction, who would own the boat-design plans? It would depend upon how the contract was worded. Be aware of such issues along the way. Sometimes a client will really desire an intermediate result and not the full project to completion. So you collect so much up-front from the client and begin construction of the yacht. Upon completion, or at certain stages of completion, the client pays a bit more of the total price. This helps finance the construction and shortens your compounding cycle.

When a customer pays up-front, in addition to collecting the money, which is great from a cash-flow standpoint, a liability is introduced. The company which has collected prepayment for the product is legally obligated to produce the product. What happens, if you have not collected sufficient capital up-front to build the product and you cannot get the extra funding in any other way? That's not a good position to be in. You could go to the client and hope he would be willing to prepay a bit more. But, if the contract is written, he is under no obligation to do so. If you must do so, be very, very nice. Acknowledge what you are asking for is beyond what you had contracted. Explain that you have misjudged production costs. Ultimately, however, this shouldn't happen. It gets back to the crucial maxim, "Know your costs."

You must know what special laws apply to your industry in regard to customer pre-financing. Just as when you are dealing with equity investors backing your business, you might find that there are laws that affect pre-financing in your industry. For example, the Federal Trade Commission has a mail-order rule, stating that after you receive an order for a product, it must be delivered within 30 days. If you will not be able to deliver within the time limit, the customer must be contacted and given the option to cancel the order.

Just from a customer service perspective, it is clearly unacceptable, if a product you advertise as available, is not delivered for one month, but that is not the issue. The issue is that you would be in violation of the law, if you did not contact the customer. You could be seriously fined by the FTC for this. Further, you cannot just tell the customer, "Sorry, guy, you will need to wait until we make the next batch next month." You must give the customer the explicit option of canceling the order.

Legal and timely fulfillment issues must be considered, when you depend upon customer financing. But, if you have these bases covered, customer financing may well be the best source of growth financing obtainable.

Chapter 23.
Going It Alone, Consulting

I'm a big fan of hiring others to grow your business. It's the way to acquire a diversity of talent, which allows your organization to undertake larger and more profitable projects. It allows the entrepreneur to grow the company to substantial size and profitability. It relieves the entrepreneur from needing to do everything himself. Not only is profitability enhanced, but the stress of running a business is actually reduced. Despite all of these advantages, there are some very bright people who understand the value of entrepreneurship who simply don't want to hire employees. They would rather be a one-person show. This chapter is designed to help them understand one-person business organizations, the benefits and the difficulties involved.

One-person companies survive and can make the consultant a decent living, but consultants rarely grow very rich. You won't find any consultants on the Forbes 400 list. The reason is simple. Consultants usually bill by the hour, and there are only so many workable hours in a year. This puts a real limit upon how much a consultant can earn in one year. A typical work year is about 2,000 hours (250 days of the year times eight hours per day), and even if you are billing $200 per hour for your services, you can only earn $400,000. Unless, of course, you are an attorney. Then you can bill several thousand more hours per year! Further, most consultants will not be able to generate a full 2,000 billable hours. The demand will often be there, but other aspects of consulting will take time away from billable hours. If you are a computer consultant, specializing in database design, for example, then the systems your are using, such as Oracle, are constantly changing and evolving. You will need to commit some time to continued learning to stay current in the field.

No matter what your area, some time will be consumed in marketing your services and doing the paper pushing required of all companies. You will need to fill out tax forms, etc… So, in practice, you might be lucky to generate 1,500 billable hours. I think 1,000 hours is even a better estimate. Even at $200 per hour, at most you will make $200,000 per year. This is a practical upper end. Half of that is much more common as most consultants bill less than $100 per hour. Now that's great income, don't get me wrong, but as stated above, you will never get very, very rich this way. But, you can achieve comfort.

Some consultants claim to make greatly in excess of this. However, they are usually personality speakers, who host seminars and talks for larger companies that can afford to throw away serious amounts of money. Sometimes, the person is buddy-buddy with an upper-level executive who encourages the company to pay an outrageous amount for the "consultant." Because one business has paid this amount, other businesses figure they can afford to hire the person at about the same rate!

While there are people who make a million a year in speaking engagements, these people are not, technically, what I would call consultants. They are not problem-solvers. They are personalities. This points out one important aspect of larger businesses. Larger businesses are often clueless as to what creates the most value for them. Do not assume, because you are exceptionally skilled in an important area (like Java programming), that you will be able to convince the firm to pay you significantly more than the going rate for similar services rendered by other consultants.

At a technical-skill level, the value of your skills will be measured as labor costs. The company will ask, "How much would it cost to get someone about equally qualified to do this job?" This is very different from a larger company wanting to get the currently hottest business consultant as one of their speakers. In this case, the company might well throw money at the "consultant." This is why talented programmers should reconsider the traditional consulting path in favor of becoming a custom-solutions-provider. Start with a base of code that provides real value to businesses. Don't market yourself as a consultant, but market your semi-custom product. Turn the marketing focus away from services rendered, based upon what the client was thinking of doing anyway. Emphasize the value that *your* product represents to the client company.

Three areas of consulting come immediately to mind. One is computer consulting. This could involve programming code for businesses, or it could involve helping smaller businesses set up computer networks, for example. It could involve creating web pages for companies. This is probably the hottest area for people knowledgeable in programming today. But, all of this changes rapidly. At today's rates, $50 or even $100 per hour is doable. The more experience you have the more you will be able to sell you services to the larger companies which are willing to pay more for skilled consultants.

Second is the area of graphic design, which often overlaps with web page development and some simple programming. Most people working in this area refer to themselves as freelancers, rather than consultants. Freelancers sound less expensive to hire than consultants whereas consultants sound more skilled and professional. It may all just be semantics, but semantics are important in how you will be viewed by your potential clients. If you say, "I'm a graphic arts consultant," your potential client will probably say, "Oh, I don't really need a consultant. I just want someone to do some simple drawings." Our consultant says, "I do that! I guess I'm really more of a freelance artist than anything." The client likes that. It sounds less expensive.

On the other hand, saying you are a freelance computer programmer makes you sound like a hack. You will be taken more seriously if you call yourself a "consultant." It has always amazed me that artists working as freelancers could charge much more than those working for others. Don't get me wrong. I don't mean to put down artists. I wish I had better artistic skills. And, the few artists I know are all great people. But, after all, there are a lot of people who are talented in drawing, page layout, and the other areas of graphic arts. If you are a skilled graphic artist and get a two-year degree from a technical college, you will probably only make $12 per hour as an employee. There are enough talented people out there that companies can pay such rates and still have an abundance of applicants. Yet, a freelancer can easily charge $25 per hour and pick up a lot of business. Some freelancers charge considerably more.

Freelancers are able to charge so much because companies hiring employees to produce art for clients add a substantial amount to the price they bill the clients. This amount covers the company's overhead expenses, such as rent, and adds a reasonable profit for the company. So, hiring a freelancer at what seems like high hourly rates can often get the client the same service at an overall lower price. Freelancers usually don't have anywhere near the level of overhead. They often work out of their homes and have no actual business rent at all. Thus, you have two people doing the exact same thing with the exact same talent. While one earns $13 per hour, the other is earning $40 per hour. The freelancers have more control over their destiny and make more money to boot!

The third area is freelance videography and photography. This is another area where people with a lifelong interest in a hobby are able to turn their hobby into a vocation. Often, the person has made a substantial personal investment in equipment and wishes to use it to generate money to help take the bite out of buying all these toys. They never meant to start a business at all, but the spouse started making ultimatums, along with the comments, "Hey, you just can't go spend $1000 for another silly camera accessory. We have bills to pay. Children to feed..." So, they found a way to support their photography hobby.

While computer skills, graphic arts, and photography are the traditional consulting areas, there are numerous others. If anything you contemplate has value to the potential client and is a personal service you can render, you can consider doing it as a freelancer or as a consultant. However, if your service is commonly available through larger companies, at an overall rate of about what you expect to charge, you will be at a disadvantage. It is best if the industry supporting the service has a substantial mark-up above the labor costs to render the service. As with the graphic arts example, it is precisely this that allows you to bill rates that make consulting profitable.

The best reason to become a consultant is that you already know what you want to do and you know there is a freelance market for this service. You could do the same thing as an employee, but you think you can make more money on your own. Usually, you have done this particular thing as an employee.

When you first become a consultant, decide exactly what you will do. For example, there are many programmers who can program in a dozen or more computer languages. Yet, it is difficult to be equally good at all of them. You might be dominant in one area and decide to go with that area. Or, you might decide the market you wish to serve has more demand for another programming language and you decide to focus upon that area. This is really an issue of positioning yourself. Try to come up with a short one-paragraph description of what you will do. If you can state this in one line, so much the better. If you start listing ten unrelated areas, this lack of focus is almost always a bad sign.

Another part of positioning yourself is deciding how you will generate clients and what type of clients you will primarily seek. Will your clients be individuals, smaller businesses, mid-sized businesses, or larger businesses? Larger businesses can pay consultants more, but are more demanding of past experience and demonstrated skills, unless, of course, you are buddy-buddy with a high-ranking corporate officer or someone on the company's board of directors. Smaller companies are often far more concerned with how much the service will cost them. They want the best price and aren't as concerned with seeing an outstanding list of past clients, references, and achievements.

This brings up an interesting point. I have heard people pose the question to a wannabe consultant, "Why would anyone hire *you* to do this?" Sometimes, the wannabe consultant cannot think of a good reason. Does this mean the person will not succeed? Absolutely not! Many people hire various freelancers with the assumption that anyone working as a freelancer knows what they are doing. Ask yourself, the last time you hired a photographer to take your portrait or photograph a wedding for you, did you really ask the person about his personal experience and skills? Or, did you just look someone up in the Yellow Pages? Don't fret if you don't have a solid list of references and clients to attest to your prowess. That will come in time, if you work at it.

A problem many wannabe computer-programming consultants get into is believing, because they have had a few classes in programming and have done well, they now understand programming. They have studied C++ (a computer programming language), and they think, "I'm good at this." Then, a company wants them to create an application program for a Windows 98 operating system and the company wants the system to have a rich graphical user interface. The "expert" hasn't a clue how to do this. They have never even heard of the MFC for windows programming, which is a necessary tool here.

It is better to pass on a project if you have serious doubts about being able to do it well. You could attempt it, anyway, but this is a tough moral boundary. I know of cases where a small consulting group has undertaken a project that was mission critical to the client company hiring them. They had to struggle to attempt it, but they knew mastery of this particular problem would have great consequent benefits, i.e., many other companies would want to buy the particular product in only slightly modified form from them. The client company never received a usable product and suffered significantly as a result. Yet, the consulting company went on to sell the technology they had developed while working on the project to another larger software company. It was sort of failing, but making a lot of money, anyway. Was it really ethical for the consultants to use the client company as a source of income to work toward the project which was never delivered? I would say "No." Yet, how do you get a start?

Do a trial run. Pretend you are a company that contemplates hiring you. Specify a problem such a client might want solved. Don't kid yourself, but word the desired result just as a client might. Then, see if you can do it. Record the time it takes you. Talk to other consultants in the same field and ask, "What are typical problems clients want solved?" Try to get some experience, before you commit to a real project. As a consultant, you really need to be an expert. You should internally feel you are an expert. It's OK to be nervous, but if you know your capabilities aren't up to speed, don't take on a project yet. Or, aim for a project you can handle. Then, grow into more complex assignments bit by bit.

So, you have chosen a field. You have practiced in one form or another. You are confident. You are all set, right? Not really. If you contemplate being a consultant professionally for any length of time, there are several things of which you need to be aware. First is disability insurance. As a freelancer, just like an employee, you depend upon your ability to render services for your regular income. What happens if you cannot work? Some studies suggest the odds of your becoming disabled are as great as one in five throughout your work career.

Many people, who are very careful in always keeping their medical insurance up-to-date, totally ignore disability insurance. In the insurance industry, disability is often called the neglected insurance. It's one people just don't think about. But, if you are injured or become ill, even as medical insurance will pay medical costs, you will almost certainly have other living expenses that are not covered. Further, without income, how will you continue to pay health insurance premiums that are so important to you now? Many people, who were doing very well financially, have been wiped out by a lack of disability coverage. Yet, disability and worker's compensation are tough areas for consultants to cover.

It is possible for people to abuse insurance in these areas, so the insurance companies will not be eager to insure you. They fear you will claim disability and refuse to work. Multi-person companies will not tend to let this happen. They don't want to see their insurance rates rise and are watchdogs of potential abuse. But, who watches you, if you are the company owner and sole employee? You will be viewed more skeptically. That's just the way it is. Some professional organizations sponsor such insurance for their members. One way or another, you really do need to be covered against losing everything you have worked for if you are temporarily disabled.

You must also consider liability insurance. This is such an unpleasant area, I'd almost rather not discuss it, but it is so important, that I will. We do live in a sue-happy world. Suppose you are a database programmer and you are working to put your client's product list on the Internet with on-line ordering capability. Your client is a small business. You are used to working with larger companies that always maintain RAID (no, this has nothing to do with bug-killing spray. This just means anything entered as data on a computer is stored, not on one hard disk drive, but on at least two. It is real time backup-of-data. As soon as something is entered, it is written to multiple drives. RAID stands for redundant array of independent disks). You don't give this a moment's thought.

Now, the small business has been getting all its orders via mail with a paper trail. And, they back up their computer records only weekly. Because of the paper, if the hard drive were to fail during the week, the records for that week, which had no data backed up yet, could still be reconstructed. It would be time-consuming, but you would know who ordered what and how much they had paid. You would know what needed to be done to fulfill the orders that came in during the week. But, on-line is different. The orders come in as bits and bytes and go to the hard drive. That is the first permanent record the company has of the order. One day, you know what happens. The hard drive fails. All the records of orders placed over the Internet for that week are lost.

Data loss is a serious business problem. Remember Henry Gump? He was done in by a fire to his list of consultants. And, he was a computer consultant who should have known better! Well, the business you consulted for is left in limbo. What orders came in for the week? At the very least, the company will lose customers who are expecting a response to their e-mail questions. The situation could be much worse, but let's assume the only loss to the company is one large order for $10,000 worth of merchandise. It was one of the business's regular clients, and the client, rather than calling to check on the order, just ordered from the competitor. Because of a lack of response, the business you consulted for has just lost a $50,000 a year client. Who is responsible for the loss of the client? Obviously, the business that trusted you to get them onto the net is disappointed with the results. They sue you for $100,000. This is a serious problem.

Now, if you had been selling packaged software, you would have been careful to put in disclaimers that your software is, in no way, responsible for any losses resulting from using it, no matter how horribly flawed it is. It is explicitly stated that the user of your program assumes all the risks. But, you just went into the company and wrote the code. If you lost a lawsuit, you could wind up owing $100,000. That's a horrible start for a new consulting business! It could be prevented, if you had purchased the proper liability insurance. This type of insurance is called errors and omissions liability insurance. If the services rendered wind up hurting the company for which you consulted, then, this is designed to cover those losses. The problem is that this insurance is very expensive and hard to get.

Remember, a programming flaw could lead to the failure of a multimillion-dollar business! And, the insurance company has no real way of knowing just how competent you are. Some companies demand that their consultants be covered by such insurance. Some consultants only purchase the insurance to cover those contracts and self-insure the rest. Self-insure, in this context, is a euphemism for, "I really hope that doesn't happen." Some consultants just absorb the insurance expense as a necessary evil. You will need to make your own call here.

Next up is retirement. You will have Social Security and will pay into this. But, most people will require more money and many employees have pension plans or 401(k) plans to supplement their Social Security. You will need to consciously set aside money. You could create your own tax-deferred retirement plan, use an IRA, or just squirrel away funds into stocks and bonds held in a non-tax-deferred account. The point is do set money aside. It is a shame to earn $100,000 a year and then wind up eating cat food in your old age. That's simply poor planning! Fortunately, as a consultant, you will have good income and good cash flow. As you will not have to reinvest most of the money you collect from clients back into you consulting business, this money will be available to invest elsewhere. Because of this, you will probably favor an S corporation business structure for your consulting business. This will allow most of the money you earn to flow out into your personal financial accounts.

Many people treat tax-deferred investment vehicles and accounts (IRA, 401(k), etc.) as the greatest thing since sliced bread. I tend to be a bit more skeptical of them. It is true you can save a good deal of money that would otherwise be paid in taxes. For regular employees, this is a form of forced savings. The money will not be squandered, as it is not readily available to squander! Put together the tax-deferred compounding and the forced savings aspect, and it seems you have a winning deal, so why am I not as enamored of them? The reason is that entrepreneurs often find really good places to put their money that are not along the conventional stock or bond investment lines. The availability of the money is the issue.

What if you choose to move from personal consulting into a larger business endeavor? The money you saved could be useful to you within your own business. Entrepreneurs tend to like keeping flexibility in how they utilize their money. Sure, the government will give you tax-deferred compounding, but along with this comes all kinds of restrictions and possible penalties, if you desire to remove the money from the retirement account prematurely. The fact that you are reading this book is a good indication you might well have a better use for your money than putting it into a collection of publicly-traded stocks and bonds. If you see an opportunity, it is best if your money is in a standard brokerage account.

Building a business above and beyond consulting is not the only reason you will want cash reserves. Here, I emphasize cash, not money invested into stocks or other volatile investments, which are better long-term growth choices. Rather, money readily available, without danger the principal has dropped significantly when it must be withdrawn. Consulting is not steady work. We have been in a great economy, but this varies. Even in good times, you might go for short periods without a client. You must have cash reserves. Three months' living expenses is an absolute minimum. It would be preferable to have four to six months' income held in a money market fund.

In addition to this, it is best if you can build some revenue streams which are not solely dependent upon your continued consulting. Some consultants do not keep cash reserves, but have, instead, steadily invested in solid dividend-paying stocks. The idea is that they reinvest the dividends when they are working and do not need the money. But, if times get worse, they use the dividends for living expenses. They follow the age-old motto of the rich, "Never invade principal." Neglecting inflation, they will not get poorer. Every $100,000 invested might give them $5,000 in dividends annually to help them weather periods of consulting inactivity. But, entirely aside from dividends from conventional investments, ask yourself, "As a consultant in my area, is there anything I can do to generate ongoing revenue streams?" One answer might be writing a book in your specialty area.

Granted, a book like, *Unix Administration Made Easier*, will probably not have the popular demand of Stephen King's latest novel, but such books not only help you establish yourself as an expert in the field, they have the potential to generate revenue year after year. The motto here is, "Do it once. And, sell it repeatedly." I know consultants who have all but given up consulting to write books— web page design, computer programming, etc., books right now are very hot. No doubt this is partly due to the current employment market in these areas. Also, revenue from books provides a form of disability insurance in that these revenue streams will continue, at least for a while, even if you are disabled.

When people first become consultants, they are often enamored by any clients they get. They tend to take all jobs that come their way. This is not a good practice to follow as you become more and more successful. One of the greatest stresses a consultant can have is needing to do too many little jobs here and there. Each saps resources and time.

Suppose you are a freelance videographer. You charge $40 an hour for your camera skills. One client wants you to shoot a five-hour training video for his company. The other client wants you to attend his wedding and get half an hour of video. That client feels this should only take one-half an hour of your billable rate or about $20. Which client is the better client? Many small jobs, like the second, will just wear you out. To be happy as a consultant is to be able to say, "No," to be able to turn down undesirable jobs diplomatically.

There are two good reasons a person might decide against becoming a consultant. One is travel involved. Many people, new to consulting, are unaware of the geographical area they will need to span in order to generate sufficient clients. This, of course, depends upon your field. I would guess that a freelance photographer could locate enough clients in a good-sized city. But, if you are a database consultant who is very, very good and, hence, very, very expensive, living out in the boonies will likely involve a hell of a daily commute. Usually, flying around the country will be typical. While this really turns on some people, it really annoys others (I'm among the annoyed). Try to make an estimate of the area over which you will need to hawk your expertise.

Beyond a certain point, you will need to become a "flying consultant." Then, the entire world becomes your geographical area. But, for companies to pay for your travel, hotel, and all the other expenses incurred will demand their really wanting *you* as their consultant. These are typically larger companies and organizations looking for the best (or, at least, second or third-tier) in the field. So, unless you are a Chris Date or a John Carlis (renowned database experts and consultants), such a broad geographical base might not be a practical goal.

An emerging area of personal consulting, which can eliminate huge travel costs, is the so-called virtual consultant. Virtual assistant, virtual secretary are all similar concepts. In virtual consulting, you work from home and interact with your client companies via the Internet. This is not fully perfected yet. In many areas, talking with the clients in person really is necessary. For example, if you are modeling a client's data, to do this most effectively involves talking with all the people who collect the data, use any of the data, or in any other way interact with the data. A question asked often leads to necessary follow-up questions and clarifications. There needs to be a rapid exchange of ideas. E-mail or the phone simply is inadequate. Video conferencing might be viable. But, being there allows you to do a better job.

But, what if you are a freelance artist, who designs book covers for smaller publishers? I haven't done this, nor do I know anyone who does, but I'm guessing heavy client interaction is not an issue here. The client could send an e-mail describing the book, its audience, and other relevant factors. The client might suggest some ideas or themes. The cover designer could generate some ideas, maybe, some rough sketches, and send them back to the client. The client makes a decision as to which idea to use, and the artist completes it. It seems all the contact could occur over e-mail and the Internet.

In fact, it would be good for the artist to create a web page displaying his ideas. This page would not need to be available for all to see. It could be a private part of the Internet used as a work space showing the ideas and designs in progress. The client could have a link for e-mailing comments and other forms of interaction could be provided. At the beginning of the project, the client would be given the address of the web site (called a URL or Uniform Resource Locator) and a password to access the page. This way the project is not observable by just anyone. It might also help to create an ongoing relationship with the company. After all, they will have *bookmarked* the page, and this can become an entry point into *all* their projects you have in progress. It helps to create a bond between your company and theirs.

Whether the type of consulting you do can be done exclusively on-line depends upon your area. Don't lie to yourself here. You might be a great data modeler and just love the idea of consulting over the Internet, but it's just not fair to the client to do it this way. It makes your job more difficult and more error-prone. Your client might not realize this. However, your goal should be to do a great job and limited contact prevents this. Yet, our cover designer could aim for pure virtual consulting. He could set up on-line and market to the world.

Just as a point to mention, our cover designer would need to target smaller publishers. Large publishers retain staff to do cover design and related artwork. A typical cover design might cost $1,000. If you can hire a talented graphic artist for $25,000 per year and he can design 100 covers in a year, it should be clear internal staff is much more cost effective than outsourcing to freelancers. You need to be aware of this type of issue, so you know where the real market for your service lies.

Another area leading many people to drop consulting is a dislike for personal selling. For example, they are technical experts who just want to write Unix code (it's hard to believe, but such people do exist). These people don't enjoy going to a new company and meeting a whole bunch of new people. To succeed as a consultant you must do what is referred to as consultative selling. This means you discuss the client's problems with them and think about how you can help the client. Then, you tell the client how you can help them and explain what you can (and cannot) do for them. This involves a lot of personal contact.

Chapter 24.
Virtual Organization,
Outsourcing

It's a great time to be an entrepreneur, if for no other reason there are a whole host of companies that stand ready to assist you in one way or another. Just as we argued that you don't need to be able to do everything yourself, but rather can hire employees, you can take it one step further. Not everything that needs to get done within your organization needs to be done by employees within the organization. Rather, you can outsource certain areas to other companies or to individuals.

Much of this book has focused upon computer consulting companies. The company sends out a skilled programmer or nerd talented in some related area. This person goes to the company and finds out what must be done. The consulting company can hire regular employees and send these employees on the jobs. There is another option. Rather than have employees at all, it is possible for the list of consultants the company sends out to exist within the company only as a list.

The individuals sent out are independent consultants, who pay the company a certain percentage of their billable hours in exchange for the company lining up the contracts. Not having employees simplifies running your organization. And, in many cases, the same results can be achieved at about the same cost.

Because not having employees simplifies things for businesses and relieves them of the responsibility of paying Social Security taxes (the independent contractor is responsible for his own Social Security), many companies have tried to abuse the independent contractor privilege. There are certain legal conditions that must be met before you can classify someone who works for you as an independent contractor.

If you contemplate hiring independent contractors, check with the government to be sure that you are classifying your workers correctly. Because this is a tax issue, you can learn more about this from free classes the IRS provides. (In fact, there are several other classes the federal government provides, free of charge, in many areas applicable to the legalities and bureaucratic details of running a business. These areas include employment taxes, forming a corporation, etc.)

Outsourcing has led to the term "virtual company." This is a company which outsources a great deal to other companies or independent contractors. A benefit of doing this is that your company is not limited by the production capacity of your internal organization. Rather, you could focus on marketing and allow another company to do your manufacturing. This can translate into faster company growth for you.

Understand that your reputation can be affected by the actions of the company or individual you are outsourcing to. The quality of your product will be judged by how well the other company produces it. Some entrepreneurs don't like giving up quality control. However, if you can clearly specify contractually what is and is not acceptable, and you are working with a reliable company, quality control hopefully won't be a problem. As with all negotiated situations, don't agree to a long-term contract. Give yourself an escape route in case you are not happy.

While production quality control is something which comes quickly to mind, many other areas are more easily neglected. For example, how quickly will the company fulfill your customers' orders? This assumes you want your orders fulfilled by the company to which you are outsourcing. Another issue is: Who owns the customer list? If orders were to be placed directly with your fulfillment company, you might not be able to build your customer list as you would like. Give some thought to the flow of orders into your company and how they should best be processed.

If you receive only a few large orders, your company should aim to process the orders and remain in contact with the client. This is another advantage of large revenue sales. You can be right on top of fulfillment, even if you are a small organization. But, what if you receive many small orders? At some point, you will not be able to keep up with processing the orders. There is really no good solution for this situation. That is why distributors or middlemen were invented. Just be sure you don't give away too much of the profit.

This happens all the time. A company, which is making excellent profits as a percentage of revenue, but whose overall sales are small, and hence, so are the overall profits, finds it can sell more and more of its product, but only if it hires a distributor to take over the basic fulfillment. The company thinks, "No problem." But, when it learns the rates the distributor demands, the overall idea is no longer tenable. If you need a distributor as you grow, learn up-front how much distribution will cost you down the road. Don't wait until the distributor is needed.

One area where the virtual organization has been a reality, even before the term "virtual" became trendy, was book publishing. Consider the typical steps in bringing a book to market. First, the publisher needs a book. One idea would be to have someone within the company write the book. In fact, there are people who start small self-publishing companies for the sole purpose of publishing just their own books. But, most publishers don't have authors on staff, at least not as authors. Rather, they encourage submissions by people who want to have a book published.

This gives the publisher a much larger pool of talent to draw from. However, there will be many poor manuscripts submitted. And, reading 100 manuscripts to find one you like is a bad investment in effort. So, many publishers have moved to selecting their authors, just as a college football recruiter would. They start with a product focus and ask, "What would we like to publish a book about?" Then, they try to find a celebrity or expert in the field who will write the book.

After the first step of book selection, the publisher edits the book and takes care of all the design issues such as designing the cover. Usually, these tasks are done by employees of the company. In this way, the publisher assumes quality control for the content of the book.

This would be classified as a core area the publisher does not want to farm out to other companies. In the case of small self-publishers often cover design and some of the layout issues are farmed out to freelance graphic artists. The big day arrives, and the book is ready for the printing press.

Now, most publishing companies don't own printing presses. They outsource the printing to another company. This allows the publisher to concentrate upon information and content and not need to worry about the business of printing and bookbinding.

Where the books go next depends upon the publisher. Many publishers have their own storage facilities. Other publishers send their books to a large book distributor, and the distributor takes over fulfillment to bookstores and other customers. Notice how much of the work of getting a book to the shelves involves outsourcing. Without outsourcing, most publishers could never even start. They would need to start, not as publishers, but rather as printers! There is no way a small *publishing* company could justify the cost of buying a printing press.

Outsourcing is a powerful technique which allows smaller and start-up companies to compete with larger and more established companies. Despite the positive aspect of outsourcing, always scrutinize what you contemplate outsourcing and the potential negative consequences of this.

Probably the worst outsourcing mistake in the history of business was IBM's decision to outsource production of the operating system for their personal computer (PC). IBM, seeing the success of smaller companies, such as Apple computer, that were producing desktop computers, decided to enter the personal computer market. Rather than acquiring ownership of the operating system outright, IBM only licensed it and allowed the proprietary nature of it to remain with the company that provided it. That company was Microsoft.

Yet, sales of PC's dominated the sales of Apple computers (Macs, at the time, were superior) *because of the reputation of IBM*. Businesses, in particular, were much more willing to purchase desktop systems from IBM rather than lesser-known companies. IBM's reputation, with businesses in particular, was one important, and often overlooked, reason that the PC came to be dominant over the Macintosh. But, IBM had also contracted out manufacture of the microprocessing chip to Intel. And, Intel had the proprietary rights to the chip. So, it was only a short time before other companies thought to themselves, "Hmm…I can buy the chips IBM uses from Intel. I can buy the operating system, running the computer, from Microsoft…and, in fact, I pretty much can get the complete specifications of IBM's PC's! I think I'll build computers and sell them for a slightly lower price than IBM."

The era of the clone computer manufacturer was here. IBM was left in the dust! It would have been easy for IBM not to contract out the creation of the desktop operating system they were to use. If they had created it (or purchased it outright), nearly all of Microsoft's present worth would be within IBM! The lesson is that, if you are going to contract out a product, it is best if you keep intellectual ownership of the product. Letting someone else keep the copyright, the patent, the secret-to-the-universe, or whatever, is fundamentally a bad idea. What's to prevent them from deciding to do business with someone else and leave you out in the cold?

This also brings up an often-neglected area to consider when starting a business. Most people, thinking of creating a company, consider what they can do for the consumer. But, they should also ask, "What is it I could do for other companies? In particular, what areas might other companies like to outsource?" Tom Golisano was working for a payroll processing company serving larger companies. He suggested that since like 95% of all businesses had under 50 employees, wouldn't it be a good idea to offer payroll processing services to them? His boss said, "No." Golisano went on to found Paychex, the premier payroll processing company today. As entrepreneurship grows, Paychex will be one beneficiary.

The opportunities for becoming a company *outsourced to* are immense. Much of the growth in computer consulting occurred after companies went through a period of reducing management information systems (MIS) and programming staff (yes, newbie programmers out there, there was a time when programmers were actually laid off!). Yet, the MIS and programming needs remained.

Rather than as employees, the individuals came back as consultants. The individuals made more money, had more independence, and at the same time, the companies also benefited. The companies only paid consultants when they were actually needed. Just as publishers don't want to own expensive printing presses that sit idle, most companies don't want highly-trained computer staff sitting around playing PacMan, Doom, or whatever computer game is popular at the time. Outsourcing benefits everyone.

Chapter 25.
The Value of Time

It is important to understand the value of time in any enterprise. Some people never seem to learn the value of time and retain a naive view. When starting up a business, they think, "I'll do it myself. Because I won't have to pay someone else to do this task, I'll have an advantage." This is true to the extent that your company resources will be most limited in only one of two areas, employee time (including your own time) or money. Initially, it may be better to do some things in a more time-intensive fashion instead of spending what precious little cash your business has. Yet, as you grow, you must drop this attitude for, by then, time will be paid for in wages.

Many people tend to ignore "sunken costs," meaning, once the investment in a project has been made, they do not worry about the cost it took for them to develop the product. By doing this, however, they are not adequately tracking their costs to develop a project. And, after all, the goal is to undertake only projects that are worthwhile financially. If, ultimately, they are not amortizing these costs effectively over sales and recouping them, they are making bad business choices.

Many people initiate projects they know are not optimal from a profitability standpoint, but choose to undertake the project, anyway. There is an ulterior motive besides greed. They are making "life-style" choices. For example, someone really into the history of the ancient world might try to create a multimedia project of ancient civilizations, assuming the person is a multimedia developer. The developer really wants to undertake the project and looks at the time put into it as more of a hobby than as a potential profit center. Sure, maybe, he will sell a few hundred copies of his CD creation, and, maybe, that will not recoup the value of his time spent creating the project, but he doesn't let this concern him. I have no problem with that. But, there is a problem if he starts thinking along the lines, "Well, I've sold 100 of my CDs at $25 apiece, that's $2,500. My direct costs of copying the master CD were only $3 per CD sold. Shipping costs were only $2 per CD sold, so I'm making $20 per CD sold or a total of $2,000."

Looking at the numbers, it looks like our developer is doing well. But, there is no attempt to amortize the author's time investment in the project. If the project took 500 hours, the author's compensation is a measly $4 per hour for the endeavor. Given that our developer could be making $30 per hour, just as an employee doing the same basic job, it is clear the project is a complete financial failure. If profits are your motive, you must be aware of this. You must recover your investment in time.

This is especially true if you wish to grow a business. It is one thing to settle for a lower personal income or wage to do what you want to do. It is quite another if you are paying employees and the projects they are undertaking are not recouping the cost of the time it takes to complete them. Your only choices here are: 1) pay your employees substandard wages for the level of work they are doing. You'd be surprised how often employers try this. "Why should I pay you $30 an hour when what you are creating is only earning us a few thousand dollars a year?" Well, the reason is that, if the skill they possess has a market worth of $30 an hour, it is not their problem if you are having them work on projects that, fundamentally, are not worth their time investment. It is the employer's responsibility to extract this worth; and 2) incur losses, until you go bankrupt.

There have been cases where science researchers have used private investors' capital to undertake projects where the potential payoff was dubious. They continued to pay themselves the going wage rate, while at the same time working on exactly the project they wanted. The costs were being absorbed by the investors. Now, if the investors are told outright that the project has limited commercial value, that's OK. Maybe, it's medical research the capital investors want to support anyway. But, if the investors are at all misled into believing there could likely be a huge payoff, where none likely exists, then, this is highly unethical. If you cannot cover your own wages via earnings and have a good chuck left over for any capital investors or reinvestment to grow the business, you are too small to justifiably seek external investors. You cannot recover the value of your own time, let alone give investors a potentially decent profit.

This may sound odd, but you cannot afford to give away any percentage of a project or company with very limited potential that you are sincere about running. Suppose what you really, truly, madly, passionately, deeply want to do can only earn you $30,000 per year. Now, this would not be a good business, but you are passionate about it, so who am I to argue with you? You can earn a living at it. But if you sell ownership of 50% of the business to get started, then you are only personally earning $15,000 per year. What was a viable way to make a living is no longer viable.

Related to needing to recoup the value of your time (and your employees' time) is the issue of the value of trying to repair things right down to the failed component level. Some people, poorer people, in general, tend to want to save money by, "Doing it themselves," rather than just pay a professional service person to repair a broken item. It is not always economically justifiable to do this. At some point, the costs incurred to repair something simply outweigh the cost to just buy a whole new one. Some people never see this. They figure, "Why can't we just repair the floppy drive that went out, rather than buy a whole new one?" The answer is that the drive costs, maybe, $20. But the cost of sniffing out the problem within the drive would, maybe, take half an hour of a service person's time, who would be billing you at a rate of $60 an hour. Plus, the new component is probably going to be more reliable than a repaired old component. Not only must present personnel costs be factored into your estimates, but also the future cost of repairs.

With any business decision, ask yourself, "What are my personnel costs incurred right now for this contemplated project? What will be the estimated costs incurred in the future, including personnel costs?" Until you start asking questions like this, you will always wonder why it seems you are making frugal choices and, yet, you are losing money.

Ultimately, if you are successful in business, you will reach a point where your time is more limited than money. You will be willing to "burn" money to save time. This is not at all unreasonable. Sometimes, you see an opportunity. You fear, if you do not seize the market quickly, someone else will. So you spend a little more to get there first. Costs that could have been absorbed in time are paid for in cash.

Most people think in terms of the value of their time via the wages they earn. "If it takes me an hour to do this job and if I earn $20 an hour and if I would need to pay a "professional" $30 an hour, then, I come out ahead." Of course, this is true if the job takes the professional the full hour that it took you. That's usually not the case. Did you ever know a do-it-yourselfer, who decided to save money on a job that would take a professional fifteen minutes, and, two days later, the job is still not completed? And, it's not from a lack of trying! Many people just never realize the value of their own time. It is an expendable commodity they reason. Money is rare and hard to get. This is untrue. In fact, the opposite is truer.

How long will you live? 70 years? 80 years? You won't live forever. Sorry to tell you that, but it's a truth most people never really accept, except in theory. "Other people don't have all the time in the world, but I do!" is ultimately what they believe. Yet, how much money can you earn in one lifetime? Well, if you cap the amount you will earn by working for a fixed wage for an employer, then, yes, it is true that your earnings are as limited as your existence. But, what if you are building your own business? Are your earnings still capped? Technically, the answer is still "yes," but the ceiling is so much higher that, for all practical purposes, it can be treated as infinite. You have unlimited earnings. At some point, the earnings from your past work will support you comfortably and indefinitely just through conservative investments made passively. You have a limited life. It is simply incorrect to assume you can linearly map the value of your time to the dollar amount you earn. You must understand this. This is why companies grow through hiring employees. This is why companies are willing to outsource jobs to other companies. This is why you see a lot of floppy drives in trash cans!

I know people, who with any given purchase, calculate the amount of their life it took to make the purchase. (If the person makes $10 an hour and buys a $10 pizza, he would say he has just spent an hour of his life to buy the pizza.) They are constantly calculating the life-cost of a given purchase. This might be a handy way for them to really evaluate if the purchase is worth the cost to them. But you must be very careful when you start translating the value of your time into money.

Suppose you value your time at $30 per hour. That's a good wage. It's $60,000 per year. Someone comes along and says he wants to hire you. He will pay you $40 per hour. "What a great deal!" you say, as you jump for joy. Secretly, you feel your time is only worth $30 per hour. After all, that's what you've been making for years. Further, the recruiter says he'll pay you up front. "Better yet!" you think. "I know the time value of money." He hands you a check for $35 million dollars. Your mouth drops open in shock. It seems like a lot. But, that's not a problem! You take it and sign the contract. Only then does your future employer tell you a bit about himself. He's the grim reaper. He has just bought 100 years of your life (full-time, 24 hours a day—no 8-hour-a-day employees for him!) Further, he wants all your time at once. He asks you to come with him. Suddenly, $35 million doesn't seem like so much. It's not like you intended to sell him *all* of your life. You were thinking only a few hours here and there. Maybe, you'd play solitaire on your PC during off peak hours! Oh, well. We all make bad business deals sometimes. Ultimately, money is cheap when compared to life because life is finite.

The value of time plays another role in starting an enterprise that is closely related to the value of action and getting started and keeping productivity high. Many entrepreneurs who fail never understand the role that overhead and fixed costs played in their companies' failure. Once you have rent to pay, once you have employees to pay, once you start absorbing ongoing, so-called period costs, then action is imperative. High-technology companies are always aware of their capital "burn" rate. Regardless of what is achieved, some costs are generated every month. You only have so long before you are out of capital. For firms demanding a significant up-front investment in research and product development, this can be the hinge pin of success or failure, and it is one you could dangerously ignore. Did we achieve anything worthwhile this month? Did we achieve what we set out to achieve this month? If not, you have a problem. Maybe you learned some interesting things in your research, but unless it can be converted into product before you run out of money, you will fail. Yet, it is easy for people to kid themselves that progress was, in fact, made.

You will be able to raise investment funds more easily, if you can show a prototype that is nearly ready for shipment to customers. If the prototype is fully workable and could be shipped, so much the better. Ideas are a dime a dozen. A workable prototype has real value. If you raise capital at this point, realize you have reduced the risk considerably for the capital investors. They no longer need to worry if you will squander your time and never create a viable product. You have the product. Because of this, you should expect equity investors to be compensated with a significantly smaller share of ownership in your company. In this way, you should be the one to benefit from sunken costs in time and money that went into developing the product. But, if all you have is an idea and you actually find venture capitalists who will back you, don't bellyache about the huge percentage of ownership they are demanding. Inventors should always, if possible, get their idea to prototype stage before seeking equity capital.

Most companies do not have a significant up-front investment in research. Computer consulting companies, dating services, and others can jump right in and start earning profits. Doughnut shops come to mind. Almost immediately after opening for business, a doughnut shop had better be profitable. Always favor businesses that will achieve profitability quickly. It is safer to put effort and energy into selling and improving products, rather than trying to invent the next great blockbuster product. How do you know if you are working hard enough? The best measure is the revenue per employee your company is generating. If your company has a low revenue per employee relative to your competition, you had better watch out. Time is being squandered, rather than being effectively used to sell and build product.

Chapter 26.
Buying a Business

A successful entrepreneur must know how to buy and sell a business. It is a valuable skill. You may never use it, but you should be aware of the thought process behind buying or selling a business, anyway. Buying an existing business can be a great entry strategy into a market. Selling a company you have built is a great "harvest" strategy for extracting the wealth you have created within your business. Buying competing businesses can be a great way to expand and grow your business. Primarily, we will be interested in the role of a business buyer.

The key issues for a business buyer are: 1) Asking yourself: "Do I really want to buy *this* business?" and 2) Being sure you do not pay too much for the business.

Whether or not you choose to buy a given business is a personal issue. It is a very important question only you can answer. We will assume you have decided you want to buy some business and now need to know how to value it properly. The main focus of this chapter is being able to come up with a reasonable estimate of a business's worth. Buying a business is always a significant financial decision which demands intensive study of the business and the industry. Because the business you contemplate purchasing is typically much smaller than publicly-traded companies and because you are going to run the enterprise, you will have an easier time evaluating the business.

The first question you must answer is "What would be the cost for me to rebuild this business from scratch?" In other words, what would be the cost if you were to assemble all the component parts that make up the business? Many business buyers cannot answer this question. They really just don't know. They sometimes argue that no two businesses are the same and so the question is irrelevant. This is a sorry excuse for not trying. Buying a company is not a trivial decision. If you treat it as such, you are better off not trying to buy a business at all. For larger companies, it might be true this question is just too difficult to answer, but if this is your first or second acquisition, you can do this analysis. In this chapter, we are not trying to value a large company, like Merck, but a much smaller enterprise.

Of course, you can't replicate the business exactly, but you can begin by asking, "What are the crucial ingredients that go into making this company?" Focus on the big picture. How does this company make its money? For example, if the company is a manufacturing firm, what is the essential machinery that would be needed to stock an equal-sized factory? That would be a start. Suppose you consider buying a small, three-person machine shop. The owner might try to sell you a song and dance that the company is worth much more than just the value of the machinery. Be skeptical of this. Ask, "Why is this so?" "Well, we have a lot of skilled employees." Hmm… The company has two employees, other than the owner who is selling. Most likely he will not be staying on, so that's really only two employees. Are they really skilled? More so than other people you can hire? Will they stay on? Remember, there is a huge difference between buying equipment and people. Equipment you own. You never own people. They can move on. Maybe, both workers are relatives of the owner and plan to go to work elsewhere. Maybe that is why he is selling! Both his employees are going to start a machine shop across the street. Ick! You probably won't know until it happens. You can always hire a small number of employees. You will be paying them in wages and, maybe, an equity interest in the business. Why pay the previous owner for them also?

You point out that you could easily find two equally-skilled machinists, if you were to start a shop from scratch. What other reasons justify a selling price in excess of the value of the plant and equipment? The owner argues, "Location. We are well-situated geographically." It looks like the owner is already getting desperate. After all, this is a machine shop which sells most of its parts to distributors. If it had been a restaurant, then location would be very important. But by understanding the business and how it functions, you can clearly see that you could do the same operation from a number of locations, all of which are equally well-situated. You ask the owner for other reasons.

The owner says, "Advertising. We have a running ad in the Yellow Pages." Humpf. You could run your own ad. The owner is not even listing an asset you are purchasing, but an expense of the business. You can generate your own expenses. That's the easy part! More likely the owner would have used that buzzword, *reputation*. "We have an excellent reputation." Now, reputation is of value. But will the reputation stay with the company or the owner? After all, a three-person shop is pretty small. Maybe, when the owner leaves, the companies buying parts from the shop will go elsewhere. Occasionally, the owner has decided it is his personal reputation that is of value and knows he loses nothing by selling out. He will immediately turn around and start another company doing the same thing. Restaurant owners are notorious for this. Some people are fond of "noncompete clauses," which prevent the owner from starting another business directly in competition with the one he is selling. Even though I am skeptical of the value of these, it might make sense to try to get the owner's reaction if you suggest such a clause. In my opinion, never pay more money for such a clause if you require one. Either the owner plans to start a competing company or he does not. You should not have to pay extra for his legally binding word of it.

Now advertising and reputation bring us to what is crucial and that is the business's existing contracts and customers. This is where much of the real value of an acquisition lies. Suppose you have a boat-building company. You wish to grow. Your company has a solid reputation, but still you would like to generate more sales of your custom yachts. If a competitor wishes to sell out and you can pick up the contracts to build, say, 20 custom yachts, then this certainly has a value to you. The value comes from the extra business you know the acquisition will generate for your company. Because you are an expert in the area, you will be able to make a reasonable estimate of the value of these contracts. If you were unfamiliar with the business, you would be at a disadvantage, and you might get duped into believing the contracts were worth more than they actually are. In particular, maybe the cost to fulfill the contracts will exceed the price of the boats. Then, assuming the obligation to fulfill the contracts would *detract* from the business's value to you.

When purchasing any business, you need to be aware of any potential liabilities that the company may be facing. You need the contract between you and the seller to explicitly take this into account. You really need a lawyer to be sure the sales contract of the business doesn't expose you to unreasonable contingencies. There have been cases where a business is sold, then suddenly, the acquired business finds itself facing million-dollar liabilities. You do not want an acquisition you intended to grow your business to become the cause of the downfall of your business. You, as an entrepreneur, have done everything right, except make a bad acquisition. Your business, before the acquisition, was growing like gangbusters and was making great profits. Then, you are bankrupt. Maybe, you eventually win in court and recover. Then, again, maybe you do not.

You must be very careful when buying a business. The seller knows this will be the only transaction between you and the seller, and he will try to get as much as he can. Sometimes, this comes in the unpleasant form of passing huge, potential liabilities your way. Never say to yourself, "I only paid $200,000 for the business, so the most I could lose is $200,000." If horribly unlucky, you could lose your multimillion-dollar company that you built before the acquisition.

Yet, most business sellers are not out to take advantage of you. They often have built a company and now just want to move on to other endeavors. They have quite a bit of money and want to spend time with their family or playing golf. They are just tired of doing the same thing. But, their business might be too small to interest larger or even mid-sized companies. This can represent a great opportunity. Such businesses are often sold at bargain rates. Some individuals have made fortunes just buying up smaller businesses, lumping them into a larger entity, and then selling them to other larger companies or by taking them public. An advantage of such a sale from the purchaser's standpoint is that, often, the seller will finance a good chunk of the sale's price. Because the seller really wants to get out of the field, you might find you are able to acquire a company whose value greatly exceeds the size of a business you could otherwise finance.

Just like when you buy a house, put twenty percent down, and pay the rest over time, you might find a business you can similarly finance. You would seldom get the financing from banks. Suppose the twenty percent is large enough to consume most of the amount you have saved for buying a business. The banks wouldn't be happy with the collateral or any other aspect of the deal. But, the business seller might well accept such a deal! So, instead of controlling a business worth the $200,000 you have saved to buy your business, you are in control of a $1 million dollar enterprise. The fact that the seller is willing to finance you is also a tremendous, positive point. It probably means the seller has faith you can run the business. And, if you do need help and advice, this person is probably willing to aid you. After all, his payments depend upon your success.

Conversely, if you are selling a business, I would avoid financing the purchaser. Get a bank to do it. After all, you took your risks. You built a company of real value. Why should your harvest amount from the endeavor, which may have taken many years of your life, depend upon the success of someone else to run the company successfully *after* you have sold it? Where are you, if the purchaser starts making bad decisions? What if the purchaser turns around and makes another acquisition and now the entire business is even more highly leveraged? A few really bad moves and the enterprise can be in jeopardy. You don't own it and have little or no say in what happens. Yet, if this clown fails, you lose all the value you have worked to create. Don't assume you will just be able to resume control of your old company. Don't assume the person will be able to pay you what you are owed. I would much rather take a lower price and get cash rather than finance someone else and get a higher price. If you buy a business and the seller has taken this risk and financed you, never forget this. You really owe this person more than a little extra money.

Reputation and current order contracts are important in valuing a company. Also crucial, especially for companies in the direct-mail business, is the ownership of the mailing or customer list. Such lists have value, although the value is difficult to calculate. The one thing you don't want is to buy a mail-order company and find out that the owner has kept a copy of the list to use with another competing business he is starting. Maybe, some employees have made a copy of the list with the hope of selling it to competitors! All of these possibilities devalue the list to you. What assurances do you have this won't happen? Not all mailing lists are of the same value. Anyone can throw together a useless list of names and addresses. At the other extreme are lists that have been acquired via blood, sweat, and tears. The customers on such lists are excellent repeat buyers. Often, each buyer contributes hundreds of dollars a year to company profits.

Customer lists are not the only lists of value. Do you remember Henry Gump? Don't feel bad. No one else does either, despite having met him repeatedly! He had two lists. One was a list of clients needing consultants. The other was a list of computer consultants who were experienced, who wanted to do consulting jobs, and who were willing to go to work making Henry more money. This list of consultants has real value. Competitors would undoubtedly like to woo such individuals away from Henry. If someone came up to Henry and said, "We need an intranet on an NT network, and we are using an Oracle database of our products that we want to put on the Internet for customer ordering. Securely, of course. Can you do it?" Henry could say, "You bet. We have the people." Henry can serve this new client because of his resource list.

Information is not the only easy-to-neglect item when valuing a company. Patents, trademarks, proprietary products, copyrights, and other intellectual capital can have significant value. After deciding the intellectual capital has *real* value and you *want* to own it, the first question to ask is, "Do the rights really belong to the current company?" Sometimes, you will find a company claims such rights when, in fact, they are essentially leased to the company. It is important to know the difference. Unless legal contracts guarantee you the use of the right, usually exclusively, you must be skeptical of the value of such intellectual capital.

Let's assume the company you are considering purchasing does own such intellectual rights and these rights will be transferred to you on sale of the company. How do you value these rights? This is very difficult. The best you can do is try to make a conservative estimate of the revenue streams that will result from such ownership. You are concerned with the amount of these revenue streams, how long the revenue streams will last, and also any new occurrences or developments that could endanger the revenue streams. Let's take a revenue stream near and dear to my heart. Book sales! You are contemplating buying Magus Publishing, Incorporated. New authors come to the firm, hoping to get their books published. Established authors come to the firm with their latest, greatest novels.

Magus has a backlist of books. Notice that buzzword *list* again. What this means is that Magus has titles that it has already published in the past that are still "in-print," which is a just a fancy term for you-can-still-order-the-title. Most likely, the books aren't being printed, but gathering dust in a warehouse until they sell. If the inventory gets below a certain point, Magus might decide to reprint, or else let the book go "out-of-print," which is just a fancy term for this-book-sucks-it's-not-selling-let's-move-on-to-something-else.

An astute reader might ask, "But, wouldn't these books on this precious *list* also be stored as inventory and wouldn't we value them as inventory?" Ah, good point, grasshopper, such books are inventory, and you should value the books *in stock* as inventory. But, we are concerned here with something more. We are concerned with the rights to reprint and sell more copies of these books down the road. A book on the backlist might, in fact, be out-of-stock (a fancy term for our $50,000-custom-written-inventory-management-software screwed up, please hold and we'll get back to you). This book *is* at the printers. It's an expense waiting to happen! But that's not a bad thing. It's a good thing. Maybe it is Stephen King's latest novel. It obviously has some value to the publisher. Other publishers would kill to have it at their printers. This book wouldn't be covered under the value of inventory.

Further, suppose one title, "Quantum Field Theory for Stupid People" has only 5,000 copies in stock as inventory, but yet, the title sells 20,000 copies a year. Hey, it could happen! What this means is that this title is reprinted four times a year, if the print runs are all 5,000 copies. The value of this book lies in the fact that it sells 20,000 copies a year and earns, say, $1 a copy for a total of $20,000 a year as its contribution to company earnings. If you simply valued the cost of the current inventory of this book, you would be missing the bigger picture. So what we are valuing here is the *right* to reprint and sell all the company's current backlist titles. We are valuing the right to turn these rights into revenue streams that generate profits for the company! It is important to value this separately from current inventory. Be especially careful not to double count when you are valuing anything. Sometimes, there are two or more ways of looking at something and appraising its worth. As the buyer, you certainly never want to inadvertently value the same thing twice in two different ways and wind up paying double. It sounds stupid, I know. But, it happens. Sometimes, to people who are used to buying companies worth tens of millions of dollars!

You might be thinking, "The copyright to a book is usually owned by the author and not the publisher. So, the author could have another publisher sell the book. So, the publisher doesn't really own the rights to this book at all. So, intellectual ownership here doesn't benefit the publisher." If you were thinking that, excellent. You are exactly correct. The copyright ownership almost certainly does belong to the author, and if there were no legally binding contract giving the publisher the right to exclusively publish the book, the value of this backlist to the company would need to be looked at very speculatively. However, publishers tend to be smarter than authors, in the same sense that people running computer-consulting companies tend to be smarter than the consultants working for them.

Publishers use legal contracts to give them exclusive rights to print and reprint the book for a given period of time. In fact, publishers often also demand the rights to the author's next-born child. I'm not kidding. Smart publishers know that, maybe, the author will be the next Stephen King. Probably not, but maybe. A best seller begets best seller, and the publishing company which published the first work almost certainly has assured that it will be the publisher for the second work. I'm sure if publishers could, they would write into the contract, "We have exclusive rights to publish anything you write ever in your entire life. If you have been reincarnated, we also own…" Of course, they cannot do this in practice. A typical contract might give the publisher exclusive rights to publish the book for, say, five years or as long as the publisher guarantees to keep the book in-print.

So the value of the backlist stems from the right to sell the titles owned by someone else. And, this right lasts for only a fixed period of time as set by a legal contract, say, five years. This means that the title, "Quantum Field Theory for Stupid People" will not necessarily generate $20,000 profits forever, but rather will, hopefully, do so for five years. We need to take the time span into consideration. But we aren't done yet. For who says that "Quantum Field Theory for Stupid People" will not become a dud next year and sell four copies? So goes our revenue stream. Or, maybe, the book will really take off and sell more than 20,000 copies. Is there anything we know we can do that the current publisher is not aware of that can increase the sales? Usually not. Is there anything that we know will endanger the sales? Maybe, the title will continue to sell 20,000 copies a year for several decades. And, maybe, the author really doesn't want to switch to another publisher and plans to keep the book with Magus. That would mean for all practical purposes that your "exclusive" reprint right would extend beyond five years. Maybe, for almost no cost, you could get the author to extend the rights for another five years. But then, again, even if the book continues to sell 20,000 per year, like Old Faithful, what would happen if your printing costs rose? You might well make less than $1 per book. All of these contingencies change the value of the revenue stream that the book generates or the profits that result from the revenue stream. Do you see how this is getting complicated?

You could use expectation values to make a reasonable estimate of the possibilities and the attendant financial consequences. In many of the cases, you would be guessing as to both the probability of the outcomes and the financial upswing or losses incurred with each outcome. But, you could make reasonable estimates for several likely cases. And, often, it is precisely these cases that are most likely to dominate the valuation of the revenue stream. In situations like this, expectation values really are your friend. They can give you a reasoned estimate of the value of a business that is more accurate than the guess of someone who tries to value the business, but is totally unaware of the need to take possibilities and the consequences into account. Further, although for any given book the actual profit result might differ greatly from the calculated expectation value, when you are dealing with several hundred books, the aggregate expectation value will probably be very valid. In a hand-wavy sense, "Things will tend to even out."

Assuming that you have made some estimate of these possibilities and have calculated expectation values for the revenue streams involved, your next formal step would be to discount these revenue streams to their present value, i.e., account for the time value of money. This step, however, is unnecessary for two reasons. First, your estimates are probably off enough to make any time value of money calculation relatively meaningless (as Butch says to Sundance, just as they are about to jump from the ledge into the river, "Hell, don't worry about not being able to swim. The fall will probably kill you!"). And, second, the time values involved should be pretty short, typically three to five years or less. If you are trying to predict any sort of smaller-sized business revenue stream beyond five years, your numbers are almost certainly meaningless. It is one thing to do a present-discount-value calculation on dividends paid by a company like Merck or Northern States Power, but it is quite another to try the same with a smaller enterprise. In particular, I have little doubt that NSP will be paying dividends ten years from now or that these dividends will grow at a conservative estimate of 5%, but I am very doubtful that "Quantum Field Theory for Stupid People" will continue to sell in any predictable amount five years from now.

I know some of you are writhing in pain, thinking, "This is too damn hard. I can't do these expectation values and get a reasonable estimate of the revenue stream generated from such a situation." But, you can. Let's do it for QFTFSP ("Quantum Field Theory for Stupid People"). Sales are strong and show no signs of letting up, so you predict that it will sell another 20,000 copies next year, in addition to this year. It is assumed you will buy the company at the start of this year. From past experience in the publishing business, you typically expect that sales will fall off to about half the present sales in the third year. This will continue for two years. Then, you will neglect residual sales after that assuming them to be small. You will also assume that your production costs, a.k.a. printing costs, will remain the same and you will make $1 for every copy sold.

$$\text{Expected Profit Stream} = \$1(20{,}000) + \$1(20{,}000) \\ + \$1(10{,}000) + \$1(10{,}000) = \$60{,}000$$

That wasn't so bad, was it? All probabilities were assumed to be unity or 100%. In other words, we have assumed sales for this year (the first term in the above sum) are for all practical purposes assured. Similarly, for next year (the second term in the above sum), we feel we can count on another 20,000 sales. For the third and fourth years (third and fourth terms in the sum, respectively), we have assumed sales of about 10,000 each year. (Aside: if we had assumed there was a 30% probability of selling 20,000 copies in the third year and a 70% probability of selling 10,000 copies, then the third term would be replaced with two terms of $(.3)(\$1)(20{,}000)$ and $(.7)(\$1)(10{,}000)$ which say we expect third-year profits to be $13,000 rather than $10,000. Similarly, we could modify the estimated profit per book ($1) by contingencies.) Notice that I said we used past experience here to help us determine what was "likely." Only when you have been in an industry awhile will you have such experience to fall back upon. This will help you value a business much more accurately, as you will know what is "typical." Finally, we have neglected sales after the next four years. We have also neglected the chance of it selling significantly more than 20,000 copies and the chance of it failing next year completely and selling only four copies. You might tend to think of these equally unlikely possibilities as washing each other out. Remember, the goal isn't to consider every possibility in minute detail. That'll drive you nuts, and it's too fine a calculation given all the uncertainties. You simply need a solid ball park estimate. In all cases, conservatism is your friend. It is better to underestimate revenues and profits than to overestimate them. If you err on the downside and the business still looks like a good buy, you have found yourself a deal! If you cannot acquire the business for a cost at or below your conservative estimate of the company's worth, pass. There are other businesses to buy.

Now, Magus was careful to choose "Quantum Field Theory *for Stupid People*" as its title. If they had tried to use "Quantum Field Theory for Dummies™" no doubt, Magus would find itself being sued by IDG books, the owner of the "for Dummies™" trademarked expression. Anyone familiar with computers knows the books I'm talking about. They are yellow and black and have a little cartoon-like character with a picket-type sign saying, you guessed it, "for Dummies™" Many of these books lack meaningful information and are not that well-written. Some are, though. For example, *JavaScript for Dummies™* is a very well-written book, I think. The reason IDG was able to trademark this expression is because of consistently developing this expression with their selection of books. The very name conjures up the image of one of these books. These books sell well. Many new programmers or computer users, who need to learn a new software program, ask themselves, "I wonder if there is a 'for Dummies™' book on this?" This gives the trademark value to IDG.

If the quality of these books slips much further, the value of the trademark could quickly be destroyed as past readers would start to say to themselves, "The last 'for Dummies™' book I got was a piece of #*&^$. I think I'll look elsewhere." It is precisely the quality of titles like *JavaScript for Dummies™* that sustains the trademark's value. This is a case of the trademark having value. How much would be difficult to assess. But, consider the case of the "for Dummies™" titles on personal finance and investing. These are written by a guy called Eric Tyson. I haven't read any of his books, so I can't say if they are good books or bad. What I can say is this, "Who the hell is Eric Tyson?" Before his "for Dummies™" titles came out, I bet no one else knew him either. This is not to say he doesn't have good ideas. Maybe, he does. Then, again, maybe not. So why did his book appear on business best-seller lists? Why did I not too long ago see a newspaper column written by Eric Tyson? The trademark. People wanted a "for Dummies™" title about money and investing. When such titles came out, the titles would sell, regardless of who wrote them. This is clearly a case of the trademark making the author.

I'm not saying this as derogatory, in any way. In fact, if Tyson saw this opportunity and submitted his concept for such a book to IDG, my hat is off to him. He saw an excellent market opportunity and knew how to take advantage of it. What if he had written a title on investment not in the "for Dummies™" stable? It could have been nearly the same book, teaching the same ideas, but its sales would not likely distinguish it from the large number of other books written about investment. It would not be a business best seller. Contrast this to an investment book written by Peter Lynch, the investment maven who built up Fidelity's Magellan's track record. Peter Lynch's book would be a best seller, regardless of its title or which company published it. It is the author's reputation that would lead to the book's success. It is crucial to be able to distinguish situations like this, when you are dealing with intellectual capital to be valued. Ask yourself, "Who is the beneficiary of the proprietary product? Who controls the ability to create value and sales from the copyright, trademark, patent, etc.? In cases where there can be two owners of the intellectual capital, such as books, both copyrighted and with a popular trademark to help generate sales, you could wind up paying way too much for a business, if you accredited the value to the wrong owner.

Now, I have bad news for you. The above valuation method for copyrights and trademarks is trivially easy, when compared to valuing patents. Some patents have tremendous value, and new ones are being developed all the time (The SuperSoaker™ squirt gun comes to mind. Something like 250 million of these great little—annoying little, depending on your perspective—toys have been sold). In many research-oriented companies, the products created are the result of many patents, sometimes involving collaboration of multiple companies. This can lead to a horrible web of confusion. Be sure, at least, if you are buying a business that depends upon such products, that you acquire all the necessary patents or the right to use them. In particular, never, *never* pay a premium for a business for which the seller demands to keep the most crucial patent. Why should you? He is trying to get your money and, at the same time, retain the company value for himself! It may seem fair to him, but it is not.

I'm not saying you should not wish to own a manufacturing company which manufactures products intellectually owned by others. Many very successful businesses do precisely this. Just never confuse the value of the manufacturing company with the value of holding the patent. Unless there is some contract to prevent it, the patent owner could go to another manufacturer. Another difficulty in valuing a patent lies in the fact that a patented product can become obsolete due to future inventions and technological change. You need to be very much aware of these issues when buying a business. I always have the motto, "When seriously in doubt, pass on the opportunity." There are too many good opportunities to become financially tied up on something you just don't feel comfortable valuing. An entrepreneur, desiring to buy a business, needs to know his limitations.

I have discussed elsewhere the need for business mentors. When buying a business, a mentor, someone you fully trust, someone who is on your side, and someone who knows the industry intimately, is a huge advantage to you.

Let's neglect intellectual capital for the moment and try to value a business which does not depend upon proprietary, intellectual property. In particular, let's value a typical custom manufacturing firm. The same methods are useful in valuing all businesses. The idea is to put a reasonable value on the business, using the one input we can usually be sure of—*sales*. When the business you contemplate purchasing also has considerable intellectual property, you can approach valuing the business in two parts. First, try to obtain the value of the intellectual property alone. Then, use the method below. Try to buy the business for the lower of the two valuations.

I have no idea who invented or discovered this method. It was probably independently "known" to many people, before it ever became well-known. It is a method used regularly by professional business buyers and also by intelligent stock investors. The method was first made widely known to the public by Kenneth Fisher who discussed this method in his book, *Super Stocks*. Kenneth Fisher used the method to value publicly-traded stocks. It works very well there, but it also has significant value to people looking to purchase a smaller, private business. I will explain the advantages of using this method over more commonly known valuation methods based on earnings. The method uses what are referred to as price-to-sales ratios, or PSR's. The basic idea is simple, but very powerful. It is well-known a company's earnings are affected by accounting methods. You could have two companies manufacturing and selling the exact same product, charging the customers the exact same amount for the products sold, and selling the exact same number of products. Further, the real costs or expenses incurred by each company to produce each product are the same.

How do the earnings of these two companies compare? It would seem that they should have equivalent earnings, for they really are identical companies in every way—sales, costs to produce the sales, etc. At some deeper, philosophical level, the companies do have the same earnings. Unfortunately, each company could be reporting very different values for their earnings. This is not due to any official lying, but rather is the result of simple (and legal) differences in accounting methods used by the two companies. Surprisingly, one company might well report *double* the earnings of the other company. The company reporting higher earnings is said to be doing aggressive accounting, while the company reporting lower earnings is said to be doing more conservative accounting. To see how these differences arise, assume each company uses a Widget-Y-Maker machine. A new Widget-Y-Maker costs $100,000 and typically lasts five years before becoming obsolete and unreliable. In other words, it is scrapped for no residual value at the end of five years. Some users of the machine might run the machine fewer hours per year and extend its yearly life. Other users may use the machine more intensively and wear it out more quickly. We are not concerned with this aspect of the machine right now, but keep it in mind. Now $100,000 divided by five is $20,000 and this is the amount that the machine physically depreciates in value each year. (There can be complications, and it can be argued that the machine will not physically depreciate linearly in value, i.e., the same amount each year, but rather might depreciate more in the early years of its use. Then, it will depreciate less rapidly in the later years of its use. This doesn't really matter for our purposes. The crucial point is that the machine really is wearing out at the overall rate of $100,000 in five years and the machine will be used until obsolete. Real machines, of course, also have some nonzero scrap cost.)

However, depreciation, as it is reported in the company's financial statements, does not have to exactly match this $20,000 annual amount. It could be higher or lower. There is no one to say that the company must use exactly $20,000 per year as the value. The company will often use its own predictions of the machine's useful life to allocate the machine's cost as an expense. Then, the company will depreciate the machine's cost over that number of years. One of our companies is using $15,000 per year, while the other company is using $25,000 per year for the current year. Let's also assume that the companies are using the same numbers, both in their tax statements and also in the regular financial reports. Yes, these may differ also! In the absence of audited financial reports, which most smaller companies lack, you will use tax returns for your analysis. Hopefully, when the machine is carried away to the junkyard, both companies have expensed a total cost of $100,000 for their machine, and both machines have worked about the same total production hours. But this doesn't help you much, as you are trying to value the business right now, and the machine is still in operation.

Let's assume each company sells 1,000 of its Widget Y's every year. Each sale brings in $50 to the company. The revenue generated by sales of Widget Y's for each company is $50,000. Because the companies are selling the same product in the same numbers and at the same price, both companies report the same revenue. The only cost of making the Widget Y's is the *physical* depreciation cost of the machine. We neglect labor costs, overhead, etc. Well, one company is saying its annual cost for this year is $25,000 and the other is saying that its expenses for the year are $15,000. The first company reports pre-tax earnings of $25,000 while the second company reports earnings of $35,000. The $10,000 difference is solely due to accounting differences. There are absolutely no operational differences between the companies.

If you tried to value each company based upon its earnings, you would get different values for each of the companies. When investing in larger companies, investors often talk in terms of PE ratios or price-to-earnings ratios. That is, a business in a given industry is worth so many times its annual earnings. For example, if you feel 10 times annual earnings is a fair valuation for Northern States Power, you would look up the current earnings of NSP, multiply them by 10, and this would represent how much you feel the business is worth. Two things are essential to know here. First, in practice with larger companies, the focus on company valuation is so earnings-based that you will see the current PE ratio of the business listed in any business newspaper. You won't have to look up earnings to see what the company's PE ratio is. You just look it up in the newspaper. Suppose it is 12. You feel the company is too highly valued. It is selling for 12 times annual earnings, while you feel 10 times earnings is more appropriate. Secondly, calculating a PE ratio to represent a reasonable estimate for how much, at most, a company should be selling for is a bit of a black art. Who's to say 12 isn't more appropriate than 10?

For larger companies, you can do various tricks to get a handle on what might be a viable PE ratio for a business. For example, you could look up the PE ratios that the company's stock has traded at over the last ten years. You could then take the average of all the values, maybe, neglecting the high and low values. By neglecting highs and lows, you hope to minimize the effect of values that may not be really representative. You could use this average as a measure of what is "normal." However, there have been cases where stocks have been overpriced or underpriced for a decade or more. So this method is not nearly foolproof. Another trick is to look up the PE ratios for other similarly-sized companies in the same industry. The idea is to compare apples to apples and not to oranges. If one large tobacco company sells at 15 times earnings and another sells at 10 times earnings, you might try to conclude the one selling at 10 times earnings is the better value. You are paying less for the earnings. Unfortunately, this doesn't help you much, if all the stocks in the industry are overvalued or depressed. Even if it worked in determining the relative value of Company A to Company B, it still wouldn't tell you if either company represented a good buy. As pointed out above, two companies doing the same thing can report wildly different earnings and that is the real crux of the problem.

Other tricks involve trying to estimate the company's growth rate in earnings, conservatively, of course. Then, use some sort of present-discounted-value-of-future-earnings method to come up with a viable guess as to the company's future worth. You would also keep an eye out for any business conditions which might enhance or threaten the company's future earnings. When you start to combine all these methods, you might get some insight. However, *none of these methods takes into consideration that companies might use different accounting methods that have a significant effect on the stated earnings*! Some investors try to find some measure of "normalized earnings." They start with stated earnings and try to work backward, putting both companies on an equal accounting footing.

In most cases, at this point, the numbers simply become hogwash. Too many assumptions are being made. Not enough is really known about the internal accounting of either company to really do this normalization. Even when there is enough known to do this, the time spent is ridiculous. This, of course, assumes you know accounting very well. If you don't know accounting, you cannot even attempt such a normalization of earnings. Well, I guess you could, but your answer would be meaningless. The problem is that you are spending a lot of time trying to understand what someone else's accounting numbers "really" mean.

Getting back to our Widget Y example, we assume a PE ratio of three is a fair amount to pay for the business (I will assume a PE of three is what *you* feel comfortable paying for the company). In the case of the company with reported earnings of $35,000, you would say the business is worth $105,000. The company with reported earnings of only $25,000 is worth $75,000. This means, based upon a simple PE analysis, the businesses appear to differ in worth by

$30,000. Now $30,000 is 40% of $75,000. This is a significant difference in valuation between the two companies! If you had relied upon mere reported earnings alone, you might wind up paying a lot more than you thought for the business. How can you prevent this? The solution is to get back to the basics. You can value the business yourself much more simply and reliably and get a truer measure of the company's value. We will still assume you feel three times earnings is a fair price to pay for the company, provided you are dealing with a real measure of earnings and not just one accounting view of earnings. You demand "normalized" earnings. Yet, you will not need to calculate them. This is the power of Fisher's method.

You begin with revenue or gross sales the company makes. While earnings are subject to all sorts of accounting tomfoolery, sales are most always what they are. It is especially rare to see sales misreported by larger companies. There is a good one-word explanation for this. *Jail.* A company president might want to report strong earnings, so he gets a nice bonus. Because of this, he might want an aggressive approach to calculating earnings, i.e., report the largest earnings possible. This is legal. However, if he were to flatly misstate sales, that is an outright falsification easily spotted and likely would be prosecutable. Some companies tend to use more aggressive revenue recognition methods than other companies, but, in general, you know revenue or sales much better than you know earnings.

Each of our two companies reports $50,000 in sales. This is your starting point. The next step is to get an estimate of what is a reasonable profit margin, given the business's industry. Remember, whereas a grocery store might be lucky to get net margins of 3%, it is reasonable for many smaller companies to generate 10 or 15% net margins. But, it does depend upon the industry. You can use your own estimates of the expenses involved to run the business to get a reasonable guess as to what the profit margin will likely be. You can ask other people in the industry what are typical margins at both the gross and net level. Through both methods you can get a very good idea of what the margins are for the business. Multiplying this guesstimate of the net margins by the revenue generated by the business provides you with a "normalized" measure of the company's earnings. This would be the earnings value you would multiply by your PE ratio, or three, to obtain what you feel is a fair price for the business.

To do this most effectively requires either accurate values for typical margins for various industries or else that you understand the business well enough to estimate expenses accurately. For larger companies, industry averages are commonly available. This is precisely why this PSR method works well for valuing larger companies. A given level of sales will convert into about so much in real profits, and the conversion factor is the industry-standard margin. Rather than comparing PE ratios for the businesses, you can compare PSR's for the businesses, using industry norms. There is a lot more to be said about PSR's as they relate to investment in larger companies, but I don't want to get into that. We are interested in buying an entire, much-smaller enterprise. So, we will assume that you have only sketchy industry norms to use. Rather, you must make an independent estimate of the expenses involved in manufacturing and selling the product of the company you contemplate purchasing.

In our case, you must know the expense of manufacturing Widget Y's. You ask yourself, "If I were to manufacture Widget Y's myself, what would be *my* costs?" You ask around. Don't just ask the person from whom you are considering buying the Widget Y company. He wants to get as much as he can for his business. You think about the costs. You learn that making Widget Y's takes only one machine. No labor to run the machine! Further, there is no marketing expense or overhead. No rent to pay. Seems odd, you figure. And, you are right! But, remember, this is just an example. Through your own research you have learned that making Widget Y's takes one machine that typically costs $100,000 new. You could also price older machines. You talk to the company which makes the Widget-Y-maker machine. You learn from the machine specifications and talking to other people, who know the Y-making machine, that the machine will produce about 5,000 units before it is useless. Because you know that the business you contemplate buying sells 1,000 widgets a year, at such a sales rate, you would need only one machine, and it would last for five years, if the production runs were the same size of 1,000 each of the five years. This means your amortized expense of the machine is one-fifth of $100,000 or $20,000 per year.

Subtracting the $20,000 annual cost from the $50,000 in sales tells you earnings are $30,000 a year. You have essentially uncovered the normalized earnings, without doing any reference to the business's accounting books! All you really needed from the business was the revenue!

Hence, if you feel three times earnings is fair, you will pay at most $90,000 for the business. When you can calculate a reasonable industry profit margin, based upon the expenses incurred to run a business, you have arrived. You really are an entrepreneur who knows how to value a company. Something should be troubling you about now. One owner wants to sell for $105,000. The other wants only $75,000. Both claim their businesses are equivalently priced, based upon earnings. Yet, are the businesses really equivalent? For this to be true, the existing Widget-Y-making machine in each company must have the same abilities to create product. In our case, each machine must be of the same age. Remember, after 5,000 units the machine is worn out and has no value. This is absolutely critical. If both businesses had just purchased the machines and each was only one-year old, you would certainly buy the company selling for $75,000. The companies are equivalent. But, what if the company selling for $75,000 has been using the existing machine for four years already? The company selling for $105,000 has only used the machine one year. Remember, the only assets in either of these companies is the one crummy Widget-Y-making machine. So, if you buy the company for $75,000, what you are really buying is the ability to make 1,000 widgets. It has already made 4,000. And, you know you can sell the widgets for $50 apiece. This means you can generate $50,000 in revenue. But if you pay $75,000 for that machine, via buying the company, you wind up losing $25,000. That's not a very good business to purchase.

Starting to ask questions like this is a benefit of trying to estimate a business's expenses independently of what the owner of the business is telling you. You become aware of issues you might not otherwise think about. When you buy a business, what you are really buying is the ability to create or build some product or service. You want to know the costs involved in building an equivalent business from scratch. Getting back to the above example, we should note that we could just buy the Widget-Y-making machine for $100,000. So, why ever pay the owner of such an existing business more? We won't pay $105,000 for the other business. There is no good reason. Further, estimating your expenses from scratch has the added benefit of giving you insight into the ease with which you can expand the business. You will see the incremental costs, if you were to ramp up production. One complication of using revenue, as the starting point, is you need to ascertain the stability of the company's revenue, but this is fundamental to properly valuing the company anyway.

In the above analysis, we estimated production expenses and, hence, margins. This allowed us to convert an existing business's revenue into "normalized" profits. These "normalized" profits are an improvement over just blindly taking reported profits, but yet, we still needed to value the profits (earnings) by using a PE ratio we felt appropriate. The PE ratio is a measure of what we feel the business is worth. There is no one right answer. In the following paragraphs, I will give you some general guidelines about reasonable PE ratios.

First, investors in larger firms often base PE values upon growth rates in sales and earnings. Buyers of smaller enterprises should be more skeptical of doing this. Suppose a small, three-person firm grows by 30% over two years. What does this say about the business's value? Unfortunately, not a lot. Basically, it says the business has grown at 30% for two years. It doesn't say that a reasonable growth estimate in future sales and profits for the business is 30%. It doesn't imply the business has any better prospects than a similar company that grows at 15%. The growth of bigger businesses is often tied more to the general economy and can be estimated conservatively with a reasonable certainty. Because such estimates are reasonable, they can enter into the valuation picture. Ultra-small companies simply haven't shown that they are capable of sustained growth at any rate. Never pay extra for higher past levels of growth, unless you have good reason to believe the growth must continue. There is no reasonable assurance that the growth rates will continue.

Further, because much of a smaller business's growth, upon sale to new management, will depend upon the actions of the new management, there is no reason to pay the previous owner for this growth. Sometimes, a business is built to a ten-person company. The founder sells out, walks away from the company, and feels smug that he has made an excellent sale. Three years later, the business is ten times its initial size and over ten times as profitable. The original founder sometimes feels he still deserves credit for the latest growth. He feels he should have gotten much more for the sale. That simply is not true. Why pay anyone else for growth that you as the entrepreneur will work to achieve?

Ultra-small companies, i.e., those with only a few employees, are never worth the larger PE valuations given to larger companies— assuming no proprietary products controlled or significant intellectual capital owned. If the seller starts asking for ten times earnings, just point out there is a tremendous difference between larger and smaller companies, both in terms of likely growth and survival. If the owner insists on an excess valuation, just walk away. Build the same business you desire from scratch. Some people start little shops and try to sell them for values way out of line with reality. These people love people inexperienced in business, and, especially, inexperienced in the industry, as inexperienced people are gullible targets for all sorts of sales pitches that simply cannot stand up to scrutiny. Knowledgeable buyers will always focus upon the resources acquired in the sale and what it would cost to acquire those resources elsewhere.

Sometimes, an owner will not be aware of where value lies within his own company. There are cases where an owner was sitting on an extended contract to lease a prime retail location. He didn't own it, but he had renewal rights, allowing him to basically stay there forever at reasonable increases in rent over the years. Such a contract might be worth more than the value of the existing business. Typically, a new and entirely different business takes over the old location. A liquor store replaces a fix-it shop, and instant value is created by using the location more effectively. You, of course, are under no obligation to point out the hidden value in his business! But, do not let the sly, old pitch of planting hidden value for you to discover mislead you either. There are some who will intentionally try to leave some supposedly large asset for you to "discover." They will want you to say to yourself, "Gosh, he's missing the huge value in…" You buy the business and feel you have made a shrewd business decision. Only later do you realize that the huge asset really isn't worth that much. When buying businesses, let the buyer beware. And, your best defense against a bad purchase is to know how to estimate expenses to run the business.

In general, you should never, I feel, pay more than two or three times the business's current earnings to buy a smaller business, and you should really be thinking in terms of "book value" or the value of assets acquired. "Book value," here, refers to the current market value of all of the assets the company *owns*. This is not the same as the reported book value, which is a measure of how long-term assets are expensed. Just like you need to determine the earnings value of the revenue, you need to independently estimate "book value." Smaller enterprises are valued by assets, whereas larger companies can be valued by sales or earnings. By assets, I mean assets the business owns. Formally, assets = liabilities + owner equity. Never let this confuse you. Assets are anything that can be used to create products or services that can be sold. Technically, the assets can be financed via either borrowing or else via equity, which is just a fancy term for the owner's money. You want to buy the equity portion of the business, not the liabilities! Don't let someone borrow $200,000, buy $200,000 worth of equipment, and turn around and try to sell you the assets and the debt for $200,000! In this case the actual owned assets are zero. Usually, you can get your own liabilities without anyone else's help.

While this seems obvious to most people, some people try to highly leverage their operations. In particular, they find some businesses with considerable total assets (and, also, considerable debt) to buy. They turn around and try to sell off some of the assets to raise money to acquire different assets or buy out other businesses. No sane lender would have borrowed them the money directly. What they really are trying to buy is debt! Similarly, in leveraged buy outs (LBOs), money is borrowed to buy a business, usually with the idea that certain of the business's existing assets can be sold after the purchase to pay off at least some of the incurred debt. I am personally not fond of these ideas. Only in cases where it is really clear that a business has considerable assets tied up unproductively and the selling price of the business is low does it even begin to make sense. Although aggressive financing of a new business allows rapid acquisition and growth, there is also a good chance that it will all come crashing down on top of your head. It is better not to hope to acquire something for nothing, but rather create a little value the old-fashioned way—through growth via selling more products profitably.

When buying a smaller enterprise, it is also important to uncover and account for costs the owner absorbs, but doesn't really acknowledge. The typical example is the wage of the owner. Suppose a guy wants to sell you his fix-it shop. It employs one person besides the owner. The owner tells you it's a great business. It earned $50,000 last year. You look at the owner's books and immediately notice wage expense for only one person. The owner is not including in his expenses any wage paid to himself. He is lumping his wages together with profits. In essence, he doesn't treat his own time as an expense. Yet, are you buying a business or a job? Suppose you wanted to manage the operations, but not do any of the repairs yourself? You would need to know how much of the owner's time is spent doing repairs so that you could employ someone this amount of time. If it turns out that a skilled repair person costs $40,000 per year and if the owner was spending a solid forty hours a week doing repairs in addition to the business management, then you would need to hire someone full-time.

This means the company earnings aren't really $50,000 but only $10,000. Now, if the owner is trying to get you to pay twice annual earnings for the business (a PE ratio of 2) and using the $50,000 figure that means he's asking for $100,000. He says, "It's a great deal. In two years, you'll have paid off the business and own it free and clear. After that, all the earnings are pure gravy to you. You can't beat that." You need to ask yourself, "Hey, wait a pea-picking minute here. There's something wrong with this plan. What is it?" It will become clear that paying off the business in two years is more theoretical (and, incorrect) thinking to encourage the sale than realistic analysis. It overlooks one crucial factor. You need to eat. You need a place to sleep. You have personal costs involved with just living. You need to cover these costs. Because of this, you are working full-time already. Suppose you are also a skilled repair person and are yourself earning $40,000 a year working for someone else. You cannot do this anymore, if you are busy running your company. This means you will give up your job and lose out on $40,000 in wage earnings.

The owner says, "Well, gosh, you need to take a risk, sometimes, if you ever want to be your own boss. It's an opportunity cost." This is not an opportunity cost. You are not just passing up one opportunity to pursue another. It is rather a fundamental issue of properly valuing the company. When you make good business valuation choices, you will become richer. When you make bad business valuation choices, you will become poorer. If you pay exactly what the business is worth, you are not any richer nor any poorer. You have simply changed the form in which your existing wealth is stored. If you were to buy into the owner's line of thought and pay $100,000 for the business, you would be making a bad business acquisition. Suppose a competitor to your present company comes to you and says, "Because you are doing such a good job, we want to hire you." You say, "OK. I'm kind of tired of staying where I was. How much will you pay me?" They offer you $40,000 per year.

If you accept the offer, you have just changed jobs. You are no wealthier nor any poorer. But, what if the company says, "There is one catch. Our jobs are so good that you need to pay for them." "Come again?" you say. You can't believe what you have just heard. They want you to pay them so that they will give you a job that will pay you money. They explain, "Well, because other people want our jobs, we charge for them. All you have to do is to borrow $80,000 from us at 10% and, then, we hire you. In two years you will have earned the cost you paid for your job." Now, I know what you tell them. It is not pleasant and involves sharp metal reaming tools and parts of their anatomy. You aren't going to make a large up-front payment to get a job. You can easily get one for free! They are asking you to absorb $80,000 in costs that benefit you in absolutely no way.

The owner who is trying to sell you his business for two times earnings, or $100,000, is no different. He wants you to pay a premium for something that should cost you nothing. He is telling you to neglect a major expense of running the business, your time as a producer. If he had said, "Well, we don't include in expenses the cost of rent and machine upkeep, so these don't really detract from profits," you would have seen his flawed reasoning right away. He can't choose what the business expenses are. They are what they are. And, that's all that they are. So if you feel twice earnings is a fair valuation, you should pay precisely that, twice earnings, or $20,000, not $100,000. Don't pay to buy a job for yourself. That's not a smart move.

Now, if you had used the method of PSR's (estimating expenses to get a handle on net margins, then multiplying your calculated margin by the repair shop's revenue to get a measure of profits), you would not have made this error. You would, for example, have made an estimate of the average labor cost per repair and have estimated your total labor cost as this average cost per repair times the number of repairs the shop makes in one year. You might have used another method to estimate labor costs for the repairs. There are many correct ways to get at the same result. Just be sure your way of estimating expenses gets to the correct result.

The smaller and more family-owned the business, the more likely there are hidden labor costs. You should watch the business closely from inside for a period of time before deciding to buy. Just ask the owner if you can help out and watch. To get the ropes so to speak. Keep an eye out for things that affect valuation. For example, the owner says there is no advertising cost, but, then, his six kids prepare ten bags of direct mail pieces. That's an expense. You will need to have your six kids do it (for free, which might not be easy if they are all in their forties, married, live away from home, and are working as engineers to boot!). I mention marketing, because marketing expenses are often overlooked. You really need to know how the business generates its sales, how it brings in those sales. For example, if you had no experience with the mail-order business and tried to estimate production expenses for a mail-order company, you might be dead on when it comes to production costs for the products, and from these you might incorrectly conclude that the business is wildly profitable. You made one mistake only. You are assuming one person in five to whom you mail one of your catalogs places an order. It turns out that only one in a hundred does so. You have neglected the significant marketing cost involved. Mistakes like this happen when you try to value a business you don't understand.

Chapter 27.
Writing a Business Plan

The business plan is a sales document. You are generally trying to sell the idea of your business to equity investors. You need capital to get started and want someone, or many people, to back you. For their money, they will get a percentage of ownership in your company. Even though a business plan is sometimes claimed to be used to seek debt financing, I don't believe banks will borrow to a start-up company, no matter how well-thought-out your business plan. Debt lenders want collateral and regular cash flow to pay down the debt. They aren't interested in debt financing a new venture.

Equity investors are interested. They want to see a business that typically can grow rapidly to around ten million dollars in sales within about four years. They expect rapid growth and hope to cash out down the road with a relatively large return. Unless your business has this potential, equity capital really isn't a viable option. But assuming your business has this potential, your business plan will be used to show potential investors you are prepared to exploit a great market opportunity. It shows your ability to make reasonable calculations and estimates of the future. Your business plan must focus squarely upon the opportunity and the profit potential your business offers the equity investors.

Like any sales tool, your business plan should address the buyer's interests. You want to strike a nerve that matters to them—profit on their equity investment. You need to clearly, accurately, and honestly show that you have a great opportunity. If you fail to do this, you won't get the money.

A captivating idea or hook helps. Something that excites the investors and makes them feel that your idea is new, original, and bound to be a big financial success. Your opportunity should be something with which they want to be associated. However, if you don't have a great hook or a story, instead of trying to think up a false one, focus upon business fundamentals.

Venture capitalists know the numbers. If you don't know what you are doing, it will be obvious to them. They expect you will be able to accurately estimate your start-up expenses. If you try to wave your hands here and avoid the work of researching and estimating your expenses, your plan will get filed in the trash can. This is so important it is worth repeating. If you cannot show that you can make a reasoned and researched estimate of the costs involved in building your product, how can they trust you to know anything? How do you know how much capital starting your enterprise will require? Why should the potential investor listen to anything else you have to say? They won't. You're wasting their time.

The investors also want to know, "Why should we back *you*?" Some people with business ideas, especially ideas they have not thought out, tend to be very afraid of sharing their ideas. They feel someone will steal the idea or do the project without them, cash in on the idea and become rich, while they are left out in the cold. Usually, their brilliant idea has already been brought to the venture capitalists who have rejected the idea for good reasons. Even if it were a good idea, it would be rare for people whose specialty is financing start-ups to try to start it themselves. They just aren't interested in running a business. In good times, the venture capital business is amazingly profitable, and they will be happy to stick to that, rather than to start a business based upon your idea!

If it is a good idea, they probably will discuss the idea with others. How can they know for sure it's a viable idea unless they consult other experts in the area? They want to find out if the idea is viable, and they probably won't share anything too valuable with anyone not involved with the venture capital firm or anyone they don't trust.

Don't assume because you are the one showing them the idea that they will instantly assume you are qualified to execute the idea. They are especially interested in knowing if you have the personal skills and experience to bring the idea to fruition. If the idea doesn't work, they want to know that your management team could take the company in a slightly different direction. So, the personal background of all key members on your management team is crucial to the success of selling your business plan.

The more experience and breadth of skills your team has the better. The combined experience of your key players should cover all aspects of running a business from manufacturing (if applicable) to sales, personnel management, etc. I know at least one person is thinking, "I've got a great idea, but no team. I'll acquire the team, after I get the financing." Although a few have been successful with this approach, most are not. Unless you already have at least some talent lined up, your plan will not be taken seriously.

In acquiring a management team, your business plan is also a good sales document. You want to show it to people you wish to bring on board and say, "If I can raise the financing to launch this business, do you want to be a part of it for such and such a percentage ownership and for such and such a salary doing such and such?" If they say, "yes," ask them if you can put them down on the document as being a committed member. If they again say, "yes," so be it. Add them to your team. That will make your business plan more sellable to investors. If they say, "No, wait until you have the financing, then you can put me down," you think to yourself, "Yeah, right. I'll take all the risks. You won't put your crummy name on the line, and you think I'm going to come back and offer you this position once I have the financing? What planet were you born on?"

To them you say, "OK. Thank you..." Don't burn your bridges here. You might want to go back to them and bring them on board later. If you bring them on later, there is usually little reason to give them as large a percentage ownership as you might have before. That you have raised the money needed without that person being listed means that your backers feel you can succeed without this person. In fact, you might be able to put this person on staff as an employee and not give up any ownership of the company or only a small amount. Some very knowledgeable people disagree with me here and have the attitude that, if the person wasn't on board from the start, they don't want them later. In any case, as you acquire resources, you will need to pay less for the resources acquired later.

The business plan should be whatever length is necessary to clearly and completely convey the idea of your business. It must provide enough information for an informed investor to decide whether or not to invest in the business. The plan should be targeted to the specific type of investor you want to attract. For example, if you want to start an Internet company and you know the venture capital firm from which you want money tends to be the vulture capitalist type who really doesn't give two bits about your business, other than getting it to the IPO market, then you could emphasize not only the prospects for the business, but also why you feel more expansion capital, needed to continue to grow the company, could be raised from an IPO. And, you would go on to show how your company could be sold to the retail investors and why it would appeal to them. Usually, this is done subtly. Show the potential investors a viable exit strategy to get cash back from their investment.

The above is all very important if you are trying to raise capital, but if you are only seeking to put together a plan of business for your own use, you can forego the personal resumes of your team members. Nor do you need to write in full sentences! A plan of business should be a collection of well-thought-out information designed to help you succeed.

It should include a full description of your product and known manufacturing issues. It should have an accurate and researched breakdown of the projected costs to make the product. Or, if you are a service company, your plan should have a full breakdown of the expenses to provide the service. If you anticipate a change in your overall cost structure as your sales grow, you should record estimated expenses at different levels of sales. The good thing about having your financial projections available is that you can go back to them and confirm that your initial estimates were valid.

Your plan should have a full breakdown of how you will market your service. The more specific you can be the better. If you are selling a high-end computer software product, a list of companies you plan to approach is good. The results of any discussions with these companies is also a good idea. For example, if you are estimating you can sell your product to 40% of these companies your first year, but you have already contacted several companies and not generated any sales, your estimates might be too ambitious.

The area that is the real bugaboo is trying to estimate sales. Entrepreneurs tend to be overly optimistic when forming their projections. Not that I'm against optimism, in general, but incorrectly anticipating more sales than you will receive can complicate your life in unpleasant ways. You should also consider the case where sales are greater than anticipated. Can you deal with this situation or will you need to sacrifice sales? How many sales can your company support before cash flow becomes a real problem? What are your growth strategies?

Don't forget, as you draw up projections of your expenses and estimated sales, create a cash flow projection for at least every month of your first year. This is probably the thing most missed by people starting a business. They get the expenses and make a stab at estimating sales, but they neglect the difference between when money will be earned and when it will be received. While you might be doing great from a profit-loss perspective, if you are dead-out of cash, you are in trouble.

A business plan lets you compare where you are to where you thought you would be at the present. It helps to psychologically reinforce sales and growth targets.

Finally, a great reason for writing a business plan is that it gives you a journal of your entrepreneurial history. It records your thinking at the time. It helps you see how you have grown as a business person. Someday, when cleaning out your attic, you come upon a stack of reports. After blowing dust off the cover of one, you chuckle and say, "I'll be damned. This was the business plan for the first venture I ever tried." You laugh and think, "What the hell was I thinking?" Chinchilla farming just never materialized into the explosive growth area you had imagined it would. Then you leaf through a couple of others—ideas you contemplated and researched, but never tried. You come upon a plan that makes you smile fondly and you think, "This was the business that first made me a multimillionaire." You remember the struggles and the triumphs. They were exhilarating and, maybe, the best years of your life.

****

I hope this book has given you the tools to realize you, too, can become a successful entrepreneur. I wish your journey to be both personally and financially rewarding. Always follow your dreams, and good luck on your endeavors.

Other books by Peter Hupalo:

How To Start And Run Your Own Corporation: S-Corporations For Small Business Owners

Becoming An Investor: Building Wealth By Investing In Stocks, Bonds, And Mutual Funds

LaVergne, TN USA
06 December 2010

207623LV00009B/90/A